REVIVING LIBERTY

Radical Christian Humanism in Milton's Great Poems

Joan S. Bennett

Harvard University Press
Cambridge, Massachusetts, and London, England   1989

Publication of this book has been aided by a grant from the Andrew W. Mellon Foundation

This book is printed on acid-free paper, and its binding materials have been chosen for strength and durability.

Library of Congress Cataloging-in-Publication Data

Bennett, Joan S.
  Reviving liberty : radical Christian humanism in Milton's great poems / Joan S. Bennett.
    p. cm.
  Bibliography: p.
  Includes index.
  ISBN 0-674-76697-0
  1. Milton, John. 1608–1674—Political and social views.
2. Liberty in literature. 3. Humanism in literature. 4. Radicalism
in literature. 5. Christianity in literature. 6. Great Britain—
History—Puritan Revolution, 1642–1660—Literature and the
revolution.   I. Title.
PR3592.L48B45 1989   88-22682
821'.4—dc19   CIP

For Miriam and Aaron

Acknowledgments

THIS BOOK has grown steadily over many years and in diverse places. Much of the work has been done in the press of other business—in administrative offices, airports, hotels, the hospital, houses full of children. Some time has been spent in the rich quiet of the Folger Library, the British Library, and the Union Theological Library, to whose staffs I am grateful. One valuable research year was made possible by a fellowship from the American Association of University Women. Four sections have been published in earlier versions and are reproduced here with permission of the publishers: Chapters 2 and 4 are reprinted with some additions from articles in *PMLA*, 92 (1977) and 98 (1983); the first section of Chapter 5 appeared as "Liberty under the Law: The Chorus and the Meaning of *Samson Agonistes*," in *Milton Studies*, 12, James D. Simmonds, Editor, published in 1979 by the University of Pittsburgh Press; the second section of Chapter 5 appeared as " 'A Person Rais'd': Public and Private Cause in *Samson Agonistes*" in *SEL*, 18 (1978); portions of the third section of Chapter 5 are extracted from my essay "A Reading of *Samson Agonistes*," which appears in *The Cambridge Companion to Milton*, edited by Dennis Danielson (Cambridge University Press, 1989), and are reproduced by kind permission of the Syndics of Cambridge University Press.

It is a happy privilege to belong to the community of Milton scholars, many of whom have generously guided my work. I wish to thank especially George Sensabaugh and Christopher Hill, who from their different vantage points have given sustained encouragement to the entire project. Very helpful criticism has also come from Stanley Fish, Austin Woolrych, and Mary Ann Radzinowicz. I am grateful for the intellectual camaraderie of Jackie DiSalvo and the openness of Joseph Wittreich. The scholarship and historical insight of Arthur Barker, whom I have not met, provide the base on which this project is built.

The community of deepest influence is my family. I am of the first generation to enter higher education; however, it was from my father, who had no opportunity to attend high school, that I learned to seek out Plato, Aristotle, and the life of the mind. I am indebted with him to the staff of the Lilac Blind Foundation, who know well the inward light brighter than the blaze of noon. My mother, who wanted all her life to find time to read, began courageously at the age of seventy-three with *Paradise Lost*. She and my sisters have shared with me child care and other responsibilities for nurturance while remaining faithful to their own callings. My husband, Robert, shares the labor both at home and in the world. I have written this book for our children, Miriam and Aaron; may they become children of reviving liberty.

J. S. B.

Contents

Thus much I should perhaps have said though I were sure I should have spoken only to trees and stones; and had none to cry to, but with the Prophet, *O earth, earth, earth!* to tell the very soil it self, what her perverse inhabitants are deaf to. Nay though what I have spoke, should happ'n . . . to be the last words of our expiring libertie. But I trust I shall have spoken perswasion to abundance of sensible and ingenuous men: to som perhaps whom God may raise of these stones to become children of reviving libertie.

—*Ready and Easy Way, CPW* 7:463

REVIVING LIBERTY

Abbreviations

All quotations of Milton's poetry are taken from John Milton, *Complete Poems and Major Prose,* ed. Merritt Y. Hughes (New York: Odyssey, 1962). Works shortened in citations include:

DDD	*The Doctrine and Discipline of Divorce*
De Doc.	*De Doctrina Christiana*
Likeliest Means	*Considerations Touching the Likeliest Means to Remove Hirelings out of the Church*
Of Civil Power	*A Treatise of Civil Power in Ecclesiastical Causes*
PL	*Paradise Lost*
PR	*Paradise Regained*
Ready and Easy Way	*A Readie and Easy Way to Establish a Free Commonwealth*
SA	*Samson Agonistes*
TKM	*The Tenure of Kings and Magistrates*

Other works frequently cited are:

CPW	*Complete Prose Works of John Milton,* ed. Don M. Wolfe et al. (from which all prose quotations are taken)
Laws	*Of the Laws of Ecclesiastical Polity* in *The Folger Library Edition of The Works of Richard Hooker,* ed. W. Speed Hill
Haller, *Tracts*	*Tracts on Libery in the Puritan Revolution, 1638–1647,* ed. William Haller
Haller and Davies	*The Leveller Tracts, 1647–1653,* ed. William Haller and Godfrey Davies
Jackson	Thomas Jackson, *The Life of John Goodwin*
Woodhouse	*Puritanism and Liberty, Being the Army Debates (1647–9) from the Clarke Manuscripts with Supplementary Documents,* ed. A. S. P. Woodhouse

Introduction

THE PUBLIC issues most urgently at hand for the Western world at the end of the twentieth century also played a central role in the struggles of John Milton and his contemporaries to achieve a just society. In 1644 Milton saw England as "a nation of prophets"; in *The Experience of Defeat* (1984) Christopher Hill asks the question of our own day: "Where are they now?"[1]

A group of American sociologists, after interviewing two hundred people, have challenged: "Is it possible that we could become citizens again and together seek the common good in the post-industrial, post-modern age?"[2] Only, they conclude, if our culture manages "to communicate a form of life, a *paideia*, in the sense of growing up in a morally and intellectually intelligible world." Such an intelligibility would not be achieved by imposing on "an abundance of sensible and ingenuous men" any version—"humanistic" or other—of a notion that they "have Abraham as their father," that their personal salvation or their cultural hegemony is permanent or successfully reified. Paideia is neither ideology nor utopia.[3] It was, however, the fundamental goal of Milton's public life and of the poetry which he offered to his original audience and to us, both of whom he was inclined to consider "these stones" (*Ready and Easy Way, CPW* 7:463; cf. Matt. 3.9–10).[4]

Some of the excitement now abroad in the intellectual world could contribute to such a paideia in our age as, in fields from philosophy of science to philosophy of literature, discussions of thought and praxis are moving "beyond objectivism and relativism."[5] One lesson of the emerging epistemology is that observers (scholars, critics) are part of the phenomena they study and that they affect the configurations they observe. Inevitably, for instance, I am a presence in this book about Milton and his contemporaries.

Those whose own theories and experiences prevent them from believing that any text or oeuvre can be read as genuinely coherent will, I hope, find it valuable nevertheless to enter with some depth and historical concreteness into the practical context—the religious and revolutionary fervor—that attended this poetry's creation. In particular, I hope that readers will not be deterred by my use of the words "Christian humanism." Non-Christians and nonhumanists may not be inclined to care about refinements within a vocabulary whose terms for them are objects of attack, having served as vehicles of a historical hegemony they oppose. However, we are usually closest to understanding a world view when we study its internal debates; and in today's intellectually fluid world, it is possible that two practitioners of the same theory—say the Christian or the Marxist—might on the whole have less in common than a pair containing one of each. I agree with Christopher Kendrick that there does not exist "a static and seamless Christian tradition as the ultimate context in which [*Paradise Lost*] should be read."[6] However, although readers will read all works in whatever contexts are most compelling for them personally, I believe that they would be considerably impoverished if they were to ignore one another's contexts and that a dynamic, multifaceted, practical, and political Christianity is a rich and even inevitable context for reading Milton.

This book focuses primarily on the public rather than the private dimensions of Milton's poetry. Christian humanism shares with Marxism and other calls to continuing social reform a commitment to see the private good as definable only in the public, or community's good—to do as Milton, on the eve of his political imprisonment in 1659, exhorted the readers of his last attempt to avert the monarchy's restoration—"to place every one his privat welfare and happiness in the public peace, libertie and safetie" (*Ready and Easy Way, CPW* 7:443). I share the hope of Richard Bernstein, who in a discussion of contemporary philosophy identifies at the heart of contemporary intellectual ferment a recognition of this need: "What we desperately need today is to learn to think and act more like the fox than the hedgehog—to seize upon those experiences and struggles in which there are still the glimmerings of solidarity and the promise of dialogical communities in which there can be genuine mutual participation and where reciprocal wooing and persuasion can prevail."[7]

That seventeenth-century England offers fertile territory in which to ground our historical and imaginative efforts has not gone unrecognized. Yet some of the most serious current attempts at such study are hindered by a tendency to read particular contemporary experiences, especially the aftermath of World War I or of May 1968, too broadly back into the aftermath of the English Revolution and to turn an assumed "fatigue and depoliticization" into a perceived "emphasis on personal, private salvation" in Milton's late poems.[8] Fredric Jameson, for instance, makes the important observation that in the revolutionaries' "burning preoccupation with the nature of collective life" something that he calls "the religious community" served "as a concrete mediator between the public and the private and as a space in which problems of institutions and power meet problems of personal relationships and ethics or private life." Assuming, however, that "the Calvinist meditation on original sin and the fall" must be a "displacement from politics to psychology and ethics," he fails to find "all these great themes of church and collectivity" in Milton's poetry, seeing there no poetic equivalent to either a political party or to what he suggests was its seventeenth-century counterpart, a "gathered" congregation.[9] Commitment to a gathered congregation, however, while one viable form, was not identical with commitment to the creation of effective communities. The picture was more complex. Particular congregations flourished and failed; and then, as now, people lived out their religious commitment in the critical service of political parties and social movements, as well as in mutable communities of the faithful. This book is largely about "the religious community" that Jameson recognizes in Milton's milieu.

In Chapter One, I discuss the advisability of a new term—"radical Christian humanism"—in the vocabulary of religio-political-literary history, acknowledging that there are limitations to what Herman Rapaport decries as "the traditional approach to Milton," which "views the poet as the last great Renaissance apologist for humanism."[10] No one in the long controversy of Milton criticism has doubted that Milton thought himself a Christian, but the question has been: How is the "humanism" reflected in his erudition related to his faith? In a 1958 consideration of "the tone and texture of Milton's poetry," Kingsley Widmer saw the question as a philosophical one: Is Milton "reasonable" or "absolutist"? "Reason" in this question is assumed to mean "a general reasonableness" derived from "the positive values of classical learning, religious and ethical moderation," and in this "reasonableness" we can see a descendent of the ancient mutation of Aristotle's "mean" into the Roman "moderation." Widmer's question implies that if Milton viewed "the world as evil" and "virtue as renunciation" of the world, he must also have ultimately rejected a commitment to action in this world.[11]

Widmer was defending the artistry of Milton's similes and his representation of Heaven. A quarter-century later the question has been raised again from a different base of concern by Andrew Milner, who wishes to incorporate the great poet into a historical schema amenable to the development of an overarching sociological theory that yields political commitment. Concerned to define Milton's "rationalism," Milner recognizes that, over against the authoritarian scholasticism which Milton rejected, "formally, there are probably an extremely large number of possible alternative criteria" of truth. But he believes that, as a seventeenth-century bourgeois, Milton had "only two major options" available: scientific empiricism or Cartesian rationalism. Milner contends that Milton is a rationalist in the latter sense (and can thus be considered seriously in the continuing development of Marxian thought). Rapaport, on the other hand, sees in Milton empiricism (or *techne*) with a vengeance; he finds "adumbrations" in fact of "the instrumentalization of reason" underlying an absolutist revolutionary state.[12]

Like Milner, I am interested in Milton's relation to what has happened since the seventeenth century to the senses in which it is possible to understand "reason" and "temperance." Milner recalls how A. J. A. Waldock (1947) found himself forced to see either a "Renaissance" or a "Puritan" Milton (Widmer's "humanist" vs. "absolutist" Christian) and chose the latter because he detected in Milton little "rational 'temperance,'" which Waldock defined as "finding happy compromises, comfortable and middle ways." In such a definition as this, Milner sees evidence that "the very meaning of the term 'reason' has been subverted" since the eighteenth century. "The rational man has given way to the 'reasonable' man, that is, the man whose refusal to draw logical conclusions, whose willingness to compromise, marks him precisely as non-rational—as, in the proper sense, non-reasonable. *The Shorter Oxford Dictionary* entry under 'reasonable' is surely significant: 'adj. I. Endowed with reason. Now *rare*.'"[13] I too reach beyond such an attenuated understanding of *ratio*: I look, however, at one of the other alternatives to scholasticism—different from either Cartesian logic or skeptical empiricism—that were available to Milton's imagination and offer a reconsideration of *recta ratio*. As we engage in the new "conversation about human rationality" that is post-empiricist and post-Cartesian,[14] it may be possible to gain imaginative access to the long and varied Christian encounter with classical phronesis and praxis in such a way as to move beyond both Milton the "poet of democratic liberalism" and Milton the "prophet of revolutionary absolutism."[15]

Throughout this book I have tried to show that Milton's Christianity did build upon pre-modern conceptions and experiences of reason that have some affinities with the post-modern and, further, that this effort resulted from, and in, a religious commitment to political process which he embodies over and over in his poetry. Chapters Two and Three look at the world view that allows for the necessary combination of a Christian humanist rationality and radical political action. They consider the Hell, Heaven, and Eden of Milton's *Paradise Lost* in the context of his commitment to the revolutionary cause. Chapters Four and Five consider the operation of individual characters' free reason in situations that are simultaneously ethical and political; they read Adam and Eve before the Fall and Samson *agonistes* in the context of Milton's humanistic and antinomian Christian radicalism. Finally, at the root of Milton's radical Christian humanism is his faith in Christian liberty. Chapter Six reads *Paradise Regained* as Milton's account of the birth of that liberty in the mind—and through the unique mission—of its creator, who was always for Milton "Christ Our Liberator" (*De Doc.*, *CPW* 6:537).

ONE

Hooker, Milton, and the Radicalization of Christian Humanism

IN 1593 the greatest of the Anglican apologists, believing the ruin of his church to be imminent, felt a need to explain his publishing *Of the Laws of Ecclesiastical Polity*: "Though for no other cause, yet for this; that posteritie may know we have not loosely through silence permitted things to passe away as in a dreame, there shall be for men's information extant thus much concerning the present state of the Church of God established amongst us, and their carefull endevour which woulde have upheld the same."[1]

Readers in later years have found the tone curious since Richard Hooker's work has for three centuries been considered a foundation stone of the (well-established) Church of England. Yet, if we are to understand Hooker's *Laws*, the first thing we must realize is that his heroic, and even poetic, vision of the "Church of God established" did pass away, though eloquently, in the very process of its establishment.

A half-century after Hooker's death the greatest English heroic poet, who was also deeply committed to a religio-political cause, testified to the passing of his own vision of a holy society in England. "Thus much I should perhaps have said," Milton concluded the second edition of his *Readie and Easie Way to Establish a Free Commonwealth*, "though I were sure I should have spoken only to trees and stones; and had none to cry to, but with the Prophet, *O earth, earth, earth!* to tell the very soil it self what her perverse inhabitants are deaf to. . . . But I trust I shall have spoken perswasion . . . to som perhaps whom God may raise of these stones to become children of reviving libertie" (*CPW* 7:462–63). Those who admire not only the beauty of Milton's poetry but also his libertarian vision have taken comfort in the thought that constitutionalism eventually brought about the establishment of his hopes for England. But the Christian liberty aimed at through Milton's *Free Commonwealth* was no more attained by the Whig victory than was the vision of Hooker's *Laws* attained in Anglicanism.

It is time to reexamine our understanding of the history of Christian humanism in seventeenth-century England. Literary historians generally show that Christian humanism appeared in England in the sixteenth century of Thomas More; flowered under Elizabeth I, finding its most magnificent prose formulation in Hooker's *Laws*; continued in the stewardship of the Anglican church; and manifested itself in a final glorious embodiment in the poetry of John Milton.[2] The political historian Michael Walzer, on the other hand, noticing the very different political allegiances in the seventeenth century of alleged Christian humanists, has traced a different line of descent in which Christian humanism after Hooker is left with the established church and Milton is viewed as the inheritor, through his Puritan commitment, of the Christian nominalism of the Reformation.[3]

The different perspectives, literary and political, theological and historical, must be integrated in an understanding of seventeenth-century British Christian humanism, which offers an essential context for a reading of Milton's poetry. The task requires that we determine which of all the qualities that have been held to be characteristic of Christian humanism are essential. Using Hooker's *Laws*, taken in their historical context, as a statement of the Christian humanist world view acceptable to theologians, literary scholars, and political philosophers alike, I shall argue that the real line of theological descent passed in Stuart England from Anglicans to Puritans, royalists to revolutionaries.[4]

THIS claim is based on the following observations: that Christian nominalism did flourish in seventeenth-century England; that it found a natural connection to newly virulent theories of divine right in ecclesiastical and state government; that nominalism underlay the absolutist political thought of both the Laudian royalists and the "orthodox" Puritan revolutionaries; and that neither an absolutist nor a nominalist deity is to be found, present or implied, in either Hooker or Milton, who both speak instead—though under radically different circumstances—for the same deeply rational Christian liberty.

Walzer thinks that Hooker, as the author of a classic exposition of natural law with its great chain of being, must have believed in a divine right of monarchy and episcopacy. Walzer contrasts an Anglican deity of natural law, who is as imperturbable and predictable as the law of gravity, with a Calvinist deity of pure will, who is constantly active in every motion of the universe, as unpredictable as an earthquake except when he reveals his will to people directly. The duty of the Anglican, according to this scenario, is to study and reason from the pattern of natural and revealed law, which automatically reinforces the monarch's authority. The duty of the Puritan is to await and obey particular orders from an unpredictable God. It is the latter "arbitrary sovereign of the universe" whom Walzer sees embodied in Milton's God.[5]

Although Walzer is mistaken about both Hooker and Milton, his political analysis of nominalism is most insightful. That a divinely sanctioned absolutism, political and ecclesiastical, could have seemed to derive naturally from a Christian nominalism may be understood as follows: If one believes that the omnipotent God is inscrutable except by direct revelation, that he is intrinsically unpredictable, then one will seek an authoritative source of that revealed will so as to observe its dictates. The medieval church had held that God was not inscrutable, that he had revealed his will in nature, Scripture, and tradition as these were interpreted by the church. It had thus provided believers the feeling that they understood God's ways with human beings as well as the comfort of knowing that this understanding was and would continue to be completely authoritative since the church was the recipient of God's continuing self-revelation. When Protestantism denied the infallibility of the church, it lost that kind of authoritativeness. Reformers then had to consider whether God's will was still to be studied by the now fallible clergy and the laity in nature, Scripture, and tradition, and to what extent it could be known and understood.[6]

Two major, and differing, solutions to the problem of religious epistemology emerged in the Britain of Queen Elizabeth. The Disciplinarians or Presbyterians, as they developed in the Marian exile and were represented in a pure form by John Knox in Scotland and the Scottish Presbyterians in England, sought to retain the comfort of an infallible source of saving faith by replacing the Roman church with a Scriptural kirk.[7] With the elimination of nature and tradition, however, the absolute assurance they regained was now based in a nominalism which held that specific revelations were given in full and discrete particulars to the kirk as it interpreted Scripture and contemporary events. In their view it was the responsibility of an absolute monarch to enforce subjects' religious and moral duty with the magistrate's sword.

Anglicans in the Tudor settlement, on the other hand, surrendered the intrinsically authoritative claim of the church, retaining rational access to the natural order, Scripture, and ongoing providence but without infallibility (though with assurance of salvation). Tudor Anglican thought, as it culminated in Hooker, is thus not philosophically authoritarian in its notion either of episcopacy or of the royal supremacy. In Stuart Britain, however, first under the pressures that led finally to revolutionary war and then during the period of its oppression under the Commonwealth and Protectorate, the brand of Anglicanism that took up the defense of the faith against the Disciplinarians came to fight fire with fire until it became like them philosophically.[8] Laudian Anglicanism and royalism became absolutist and, in spite of its habitual invocation of "right reason," as nominalist as the Westminster Assembly.

It is not logically possible to believe both in the rationally accessible God of Christian humanism and in the divine right of kings. The matter is confusing because it *is*, on the other hand, possible, without betraying the ancient and Christian notion of right reason, to defend—as Hooker did—the powerful monarchy of a particular Christian nation. Such a defense is possible when such rule is held to be humanly chosen, not divinely ordained. At this point we must consider Hooker's conception of "the politic society," which enabled him to give significant religious status to the English government without claiming its positive legal basis to be divine or its powers absolute.[9] If we can appreciate his desperate consistency in this endeavor, we can understand why Anglicanism after Hooker abandoned the essence of Christian humanism and why the last great Christian humanist in England had to be a political revolutionary.

Beginning with Aristotle's dictum that society's purpose is the promotion of the good life, Hooker gave the principle a Christian content in agreement with medieval tradition. The "good" is to be sought for human beings in accordance with their "triple estate," as they are natural, civil, and spiritual beings (327; bk. 8, ch. 1, sec. 6), as they are "domestic," "civil," and "religious" in the terminology of Milton's *A Defense of the English People*. The "religious" goal of society is pursued by a leadership that is at once political and religious. There is no separation of church and commonwealth as long as her citizens and rulers are all Christians. The ruler of the politic society, the English church/state, has no infallibility or inherent, absolute authority since his or her authority originates in the consent of free Christians; and Hooker nowhere presents the particular ordinances of Elizabeth, her parliaments, or her bishops as *necessary* consequences of the eternal laws of nature and God.[10] Further, obedience of ordinances requires that the positive law must be inherently reasonable. The key to a distinction between an allowable absolutism and the impossibility of divine right lies in God's own rational nature as an absolute monarch voluntarily accountable to law, as one who is the divine pattern for the rationality and hence the free choice of human beings made in his image. On the other hand, since order itself is good according to natural law (331; 8.2.2), reason demands that the existing government be obeyed up to the point where it does transgress any part of natural law.

The most recent scholars of Hooker's work are not alone in noticing that the Stuart (not Tudor) doctrines of divine right of episcopacy and of monarchy effected a complete abandonment of Hooker's principles.[11] Peter Munz wondered whether the constitutionalism of book 8 was what had kept it from being published when it was written.[12] The Smectymnuans in the 1640s taunted the prelates with the suggestion that Hooker's seventh book remained unpublished because it did not support the divine origin of episcopacy.[13] And the Royalist spokesman for divine right of kings, Sir Robert Filmer, made clear that he considered Hooker inadequate as a political thinker: "The profoundest scholar that ever was known hath not been able to search out every truth that is discoverable—not even Mr. Hooker in divinity," whose failure to "confute this first erroneous principle . . . the natural liberty and equality of mankind"[14] carried him a dangerous step beyond the bounds of faith. In 1660 the Restoration prelate who, thinking to bolster the renewed episcopacy, had sanctioned the publication of book 7, was so shocked to find out, after its publication, that Hooker had denied the divine right of bishops that he commissioned Walton's fictionalized *Life* to claim that Hooker's manuscript had been contaminated by the Puritan clergy in collusion with the (from then on) infamous Mrs. Hooker.[15]

W. Speed Hill, in his study of the *Laws*'s publication history, demonstrates that Hooker wrote and rewrote the last four books in an attempt, without betraying his own theological principles, to meet the needs of his parliamentary and ecclesiastical patrons, who feared the political effects of religious dissent.[16] Hooker's own motivating fear was even more fundamental than the Parliamentarians'. It was a fear that the hearts and therefore inevitably the minds of Christian contenders on all sides would become warped and hardened by controversy to the point where, whatever labels anyone used or ceremonies anyone performed, nothing would come of contention "but the mutual waste of the parties contending, till a common enemy [atheism and apostasy] dance in the ashes of them both."[17] His only tool therefore was persuasion. A resort to force would mean that the cause was being lost, that the church established was passing away. In the years that followed Hooker's untimely death, both Anglicans and Disciplinarians became "forcers of conscience."[18]

A minority of Anglican historians, uncomfortable with this discrepancy between Hooker's theory and the church's practice, have traced the descent of Hooker's vision not to the Laudians who came to dominate the church, but to the early "Latitudinarians," Christian rationalists like the members of the Falkland group, many of whom opted out of political activity altogether.[19] John Hales of Eton, for instance, was, like Hooker, deeply irenic in his desire for a broadly tolerant church. But by the 1630s the governors of church and state had hardened the establishment's enforcement of religious conformity and its philosophical lines of defense, so that at this point in history the Christian rationalist had to choose between the effort to preserve the reasonable order of the state/church and the effort to preserve free if mistaken consciences. Hales chose in favor of order in a national church. He did so not because he believed Stuart claims of divine right, nor for any personal gain under Laud's ascendancy.[20] He did so because the same philosophical struggles that had established in his own mind grounds for a belief in toleration for conscience's sake had left him without the straightforward assurance of the church's authority held by the Laudians and the Presbyterians *and* without the radicals' faith in the coming of "more light." He was a courageous man who had to act on the courage of his *in*conviction or minimal conviction. And, as a biographer of Samuel Rutherford remarked on the source of the Scot's single-minded courage, "It is hard to lose one's life for a 'perhaps.' "[21] For men unable to sustain Hales's personal level of life-long searching after truth, the decision of such a man as Hales for political conservatism pointed the way toward fideism as a resolution of the tension between the pulls of faith, intellect, and political life.[22] The effect of latitudinarian intellectual skepticism was to aid in the evolution of the term "reason" and its meaning for human nature; in the loss, that is, of the Christian humanist faith in right reason and in the consequent restriction of reason to mean simply ratiocination, logic—to be exercised not, as in Hooker's grand vision, about and in cooperation with God and an eternally existing natural law, but merely about material phenomena.

The case of Jeremy Taylor, an Anglican "rationalist" who did not withdraw from activity in the Laudian establishment, illustrates how a skeptical nominalism made possible a sincere belief in divinely sanctioned political absolutism. It also suggests that a desire for the anticipated benefits of political absolutism could encourage the development of a nominalist religious belief. A protege of Laud, Taylor was chaplain to the king and was after the Restoration made a bishop, as he believed, by divine right. F. L. Huntley, who treats Taylor in his role as a controversialist, sees no essential difference between his religious thought and that of Hooker or Milton.[23] But if my thesis is correct, from Taylor's politics we should expect a fundamental difference at the philosophical core. And, indeed, without considering politics, both Robert Hoopes and Herschel Baker were surprised to discover from studying *The Liberty of Prophesying* and *Ductor Dubitantium* that, though Taylor was "devoted to the ideal concept of right reason" because of its insistence on conscience, he did not actually accept "the premises upon which that concept must logically rest."[24] Hooker had insisted that "they erre . . . who thinke that of the will of God to do this or that, there is no reason besides his will" (61; 1.2.5), for there is a "law eternall . . . which God hath eternallie purposed himselfe in all his works to observe" (63; 1.3.1). We find Taylor, in contrast, asserting the voluntarist view that there is no rationally accessible natural law, that the only reason we can be sure "God cannot do an unjust thing" is "because whatsoever he wills or does is therefore just because he wills and does it."[25] To corroborate his view, he quotes the originator of Christian nominalism, William of Ockham.

Baker suggests that Taylor must have been yielding to the pressures of the new secularism which made it no longer possible to "construe nature in sacramental terms" as Hooker had done.[26] On the contrary, the explanation is primarily political, not scientific. In the seventeeth century it was possible to believe in the natural law of Christian Platonism, but a nominalism like Taylor's was a predictable and necessary philosophical base for high church Anglicans to adopt because of their alliance with the Stuarts. The choice of these Anglicans to try to preserve political and ecclesiastical order was made at the cost of what had been held by Hooker to be the metaphysical source of all physical and moral order, the rational deity's eternal law.

Thus it is misleading to call Taylor or any Laudian Anglican a Christian humanist, to hold that his version of "Arminianism" is identical with Hooker's belief in free will, or that the term "reason" or "right reason" in his writing retains the meaning it held for Hooker.[27] In the seventeenth century it was no longer possible for a Christian humanist even to try to see the British monarch as a Gloriana in voluntary obedience to the rational natural law. To remain a royalist under the Stuarts was to abandon the historic Christian humanist world view in which there can be no Christian freedom without the possibility of individuals' rational choice and no purpose for human association—no state or society—that is not centered in the exercise of that Christian freedom. Two characteristics would be displayed by a genuine heir to Hooker's humanism: an active political commitment to build a Christian society that is at the same time both holy and free; and a faith in right reason (God's and humans') that fires and shapes that political commitment.

This same deeply idealistic Christian humanism did lead one peer of

Falkland's generation to speak out for reform on the floor of Parliament—and to ride into battle against the Cavaliers. The true heirs of Hooker's *Laws* were such men as Robert Greville, Lord Brooke, that member of the Puritan nobility in whom "the spirit of the age of Sidney lived on,"[28] and the great middle-class Puritan who has been recognized as Brooke's philosophical heir, John Milton. The deep bond that exists between Hooker and Milton is manifested in both men's unwillingness to relinquish either individual "consent" or "liberty," on the one hand, or some form of church/state—holy society—on the other. In Milton's Christian humanist view, a nominalistic practical theology such as Taylor's brought about in the individual Christian no spiritually informed morality but only at best an effeminate pietism that left the way open for intolerable political oppression. In order to survive, the powerful root of the Christian humanist tradition in England had to undergo a radicalization of its external form. Originally aristocratic, by the mid-seventeenth century it had become Puritan.

To experience the dynamics of a poetry based in the new Christian humanism, it is important to realize that Milton's free commonwealth, rather than Laud's High Church or Hales's Latitudinarian one, is the heir of Hooker's "politic society." To grasp this evolution, we must distinguish the society Milton envisioned from the Covenant society of the Presbyterians with whom he briefly aligned himself at the beginning of his political career.

Milton had early been attracted to the outspoken courage of the Scottish reformers in placing God above all worldly power, enduring persecution and exile for religious freedom. He called John Knox and his fellows "the true Protestant Divines of *England*, our fathers in the faith we hold" (*TKM, CPW* 3:251). But Milton soon decided that the single-mindedness of his Scottish contemporaries had no base in right reason and hence no genuine concept of human liberty. His 1646 sonnet "On the New Forcers of Conscience under the Long Parliament," well-known as an announcement of his break with Presbyterianism, accuses among the offending Scots, "Rutherford," who argues for *The Divine Right of [Presbyterian] Church Government* (1646). Milton scholars have regarded this same Rutherford's thought as essentially analogous to Milton's, which suggests that the Christian humanist basis of Milton's political thought has not been sufficiently distinguished from the nominalistically based thought of orthodox Puritanism.[29]

Samuel Rutherford's belief that Parliament was justified in waging war against King Charles was based on the Presbyterian ministers' view, not that the king had failed to observe the natural law of human freedom but

that he had failed to "swear a Covenant" and "Build the Lord's House"—
to establish a Presbyterian state church. In light of his crimes, "the ministers of *Christ* are to say, *The King Troubleth Israell*, and they have the
keyes to open and shut heaven to, and upon the King, if he offend."[30]
When Rutherford comes to answer the second of his "questions"—"In
what sense Government is from the law of nature"—he does not focus on
the liberty of human beings made rational in the image of God, or on an
eternal law to which God's goodness requires submission. Rather, he
believes that while God did not prescribe a monarchy for the state (as he
did a presbytery for the church), God did command that there be a civil
government and that human duty is to follow God's revealed commands.
Rutherford fits Walzer's picture of the nominalist saint. To follow the law
of nature is, for him, to obey God's express commands as a form of
self-preservation: "It is against nature's light to resist the ordinance of
God"—it is only "reasonable" to seek reward and avoid punishment.[31]
What is left to human beings by "nature's light" in Rutherford's vision is
not right reason and not liberty: "By nature's light man now fallen and
broken, even under all the fractures of the powers and faculties of the soul,
doth know, that promises of reward, fear of punishment, and the co-active
power of the sword as Plato said, are natural means to move us, and wings
to promote obedience and to do our duty."[32] Such a lack of faith in human
moral reason as the basis of society contrasts noticeably with that of
Hooker, who holds that human as well as "natural agents" are designed to
operate ecologically as well as individually. According to him, just as
natural agents have their law, which "directeth them in the meanes
whereby they tende to their owne perfection: So likewise another law
there is, which toucheth them as they are sociable partes united into one
bodie, a lawe which bindeth them each to serve unto others good, and all
to preferre the good of the whole before whatsoever their owne particular"
(69; 1.3.5). Therefore, "two foundations there are which beare up publique
societies, the one, a naturall inclination, wherby all men desire sociable life
and fellowship, the other an order . . . agreed upon, touching the manner
of their union." Hooker invited the reader of his *Laws* to "consider how
nature findeth out such lawes of government as serve to direct even nature
depraved to a right end" (96; 1.10.1).

How, under Rutherford's more constricted definition of natural law,
can the sovereignty be seen to be in the people? Not because of their
participation as rational creatures through faith in the divine ordering, but
"because if every living creature have in them a power of *self-preservation* to
defend them selves from violence, as we see Lyons have pawes, some
beasts have hornes, some clawes; men being reasonable creatures, united

in societies, must have power in a more reasonable and more honorable way to put this power of warding off violence, in the hands of one or more Rulers, to defend themselves by Magistrates" (*Lex Rex*, p. 10).

Rutherford's argument for a social contract, unlike Milton's, is based in a view of human and divine nature that resembles Jeremy Taylor's. This is true even though Taylor believed in the divine right of bishops instead of presbyters. Holding, like Rutherford, that there is *right* of nature, *jus naturae* in "natural, wild, or untutored" man as in animals for individual self-preservation, Taylor believes that the only *law* of nature is the will of God, revealed in Scripture and inscrutable in nature. The *lex naturae* is God's commandment, dependent on His will, not God's nature consistent with His reason. Like Rutherford, he holds that human reason is not a participant in divine truth, but only a tool for carrying out divine orders: "God is the law—given, practical reason or conscience is the record."[33]

We cannot remind ourselves too often that a seventeenth-century author's basic views cannot be predicted with certainty from his terminology. Certainly Taylor's version of "Arminianism" has very little in common with Hooker's belief in the free reason and will. And, on the other political hand, we should notice the bitter frustration it cost Richard Baxter, an orthodox Puritan more moderate than Rutherford, to be stigmatized as a theorist of rebellion, while he saw Richard Hooker, whose views on liberty seemed to Baxter to be inexcusably radical, stand as an honored name in England and the Church of England. Baxter quoted Bishop Bilson, an Elizabethan precursor of Stuart divine right theory, *against* Hooker.[34] Baxter was quite right about this irony; his definition of natural law is the same as Taylor's (and Rutherford's): "natural law is nothing but the 'signification of God's governing will . . . in which God declareth to man his duty, and his reward or punishment.' "[35]

One more distinction needs to be made in a survey of seventeenth-century religio-political belief that attempts to sketch the evolution of *recta ratio*. Although Milton's politics were more radical than Rutherford's or Baxter's, his fundamentally motivating belief in reason was also very different from that of another group of Puritans, the religious separatists, with whom he was politically most closely attuned, such as his friend Roger Williams. In the view of the Calvinist separatist, it was too much to hope from sinful human beings that, as in Hooker's vision of natural law, "truth and goodness [would] coalesce, not only in the conduct of each man's daily life, but in the very fabric of his social institutions."[36] The Calvinist separatist is, for the purpose of the philosophical distinctions being drawn here, like the Anglican Latitudinarian in his resignation of the political world to the realm of "things indifferent," by which was now meant things not only—as for Hooker—open to reason, but also—in defeat of Hooker's vision—closed to faith. Both separatists and Latitudinarians abandoned the effort to build a holy society and they abandoned the full belief in right reason. The "visible" church/state of England urged by Falkland was no more considered holy by its seventeenth-century advocates than was the secular state in Rhode Island, in which a practical, reductionist reason was conceded the magistrate for the task of governing the unredeemed portion of humanity. On the Latitudinarian side, reason tacitly gave up being right reason when it gave up trying to save the Dissenters' conscience from force. While a "reasonableness" was still claimed by Latitudinarians, the meaning of "reason" was changing to mean the uses of mere logic and a skeptical prudence to stabilize an institutional church in the face of threatened "mutations in government."[37] On the separatist side the meaning of reason was confidently and avowedly changed in the same direction: "reason" was simply utilitarian logic, a (fallen) limited and makeshift tool for the temporal meanwhile, having no necessary connection to ultimate truth.[38]

Having distinguished the Christian humanism of Hooker and Milton from the beliefs and commitment of Laudians, Presbyterians, Latitudinarians, and separatists, we may now consider J. W. Allen's question concerning the deepest problem with Hooker's thought: "If the whole commonwealth doth not believe [uniformly], how can it, as a Church, have authority to bind the consciences of its believing members? How can it, even, be regarded as a Church?" (p. 198). A genuine answer, in Hooker's own terms, was attempted by Milton. Like Hooker, he tried in the face of a changing political world to revise and re-revise plans for a practical political embodiment of the natural Law so that, whatever institutional form that embodiment took or let go of, it would remain internally consistent with human nature and freedom.

Milton's attempt to realize a holy society in Britain gave form, substance, and energy to his poetry. But Milton, as well as Hooker, has been accused of time-serving or at least of finding his Christian humanistic principles inevitably warped in the process of serving a political party. William Empson, following Phelps Morand and others, remains the most well-known spokesman for the view that Milton came to conceive of God as a *dieu de parti*. Herman Rapaport has assumed, in a more recent reading, that for all of "Caroline England" Charles I must have represented "a transcendental signified, the image of transcendence, the beyond in terms of the here and now." Is it possible, as Rapaport believes, that "what Milton wishes to justify [in his regicide tracts] is the . . . removal of the transcendental imperative" from human government?[39] Did Milton's defense of the execution of Charles I mark, as Morand had felt and Walzer implied, the beginning of a subconscious abandonment of the traditional order?

What exactly was Milton's view of the relation between heavenly and earthly rule? between God, governor, and governed? And how, exactly, does Milton's position stand in relation to the seventeenth-century royalist definition of an "order of things" of the kind assumed by these literary critics to be "traditional"? Though Milton propounded a world view which is the same in its essentials as Richard Hooker's, he did not, as we have seen, begin his arguments on the same theoretical footing as did the "traditionalists" of his own day, half a century after the Tudor reign. In Milton's disputes with the royalists' international spokesman, Salmasius, the reason for the lost common ground between Hooker and his Anglican successors becomes clear. Salmasius was making Morand's mistake; he was identifying the "order" not with God's natural law and plan for human beings in society but with a royal family that had for two generations claimed a prerogative to embody that plan in themselves. By examining Milton's grounds for opposing this royal claim, we are able to discover the transmission and the radicalization of the Christian humanist vision of right reason.

MILTON opened his defense of regicide, *The Tenure of Kings and Magistrates*, by reference to human creation. "All men naturally were borne free, being the image . . . of God . . . above all the creatures, born to command and not to obey" (*CPW* 3:198). Freedom, he explains, is the theological meaning of human existence. The first man was created to be lord of himself and all lower creation, but not of other persons. The foundation of free human relationships, that is, of ethics and politics, had been treated by Milton four years earlier in his discussion of the first form which human society took, the marriage of Adam and Eve. "It is not good for man to be alone," Milton had quoted from Scripture in the *Tetrachordon*, and then had reasoned, "Hitherto all things that have bin nam'd, were approv'd of God to be very good: loneliness is the first thing which Gods eye nam'd not good" (*CPW* 2:595). Hooker treats this same passage from Genesis as an example of the way God's goodness, in accordance with natural law, directs his omnipotence: "His will had not inclined to create woman, but that he saw it could not be well if she were not created, *Non est bonum, It is not good man should be alone, Therefore let us make a helper for him*. That and nothing else is done by God, which to leave undone were not so good" (60; 1.2.3). The law of human freedom makes necessary the creation of human society. Human freedom can be exercised to the fullest extent only in relationship with other humans; for it is only an equal, as Adam discovers in book 8, whom one can fully love. Such love of human beings for one another is in fact what constitutes active worship of God, is what human freedom is for. The whole of Christian doctrine, according to Milton, is an elaboration of the ways in which human beings' two divine qualities—reason and will—are to be used. All of "Christian doctrine is comprehended under two divisions: Faith, or the knowledge of God; and Love, or the worship of God" (*De Doc., CPW* 6:128). All of a Christian's life is to be a willed act of worship (love) based upon the rational understanding of who and whose one is (faith). Human love is the right and rational exercise of human freedom.

At this start of his analysis, and for a long way into it, Milton's thinking is identical with Hooker's. To lay the foundation for his discussion of "laws politic," Hooker goes back to the Creation to establish the importance of human freedom in God's design. The "general law of nature" by which God ordains the good for every creature, consists in each performing "only that worke which is naturall unto it" (93; 1.9.1). But "amongst the creatures of this world" only the human performs voluntarily. "Man in perfection of nature being made according to the likenes of his maker resembleth him also in the maner of working; so that whatsoever we worke as men, the same we doe wittingly worke and freely, neither are we according to the maner of naturall agents any way so tyed, but that it is in our power to leave the things we do undone" (77; 1.7.2). A person who is forced to do something ceases to function as a person, and instead is acted upon as an object, "as if a winde should drive a feather in the aire."[40] For Hooker, as for Milton, freedom defines the human identity as the rational creature of this world. Since freedom can be fully exercised only in the company of equals, Hooker goes on to discuss society: "to supply those defects and imperfections, which are in us living, single, and solelie by our selves, we are naturally induced to seeke communion and fellowship with others" (96; 1.10.1).

Once the divine origin of human society has been established, Hooker and Milton admit the complication of the Fall. People, they say, are drawn to seek human society out of a natural need for fulfilment, for "becoming" by the exercising of a righteous will. Since the first misuse of human freedom, however, they also seek company for protection. Their Christian humanist version of the origin of government—unlike Rutherford's— makes sense only against a background vision of unfallen society. God's direct role in shaping society consisted of giving man woman, and thus the human race. But it was people who together, in the exercise of the natural freedom remaining to them after the Fall, shaped the first model for all subsequent government of society, the social contract. Anyone who seeks to understand the relation between Milton's political and religious views, and the life of these in his poetry, must understand the nature of his particular belief in this widely used republican doctrine. "All men naturally were borne free, being the image . . . of God . . . above all the creatures, born to command and not to obey. And, he continued, "they liv'd so. Till from the root of Adam's transgression, falling among themselves to doe wrong and violence, and foreseeing that such courses must needs tend to the destruction of them all, they agreed by common league to bind each other from mutual injury, and joyntly to defend themselves against any that gave disturbance or opposition to such agreement. Hence came Citties, Townes and Common-wealths" (*TKM, CPW* 3:198–99). Before the Fall, the right reason of individual man and woman had been sufficient to maintain society as the natural fulfilment it was meant to be. Afterward, the right reason and will remaining to an individual were not by themselves strong enough to prevent recurrences of moral "wrong" and its attendant "violence." So, for human survival, government was contracted.[41]

While the physical and moral survival of humanity depended upon the existence of governed society, the question of who should maintain order, how, and on what terms, remained a complex one; for though an externally applied order can make possible harmony, it can also threaten liberty. How was order to be achieved without violating the freedom which was the purpose for that order? The same condition for all subsequent reasoning was accepted by both Hooker and Milton: whatever the governmental system agreed upon, both the governor and the governed must be and remain free.

This condition of liberty had to be written into all stages of any definition of "power" or of "obedience." As theory was compared to history, Hooker and Milton saw that the first men had to have *agreed by common league* to bind themselves under governors, "Not to be thir Lords and Maisters . . . but, to be thir Deputies and Commissioners, to execute, by vertue of thir intrusted power, that justice which else every man by the bond of nature and of Cov'nant must have executed for himself." Milton concluded insistently: "And to him that shall consider well why among free Persons, one man by civil right should beare autority and jurisdiction over another, no other end or reason can be imaginable" (*TKM, CPW* 3:199). Hooker too, though he had been commissioned to defend a position of the monarchy, could see no way around the necessity to assert this initial source of a governor's power in the consent of those to be governed:

"without which consent there were no reason that one man should take upon him to be lord or judge over another" (99; 1.10.4).

Granting the people's consent to be the source of a governor's power, the question remained: How did the social "contract" maintain the right relationship between power, obedience, and liberty? Hooker and Milton reached the answer by hypothesizing a point in time at which the freedom of the governed was first abused. Milton continues his account of the first to whom power was entrusted: "These for a while govern'd well, and with much equity decided all things at thir own arbitrement: till the temptation of such power left absolute in thir hands, perverted them at length to injustice and partialitie." In the face of abuse, power returned by right to its source for redirection: "Then did they who now by tryal had found the danger and inconveniences of committing arbitrary power to any, invent Laws either fram'd, or consented to by all, that should confine and limit the autority of whom they chose to govern them: that so man, of whose failing they had proof, might no more rule over them, but law and reason abstracted as much as might be from personal errors and frailties" (*TKM, CPW* 3:199–200). Human reason, once fallen, cannot be depended upon to be consistently "right reason," always to see and choose what is morally best according to natural law. The closest that humans can now come to upholding what was once consistently embodied in the law of their own natures is to invent and enforce what Hooker identified as "positive law": a code of behavior that will constrict those in power to act always in accordance with "reason abstracted as much as might be from personal errors."

Hooker's description of the origin of positive law recognizes just as thoroughly the necessary separation, by law, of power from the persons who hold it. For all who possess freedom to act, whether general rulers or governors only of themselves, also possess some power: "At first when some certaine kinde of regiment was once approved, it may be that nothing was then further thought upon for the maner of governing, but all permitted unto their wisdome and discretion which were to rule, till by experience they found this for all parts verie inconvenient, so as the thing which they had devised for a remedy, did indeede but increase the soare which it should have cured. They saw that to live by one mans will became the cause of all mens misery. This constrained them to come unto lawes" (100; 1.10.5)

Up to this point the views that Hooker and Milton hold of the nature of the state are identical: the state is postlapsarian humanity's collective effort to maintain what is left of the freedom with which and for which God created it. The power to exercise freedom, which always by its nature needed *society* for its fulfilment, can in our world exist only in the *state*. The positive law is what preserves at the same time the order of the state, which is necessary to preserve liberty, and the liberty of society, the preservation of which is the purpose of order. Positive law preserves the liberty of the governor and of the governed, just as God's voluntary binding of his own will to natural law preserves his divine liberty.

Hooker and Milton further understood that a social contract under law could not in itself prescribe any one particular form of government to the exclusion of all others (*Laws* 100; 1.10.4). The only inadmissable "regiment" would be one that betrayed the natural law that had called it into being, that took away the liberty of the people; and such abuse does not inhere in any particular form—it can only be the action of some person or persons. "Monarchy unaccountable" to law was "the worst" (*TKM, CPW* 3:204) but not the only form of tyranny, as Milton remarked after his experience with Anglican and Presbyterian church government; and even while he attacked the king, it was always what he saw as the tyranny and not the kingship of the man that he condemned.

It is not until this final stage, the application of religio-political principle to a particular situation, that the two great Christian humanists diverge. Milton summarizes the theoretical basis for all practical reasoning about government thus: "While as the Magistrate was set above the people, so the Law was set above the Magistrate" (*TKM, CPW* 3:200). And both men try to apply this principle to their own situation, the rule of a monarch in a Christian nation. In book 8 of his *Laws* Hooker provides what could have been a model for Milton's thinking about the relation between the ruler's power and the law: "Where the lawe doth give Dominion, who doubteth but that the king who receiveth it must hold it of and under the lawe?" (332; 8.2.3).

But the kind of monarch and the England to be ruled had changed a great deal in the forty-two years since the end of the Tudor monarchy. And in carrying out their shared principles to answer the final question about theory and practice, it was Hooker, not Milton, who was inconsistent. Hooker's logic had led him to pose the question in book 8: "May then a bodie politique at all times withdrawe in whole or in part that influence of dominion which passeth from it, if inconvenience doth growe thereby?" The answer which survives in his (much tampered with) manuscript would have been judged by Milton as evasive, weak, and even false: "It must be presumed, that supreme governours will not in such cases oppose them selves, and be stiff in deteyning that, the use whereof is with publique detriment. But surely without their consent I see not how the body should be able by any just meanes to helpe it self, saving when

Dominion doth escheate" (339; 8.2.10).[42] Removal of such a ruler's power, Milton would have replied had Hooker been a contemporary opponent, would be in such a case the only "just means" of preserving that liberty for which, as you have rightly argued, the order of the state exists. Christian humanist political thought required, in 1649, revolutionary action.

In the *Tenure of Kings and Magistrates* Milton proves this same point from Scripture. After analyzing *Deuteronomy*, *Samuel*, *Peter*, and *Romans*, he summarizes his refutation of the argument that God wills the order of the state to be preserved at all cost: "*There is no power but of God*, saith *Paul*, *Rom.* 13. as much as to say, God put it into mans heart to find out that way at first for common peace and preservation, approving the exercise thereof. . . . It must be also understood of lawfull and just power, els we read of great power in the affaires and Kingdoms of the World permitted to the Devil." If the powers in question do not in fact "beare the sword" to liberty, "then doubtless," he reasons, "those powers . . . are no powers ordain'd of God" but "of the Devil, and by consequence to bee resisted" (*CPW* 3:209–11).

The difference between the two Christian humanists lies solely in the application of one point of principle. And we do not know what Hooker would have said on that point, had he written in 1649. But the difference between Hooker and those Anglicans who were Milton's actual contemporary adversaries is so fundamental, growing out of their different conception of the deity, that there is no point at which they touch.

TO UNDERSTAND the political views of the royalists who were Milton's contemporaries, we must go back to their way of reading the Biblical account of the Creation. As important to observe as their differing conclusions are their different methods of thinking through the problem. Generally the humanists, because of their belief in a rational and good Creator, hold as an inevitable assumption that God cannot contradict himself. Thus, they reason, there can be no contradictions within the Scripture or between that Book and the Book of Nature; and since there can be none in reality, there should be none in the thinking of human beings who were made rational in God's image. Milton states the principle in the *Christian Doctrine*, chapter II, "Of God," when in discussing God's omnipotence he first points out the reason that Aristotle seems mistaken in applying to God the term "Actus Purus": "for thus he could do nothing except what he does do, and he would do that of necessity, although in fact he is omnipotent and utterly free in his actions." Immediately following, he says: "It should be noted, however, that the power of God *is* not exerted in those kinds of things which, as the term goes, imply a contradiction: II Tim. ii. 13: *he cannot deny himself*; Tit. i. 2: *God, who does not lie*; Heb. vi. 18: *in which it was impossible for God to lie*" (*De Doc., CPW* 6:146; emphasis added. Cf. *Laws* 62; 1.2.5). God, as omnipotent, could do anything but, being reasonable and good, imposes upon himself the precondition that he will not contradict himself.

Milton's belief in God's strict truthfulness (the divine attribute that demands "consistency") underlay his argument for legalized divorce, which says that Jesus' words "what . . . God hath joyned, let no man put asunder" could not have been meant to forbid divorce since, if so interpreted, Jesus would have been contradicting both Moses and the natural law defined in God's own provision for human marriage. In its insistence that God cannot allow self-contradiction in himself or his people, Milton's argument for divorce is exactly like his argument for resisting a tyrant. Paul's saying "There is no power but of God" can only refer to "lawfull and just" powers; if unjust, "then doubtless those powers . . . are no powers ordain'd of God . . . and by consequence to be resisted." When reading Christ's words "what . . . God hath joyned," we must "consider what God hath joyn'd": "Shall wee say that God hath joyn'd error, fraud, unfitnesse, wrath . . . ? In a word, if it be unlawful for man to put asunder what God hath joyn'd, let man take heede it be not detestable to joyne that . . . which God hath put asunder" (*Tetrachordon, CPW* 2:650–51).

The logicality with which Milton and Hooker approached all specific questions of human belief and behavior, it must be realized, is a result of that first great precondition defined by the purpose of human creation, human liberty. In chapter III of the *De Doctrina*, "Of Divine Decree," Milton makes it his first task to define the relation between God's will and ours. Unlike the proponents of divine right, he reasoned "that God [could have] made no absolute decrees about anything which he left in the power of men, for men have freedom of action. . . . Here we have a rule given by God himself! He wishes us . . . always clearly to appreciate the condition upon which the decree depends" (*De Doc., CPW* 6:155). We have seen that justice is "the condition upon which the decree" of power depends, and spiritual love is the condition of marriage. For this reason, "if the decrees of God quoted above, and others of the same kind ['general decrees'] . . . were interpreted in an absolute sense without any implied conditions, God would seem to contradict himself" (*De Doc., CPW* 6:156).

But Milton's contemporary opponents were just the sort of "absolutists," in their way of reasoning as well as in their beliefs, that are here judged irrational and untrue. The royalists claimed to accept as absolutely enjoined all divine decrees read by themselves and tradition as relevant to a particular issue, even if the demands appear to be self-contradictory; they would not admit of "understood preconditions." Their method is the same as that used to argue for the divine right of presbytery or episcopacy. For Milton and Hooker, God in the world's beginning gave expression to his own goodness in his creation of natural laws which he would not afterward break: "that law eternall which God himself hath made to himselfe, and therby worketh all things" (*Laws* 62; 1.2.5). Seventeenth-century royalists argued just the opposite. Theirs was a voluntarist position, holding that God can break even his own laws because he can do anything, being God and therefore omnipotent. The problem of reconciling God's goodness and rationality to his omnipotence they held to be beyond mere human comprehension—a forbidden question. Milton's answer to the royalists was like Hooker's to the Disciplinarians: you lay down as God's primary attribute omnipotence; I lay down goodness, which demands that I reconcile all else to it.

Turning to the royalist interpretation of the Creation story in which, for them as well as for Milton, the fundamentals of human government were laid down, we are shown a basis not for a development of social contract out of natural law, but rather for patriarchalism. The theory of the original kingship of Adam had become a canon of the Stuart Church of England in 1606.[43] It is conveniently summarized in its most fully developed form in a tract written by Sir Robert Filmer (died 1653) in response to Milton's *Defence of the English People*. The *Patriarcha: A Defense of the Natural Power of Kings against the Unnatural Liberty of the People* (published 1680) teaches that when God created Adam at the same time first father and first ruler of all Creation, he instituted the divine right of hereditary kings: "creation made man Prince of his posterity. And indeed not only Adam, but the succeeding Patriarchs had, by right of fatherhood, royal authority over their children. . . . For as Adam was lord of his children, so his children under him had command over their own children, but still with a subordination to the first parent, who is lord paramount over his children's children to all generations." The identification of "all those in authority" with the "father" of the fifth commandment, a traditionally accepted analogy, was asserted to be literally true. "I see not then how the children of Adam, or of any man else, can be free from subjection to their parents. And this subordination of children is the foundation of all regal authority, by the ordination of God himself. From whence it follows, that civil power, not only in general is by Divine institution, but even the assigning of it specifically to the eldest parent" (p. 57). As Filmer points out, this view of history's beginnings does not leave "any place for such imaginary pactions between Kings and their people as many dream of."

In place of a social contract, developing at some point after the Fall, the following course of events was held to have occurred: Adam's right to lordship descended from him to the next Father/Kings, the patriarchs. After the flood, divine right reverted to Noah, who divided his kingdom among his three sons, who became the Father/Kings of new kingdoms. The sons and nephews of Noah were scattered abroad after the confusion of Babel and headed seventy-two new kingdoms, each with its own language. But "even in the confusion God was careful to preserve the fatherly authority by distributing the diversity of languages according to the diversity of families" (p. 58). The lines of royal descent are traced through Biblical and other historical figures to reach the kingdom of England in the person of her rightful king, Charles Stuart. This view gives a somewhat literal basis for the term "parricides" as it was applied by the royalists to the king's executioners, even though, as Filmer acknowledges, "After a few descents [from Adam], when the true fatherhood itself was extinct, and only the right of the Father descended to the true heir, then the title of Prince or King was more significant to express the power" (p. 61).

The most eminent man to cry "parricide," and the one whose accusations Milton sacrificed his eyesight to answer, was the French scholar Salmasius, who affirmed in the opening chapter of his *Defensio Regia* (1649) that kingship "began with the first man and with the new-born sun."[44] This was true because the first man was both king and father: "we know that the great race of off-spring, whether descended directly from this first father, or descended from him by succession during his life, always held respect for him as their king, as the first author of their race." Adam lived for 930 years, long enough to see the seven or eight descents from himself which made up the first kingdom.[45] After Adam's death, Salmasius' account continues: "we see that by [the example and authority of] this original of sovereigns and of men have been chosen since other kings, who though they were neither of the immediate family nor of the parentage of these first; were ordained nevertheless for the government of the people, who receive them as their fathers, and who accordingly have been called the fathers of their countries." This royalist concept of a Father/King, moreover, was made the more absolute by its implied reference to a particularly powerful sort of father, the paterfamilias of ancient Roman law. Such an implication lies behind Salmasius' claim that God forbids the opposition of even a tyrant. "And just as natural fathers, Kings who hold the place of fathers, are not always of the same temperament or inclination. There are among them some of a sweeter humor, more indulgent, more patient; others more harsh, severe, hard, sometimes even cruel. But the son who killed his father even though he had been rude and harsh, would nonetheless deserve the punishment of a parricide: and a subject is likewise nonetheless blameable for the crime which kills a king, that is to say, the common father of a country, even though he be proud, capricious, unjust, cruel, and though he command with tyranny" (p. 19).

Milton never considered the patriarchalists' literal interpretation of Adam's absolute kingship to be worthy of lengthy refutation. As the first-born human being, Adam was king of lower creation, but not of other human beings; in him "*all* men were naturally borne free . . . born to command." But Milton took care to point out what he considered a fallacious pattern of thought informing the whole royalist position. Salmasius was claiming to be literally true, he asserted, a thing discoverable not by natural observation or any literal statement in Scripture nor by any logical deduction from such a statement, but only by means of an unliteral, and, indeed, mixed metaphor. Salmasius was using a "forced comparison of a kingdom with a family to allow an analogy of a king to a family head" (*A Defence, CPW* 4, pt. 1:428).

The process of thinking about such issues in analogies was by Milton's time an old and traditionally accepted one, based upon a belief in correspondences among the parts of an hierarchical creation, the "corresponding planes," Tillyard called them,[46] of the great chain of being. That Milton, like Hooker, conceived of creation as a hierarchy of being descending like a vertical chain from God, in which each link but the first shares some of its attributes with the link above it, is clear from all of his writings and is uncontested. However, literary critics who draw a parallel between God and the King, on the one hand, and Satan and the Puritans, on the other, claim that as a result of his involvement in the "Great Rebellion" Milton subconsciously abandoned his professed belief. The moral corollary to the chain's existence was the duty of every creature to maintain its place in the chain—as Hooker phrased it, to perform "only that worke which is naturall unto it" (93; 1.9.1). That this corollary must have ruled out political revolution for a true believer in the chain is the supposition of Walzer, Morand, and Empson *and* of the seventeenth-century royalists (as well as of standard Tudor propagandists). Yet, as Milton would have said, such a supposition could be based not on any reasonably held belief in the chain, but only on mistaken interpretations of correspondences between the links, on false and heretical analogies which, rightly understood, contradict the essence of the chain whose workings they seek to interpret.

To see more fully what Milton was calling "forced comparisons" we can look at a few more samples drawn from typical royalist thought. First we should be aware of the grand analogy which allows the others. It is set out by Robert Weldon, who, in *The Doctrine of the Scriptures Concerning the*

Originals of Dominion (1648), asserts that God in creating this world to be a microcosm of the universe made Adam, as first human king, to represent him as a ruler to be obeyed and glorified: "GOD had built the world in such *absolute sort*, that there was no *degree* of *possible perfection* wanting to the *beauty* of the *Universe*, but it had a *seat* in some *creature* or other; save only, that to make the *Earth* a *resemblance* of *Heaven*. . . . there was not a *creature* to *represent him*, for the *managing* of the earth" (pp. 2–3).

Salmasius makes the same claim: "If we lift up our eyes to the sovereign patron of all things, we will find that this fashion of commanding [absolute monarchy] is copied from that of God, who is the sole Sovereign of the world as he is therein the sole maker of it" (p. 136). But, as Milton reasoned, it is not logical to claim the same sovereignty for a creature that exists in the Creator by virtue of his power to create. Furthermore, we know from Scripture that God did not choose to glorify himself in one man only, but in every man created in his image. Absolute sovereignty could be given by a just God only to one absolutely worthy of it, to one perfect; and God would not sacrifice the essential justice which defines the natural hierarchy in order to gain an empty imitation of it in the form of superficial correspondences. "As to your saying it [monarchy] was 'patterned on the example of one God,' who, in fact," he demanded, "is worthy of holding on earth power like that of God but some person who far surpasses all others and even resembles God in goodness and wisdom? The only such person, as I believe, is the son of God whose coming we look for" (*A Defence, CPW* 4, pt. 1:427–28). Milton further chided Salmasius for failing to be a true protestant in civil as well as ecclesiastical affairs. Referring to Salmasius' attacks on the papacy, which had gained him his international scholarly reputation, Milton charged: "You call the greatest heresy that by which a single man [the pope] is thought to sit in Christ's place, for there are here the two marks of Antichrist: spiritual infallibility and temporal omnipotence. . . . Surely kings are not infallible? Why then should they be omnipotent? Or if they were, why should they be less ruinous to civil life than the pope to spiritual? . . . [God] does not enjoin such patience in civil affairs that the state should put up with the cruelest of tyrants while the church should not" (*A Defence, CPW* 4, pt. 1:398). Salmasius' own arguments, Milton says, lead to revolution: "The people furthermore do with God's approval judge their guilty rulers, for He conferred this office on his chosen ones when, in Psalm 149, he says that those who sing the praises of Christ their king shall cast in chains the kings of the gentiles, all of whom the Gospel terms tyrants, and apply the letter of the law to those who boast of their freedom from all statutes and laws" (*A Defence, CPW* 4, pt. 1:359).

The basic mistake in reasoning which permitted the false analogy between a human king or pope and the ruler of the universe occurred when things that bore only a partial resemblance to one another were assumed to be alike in their essences. Such a mistake in reasoning, especially if the motives of the reasoner were suspect, would itself have been reprehensible misuse of a divine faculty; but when it was applied to interpreting the chain of being, it came close to blasphemy. For by it, a man claimed absurdly to break the chain of being itself, to act as only one with divine perfection could, to think himself God. The literal truth of the human position on the chain, that is, dependency from and upon God, makes the absolute sovereignty of any human being over another impossible.

It is a literal explanation of the chain of being, not a loose metaphor about deity, man, and beast, that we read in Milton's argument against a "monarchy unaccountable": "And surely no Christian Prince, not drunk with high mind, and prouder then those Pagan *Caesars* that deifi'd themselves, would arrogate so unreasonably above human condition, or derogate so basely from a whole Nation of men his Brethren, as if for him only subsisting, and to serve his glory; valuing them in comparison of his owne brute will and pleasure, no more then so many beasts . . . among whom there might be found so many thousand Men for wisdom, vertue, nobleness of mind . . . farr above him" (*TKM, CPW* 3:204–05). Only such men in a true natural hierarchy deserve to govern; and the virtue of such men is their governing by the wisdom of the law. One who claims on the other hand to rule absolutely, above the law, steps violently out of his human link in the chain; in seeking to rise unnaturally he can only fall. By claiming for himself divine right, he abuses his power to reason and will—that spark of divinity which was truly in him—and retains only the power of force which belongs by nature to the beasts. "For if they may refuse to give account . . . we hold then our lives and estates, by the tenure of his meer grace and mercy, as from a God, not a mortal Magistrate" (*TKM, CPW* 3:204)—*as* from a God, but in fact from one without divine power, and thus "he that bids a man reigne over him above Law, may bid as well a savage Beast" (*TKM, CPW* 3:206).

When Weldon tried to show that the revolutionaries sought to break the chain of being, he set up a true premise which he then ignored to reach his conclusion: "of *Created Things* there can be but one Original; and the *reasonable Creature* must needs acknowledge the original of his *Power* to be from him, from whom he had the *Original* of his Being."[47] So much is common ground with Milton. But whereas Weldon went on to claim that God by special "Dispensation" to Adam imparted his own power of rule to an absolute monarch, Milton claimed of that original power a second precondition, justice. And "that a master superior to the law should be endured by all men . . . was never commanded by any law, nor could it be, for a law which overthrows all laws cannot itself be law" (*A Defence, CPW* 4, pt. 1:401). The great chain of being was itself the foremost law of nature; and a king who claimed to rule above the law was seeking to break the chain.

The strength of his belief in the chain of being led Milton finally to feel that monarchy of any kind is not truly the most desirable form of government a people can choose, even though we find him drawn to Spenser's wish for a Gloriana in his admiration for that rare phenomenon, the accountable monarchy of a good ruler such as Queen Christina's in Sweden, which he felt could provide "well-nigh divine" leadership (*Second Defence, CPW* 4, pt. 1:604). In his reading of Old Testament history, Milton saw that God had been angry with the Jews when they first asked for a king such as the other nations had.[48] Kingship, God had warned his people through his prophet Samuel, lends itself too readily to a confusion in the minds of both people and king of the merely human magistrate with the divine majesty of God. Such, he felt, had certainly happened in England under Charles; and now, with the revolution, "as God was heretofore angry with the Jews who rejected him and his forme of Government to choose a King, so . . . he will bless us . . . who reject a King to make him onely our leader and supreme governour in the conformity as neer as may be of his ancient [Jewish republican] government" (*TKM, CPW* 3:236).[49]

The first mistake of traditional analogies lay in their joining unlikes, in comparing natural bonds with a civil covenant. Now, "covnants are ever made according to the present state of persons and of things; and have ever the more general laws of nature and of reason included in them, though not express'd" (*TKM, CPW* 3:232); and when they cease to fulfill the purpose for which they were made, they can and should be broken. The state of England in 1649 was such that the "person," Charles Stuart, had failed to be the "thing," king, to fulfil the terms of the office of kingship, and so caused the covenanters, the people, to withdraw their subjectship. This is the meaning of a civil relationship: "We know that the King and Subject are relatives, and relatives have no longer being than in the relation; the relation between King and Subject can be no other than regal authority and subjection. Hence . . . if the Subject who is one relative, take away the relation, of force he takes away also the other relative" (*TKM, CPW* 3:229–30). The people, having chosen to defend themselves against Charles's armies, took away their subjectship; and Charles, having made war on his own people, was no longer their king, but a private person and enemy of the state. Since God gave to the people the source of the covenant's power, they can withdraw their power at will: "then may the people as oft they shall judge it for the best, either choose him [king or magistrate] or reject him, retaine him or depose him though no Tyrant, meerly by the liberty and right of free born Men, to be govern'd as seems to them best" (*TKM, CPW* 3:206). And Milton felt that it would be wise to do away with the dangerous form of monarchy now and exercise as directly as possible "that power, which is the root and sourse of all liberty, to dispose and *oeconomize* in the Land which God hath giv'n them, as Maisters of Family in thir own house and free inheritance" (*TKM, CPW* 3:237).

The second and more serious mistake of the royalists was in their trusting to argument by analogy at all. For even if the king-subject relationship had been a natural one like that between father and son, or even God and universe, its terms would have to have had "ever the more general laws of nature and of reason included in them." Those "more general laws of nature and of reason" are characterized by Hooker as "the rule of voluntary agents on earth," the activation in this world of "God's own wisdom." Hooker believed it necessary always to hold in mind that God's law is a unity and to be conscious, in any disputed decision, of the general laws that frame the situation: "The sentences which reason giveth are some more some less general, before it come to define in particular actions what is good." Because the law is a whole, "wisedome . . . groundeth her lawes upon an infallible rule of comparison." We are not free to make loose analogies when wisdom calls for literal comparison; rather, "the greater good is to be chosen before the lesse" (85; 1.8.5).

What is to happen when a specific case turns out to conflict with a greater good? According to Hooker, "momentarie benefites, when the hurt which they drawe after them is unspeakable, are not at all to be respected" (85; 1.8.5). Milton applied this concept to England's father-king: "We endure a father though he be harsh and strict . . . but we do not endure even a father who is tyrannical. If a father kill a son he shall pay with his life: shall not then a king too be subject to this same most just of laws if he has destroyed the people [by making civil war against them] who are his sons?" (*A Defence, CPW* 4, pt. 1:327). Corresponding to the chain of being, there exists a hierarchy of natural law: "Thou shall not kill" is a higher law than "Honor thy father" because it is a condition of all human relations, including that of father and son. Thus, Samuel slew the tyrant Agag, and "mark the reason. *As thy Sword hath made women childless*; a cause that by the sentence of Law it self nullifies all relations. And as the Law is between Brother and Brother, Father and Son, Maister and Servant, wherfore not between King or rather Tyrant and People?" (*TKM,*

CPW 3:215). Likewise because of the hierachy inhering natural law, an *unjustified* rebellion can properly be given the metaphorical term "parricide" since the comparison is in this case valid. So "Ishmael the slayer of Gedaliah the governor was, you say, called parricide by Jerome, and rightly so; for with no justification he slew the governor of Judea and a good man" (*A Defence, CPW* 4, pt. 1:395). God has so willed it that he, himself, must be worthy of his "God-ship" to merit the service of free and moral members of the universe; otherwise, the Christian faith would be no different from the "barbarism" reported of the American Indians, who "worship as gods malevolent demons whom they cannot exorcise" (*Second Defense, CPW* 4, pt. 1:551). According to Milton's Christian humanist view, "it was not" even "permissible and good to put a tyrant to death because God commanded it, but rather God" could only have "commanded it because it was permissible and good" (*A Defence, CPW* 4, pt. 1:407). We may contrast the Anglican royalist Jeremy Taylor's voluntarist view that "whatsoever [God] wills . . . is therefore just [simply] because he wills" it, and the Presbyterian revolutionary Samuel Rutherford's same voluntarist view that things "are just and good because God willeth them . . . and God doth not will things because they are good and just."[50] The difference from the Anglican Hooker and the Puritan Milton is striking and real. In the same vein, we should notice that the depth of Milton's faith in right reason made it impossible for him to judge the rightness of his cause according to its ability to succeed: "a cause is neither proved good by success, nor shown to be evil. We insist, not that our cause be judged by the outcome, but that the outcome be judged by the cause" (*Second Defence, CPW* 4, pt. 1:652; cf. *Eikonoklastes, CPW* 3:599).

The law that for Milton and Hooker defined the relationship between governor and governed was reflected in positive laws and was itself part of the reasoned, ordering principle of the universe, which neither God nor any human creature could overrule. "Let every soul be subject to the higher powers," royalists quoted. Milton replied: "the law is always considered the highest and ultimate power" (*A Defence, CPW* 4, pt. 1:383)—for subject, king, and God.

Some recent interesting political approaches to Milton have been handicapped by a failure to deal with the history and radicalization of Christian humanist *recta ratio*. Christopher Kendrick expresses surprise upon discovering that Milton's God (*PL* 2.87–119) "submits his own activity, which must on any orthodox view justify *itself,*" to what Kendrick can only see as "an external imperative." Not having taken into account the powerful role that natural law—as God's own *ratio*—has exercised in Christian imaginations, he thinks that that law must be "fate" and concludes: "there are few moments, I think, in which the poem is so embarrassing . . . to all Christian theology." Kendrick himself is working under the constraints of a theory determined to find "a secret fissure within Protestant theology" and a God inevitably conceived "in terms of unalloyed willful power"— Walzer's "arbitrary sovereign of the universe."[51] The deployment of such a severely oversimplified historical Christian theology in a treatment of Milton seems hard to justify, especially after the publication of *Milton's Good God*, in which Dennis Danielson successfully addresses the danger of what he calls "theoretical reductionism."[52] Such reductionism has more than once stopped literary critics from seeing that—far from using literary skills, consciously or unconsciously, either to mirror or to gloss over theological problems—Milton avails himself of specifically literary means to work toward their solutions.

Milton takes this approach to problems in political (and sociological) theory as well as to problems in theology. Jameson suggests that *Paradise Lost* should be ideally suited for testing Pierre Macherey's theory of literary production (which says that artistic representation unmasks the structural incoherence of an ideology it presupposes) because in his epic Milton "explicitly sets out to celebrate, dramatize and justify a preexisting ideology, namely that of Providence."[53] However, the point Danielson makes about theological reductionism needs to be made about reductionism in political theory as well. Far from using literary means to mirror or "dramatize and [thereby] justify" a doctrine or theoretical construct (named "Providence" by Jameson, conflated with "Predestination" by Kendrick, and roughly paralleled by "historical determinism" in Marxism), Milton uses literary means to capture, work through, and understand the same human experiences—"the ways of God to man"—that have been addressed less effectively by (competing) ideologies.[54] Thus, even if one's own goal is theoretical system building rather than literary readings, it should be worthwhile to recognize that no system involving Milton— however internally interesting—will have the value it might have if it were to read the poetry closely and in context.

TWO

Satan and King Charles: Milton's Royal Portraits

MILTON's conception in *Paradise Lost* of the fall of Lucifer has always been recognized as political in nature. Because of the poet's twenty years' service to the English revolutionary cause, his readers have sought to understand what relation Milton saw between human and demonic revolution and rule. Romantic attempts to link his God with Charles I as monarchs and Satan with Cromwell and Milton as revolutionaries[1] are widely considered to have been mistaken, although Christopher Kendrick's recent effort to "read the epic Satan as the symbolic expression or fulfillment of Milton's revolutionary desire," his "political libido," assumes an "undoubtedly" established "analogy between God's monarchy and the [Stuart] absolutist monarchy."[2] Merritt Hughes and Stevie Davies have pointed out the many allusions in the poem that associate Satan, not with revolutionaries, but with the notorious tyrannical rulers of human history.[3] Hughes was wary of comparing King Charles with Satan because of the danger of turning *Paradise Lost* into a roman à clef. Although *Paradise Lost* is not a political allegory, Charles was the tyrant with whose ways Milton was most familiar, whose actions and motivations he had devoted crucial years to depicting and analyzing.

It is important to realize the extent to which the King Charles of the prose pamphlets was Milton's own literary creation. The tract in which Milton began Charles's character development in a sustained way is *Eikonoklastes*.[4] It was his answer to the royalist *Eikon Basilike*, a publication appearing shortly after Charles's execution that attempted to picture him as a Christlike martyr-king. Concerned with counteracting the great popular impact of the *Eikon*, Milton recognized that what moved the people in the royalist work was not any power of logical argument or historical accuracy but a fictional character with an emotional rhetorical appeal. He suggests this when he pauses at one point in *Eikonoklastes* to respond to the *Eikon's* style: "The Simily wherwith he begins I was about to have found fault with, as in a garb somwhat more Poetical than for a Statist: but meeting with many straines of like dress in other of his Essaies, and hearing him reported a more diligent reader of Poets, than of Politicians, I begun to think that the whole Book might perhaps be intended a peece of Poetrie. The words are good, the fiction smooth and cleanly" (*CPW* 3:406). To answer the *Eikon's* interpretation of the king's role in the civil war, Milton drew his own character study of the king, based on this historical plot—not as a Christian martyr, but as a tyrant and usurper of divine authority. This task required that, unlike *Eikon Alethine*, the other well-known parliamentary answer to the King's Book,[5] Milton's reply regard Charles as the *Eikon's* real author and that, unlike the parliamentary historians from whom he drew his factual information, he assign full responsibility for all the royalist actions to the king himself.

George W. Whiting notices the different stress in the treatments by Milton and the parliamentary historian Thomas May of responsibility for the events of the war. Typical are the contrasting discussions of the royalist plot to free the Earl of Strafford, condemned by Parliament for treason, from the Tower of London and then to invade England with a French and Irish army. Whereas May's *History* goes at length into the roles of all the conspirators, Milton's treats the plot as the king's. The king, he says, was "soon after found to have the chief hand in a most detested conspiracy against the Parlament and Kingdom . . . that his intention was to rescue the Earle of *Strafford*, by seizing on the Towre of *London*." Compare May's description, which begins in the passive voice—"For to prevent the Earle of *Straffords* death, an escape for him out of the Tower was contrived. To further which . . . a great conspiracy was entred into by many Gentlemen of ranke and quality"—and which goes at length into all the conspirators' roles, saying of the king only that he was "privy to this conspiracy," not that he directed it. May was writing a general history; Milton was exposing a central character.[6] Thus, Milton explains in his Preface, "what is properly his own guilt, not imputed any more to his evil Counsellors, (a Ceremony us'd longer by the Parlament then he himself desir'd) shall be laid heer without circumlocutions at his own dore" (*CPW* 3:341).

Eikonoklastes, Milton's "Idol-breaker," is a study of the true nature of a character already, in Milton's view, fictionalized, either by the king himself or by a royalist author, for the purpose of carrying on a real tyranny in life.

But to tackle the problem in this way was to write another fiction; not, to be sure, to tell a lie—the "plot" in each account was literally true—but to reveal the leading character's nature in a depth that could be known only by his creator. Because Milton's treatment of Charles as a fictional character originates in the confines of pamphlet debates that require answering one's opponent point by point, it occurs in pieces as a sketch containing some direct dramatization and considerable abstract analysis. Though the character study is not sustainedly worked out, it achieves moments of depth, very valuable as answers to what was for Milton, if not for all of his political colleagues, a question at the core of the controversies: Who is a tyrant? What motivates him? confuses him? perverts him? strengthens him? gives him his power over others? Developed in *Eikonoklastes*, the sketch that answers these questions is extended in Milton's *Defences of the English People*, and these prose works provide an illuminating gloss on the role of Satan and of tyranny in Milton's poem.

The fundamental similarity between Charles and Satan can be understood by analyzing their claims to divine right to power. Whereas seventeenth-century royalists argued that the English king was a representative of God's power, Milton argued that the man Charles was, like Satan, a usurper of that power. The comparison occurs, for example, when Milton criticizes Charles's violations of religious liberty: "He [King Charles] calls the conscience *Gods sovrantie*, why then doth he contest with God about that supreme title? . . . usurping over spiritual things, as *Lucifer* beyond his sphere" (*Eikonoklastes*, *CPW* 3:501–02). Though Charles had not possessed the full strength of Satan, he had been, in Milton's view, a servant of the archrebel. When a state is governed tyrannically, "those in authority are both human and fiendish. . . . Thus, the fiend is termed prince of this world; and in Revelation 13 the Dragon gave the beast his own dominion and throne and mighty power" (*A Defence*, *CPW* 4, pt. 1:384). Although the beast was not equal to the Dragon in magnitude or complexity, the imitator shared traits with his model; and a tyrant like Charles was an imitator and servant of the devil. Accordingly, we should not be surprised to find parallels between Milton's prose treatment of Charles and his poetic portrait of Satan. Just as Milton turned the literal devil into a literary character, so also did he subject the historical king to the power of his artist's imagination. An understanding of the parallels between the tyrants of prose and poetry can sharpen our perception of the appropriateness of certain details in the poem—in imagery and in characterization—and it can further illuminate Milton's thematic conception of true political liberty in the archetypal revolutions that the poem dramatizes.

IN HIS portraits of Satan and Charles, Milton uses imagery to reveal and comment on aspects of their characters. One such image, possessing complex and powerful associations for the character of a ruler, is the sun. The sun has a specific and controversial symbolism in seventeenth-century political writing. Believers in the divine right of kings argued by analogy from the chain of being that, as one God rules absolutely over heaven, one father over a family, and one sun over the planets, so one king should rule absolutely over England. Milton, however, explaining that the royalists were employing a false analogy, argued from the same chain of being, but by a more complex logic: The right to exercise power belongs to those whom nature has given power to exercise. God, since he created and sustains the universe, naturally has power over it; the sun by its nature imparts life-giving influence on the earth and so naturally controls her fertility; nature has given a father power to beget sons. But no one man can create or has been created as essential to the life of all other men; and a king does not have the power to create his subjects. In fact, just the opposite occurs. The people, by virtue of the power of self-government in creatures made rational in God's image, together create a governor whose power is lent him as custodian of the law, not inherent in his person or absolute, a governor who is the people's servant and natural inferior— natural according to the true operation of the chain of being.

When the king claimed divine right, he was, in Milton's view, claiming absurdly to break the chain of being itself, to act as only one with divine perfection could, to think himself God. Thus, when the *Eikon Basilike* had Charles compare his royal prerogative to the sun's light, Milton drew the analogy out ad absurdum to point out the overwhelming egotism of the man whose reasoning about his prerogative could be led so far astray by his desire for power. If Charles were, as the *Eikon* claimed, the sun and father and if Parliament his co-ruler, were the earth receiving his influence, then this mixture of metaphors would have to be reconciled with Parliament's genuine role as the king's mother, since the people, whom she represents, out of their own inherent power of self-government create the king: "And if it hath bin anciently interpreted the presaging signe of a future Tyrant, but to dream of copulation with his Mother, what can it be less than actual Tyranny to affirme waking, that the Parlament, which is his Mother, can neither conceive or bring forth *any autoritative Act* without his Masculine coition: Nay that his reason is as Celestial and life-giving to the Parlament, as the Suns influence is to the Earth: What other notions but these, or such like, could swell up *Caligula* to think himself a God" (*CPW* 3:467).

In response to the king's attempted use of the royalist sun symbol to claim that there will follow for the people "*much horror and bad influence after his* [own] *eclipse*," Milton assigns the sun a different meaning, one that removes from Charles's character a false symbolic prop and that judges him: "He speaks his wishes: But they who by weighing prudently things past, foresee things to come, the best Divination, may hope rather all good success and happiness by removing that darkness which the mistie cloud of his prerogative made between us and a peacefull Reformation, which is our true Sun light, and not he, though he would be tak'n for our sun it self" (*CPW* 3:455). And when the *Eikon*'s Charles envisions his future glory, foreseeing "*much honour and reputation that like the Sun shall rise and recover it self to such a Splendour*," Milton insists that "those *black vailes* of his own misdeeds" will "keep *his face from shining*" (*CPW* 3:502).

Holding in mind Milton's prose use of the sun's political significance to reveal the tyrannical character of Charles, his mania for power, and his warped analogical reasoning, we may turn to book 1 of *Paradise Lost*, where the fallen Satan is described as an eclipsed sun in a simile that refers us to the fate of earthly rulers. Satan stands before his troops, "As when the Sun . . . from behind the Moon / In dim Eclipse disastrous twilight sheds / On half the Nations, and with fear of change / Perplexes Monarchs" (594–99). Charles II's censor, presumably reading the poem with the royalist king/sun symbolism in mind, is said to have taken these lines as a threat to the new king, veiled in the traditional interpretation of an eclipse by monarchs who think of themselves as ruling on earth as the sun rules the heavens. However, the political references to the sun that Milton provides in the poem actually develop a concept of government's relation to the chain of being that is more literal and logical than the simple correspondence assumed by seventeenth-century royalists and by Milton's Charles and his Satan. In book 2, lines 488–95, Satan is again compared to the sun, this time the setting sun, which gives temporary, but "false presumptuous hope" (521). In book 3, after Satan has confirmed his intention never to submit to the rule of God, Milton abandons the traditional analogy and describes him as a spot or blemish on the surface of the literal sun (588–90). Thus, in the first three books, Milton leads us away from a false analogy between the physical power of the sun and the governing power of a rational creature. A false ruler, he implies, can be compared (like the Charles of *Eikonoklastes*) to a sun that fails to shine with the light given it. But a true ruler is genuinely comparable to the shining sun only if he does not claim absolute power (the claim of "prerogative" is what darkens the sun)—just as the literal sun has no absolute power over earth apart from its physical light. The ruler's "light," like the sun's, comes from God, whose vehicle he is; and the light originates not in the personal character of the ruler but in God's law and spirit (in "a peacefull Reformation"). Once we are aware of the use Milton made of the controversial sun symbolism in his prose sketch of Charles, we can recognize an invitation from the poet for us to compare the fallen Satan's and the unfallen Adam's addresses to the sun in books 4 and 5.

As Lucifer in heaven, while he kept God's law, Satan had shone as the brightest star, crowned with "surpassing Glory." When he defied divine law, which his personal abilities were created to execute, and claimed a right to "sole Dominion," Satan removed the ground for a genuine sun/ruler analogy and substituted instead Charles's royalist basis for comparison, in which the ruler is like a god. In his confession of despair at the beginning of book 4, Satan cannot remove the royalist analogy from his tortured mind, even when he is forced by his defeat to recognize that he himself can no longer stand as the object of even this comparison:

> O thou that with surpassing Glory crown'd,
> Look'st from thy sole Dominion like the God
> Of this new World; at whose sight all the Stars
> Hide thir diminisht heads . . .
>   . . . I hate thy beams
> That bring to my remembrance from what state
> I fell. . . .   (32–39)

By contrast, instead of attributing absolute power to the sun in its realm, "like the God" in his, and then claiming an analogous power for his human rule over earth, Adam's right reasoning about his own role as God's creature leads him to recognize the sun for what it literally is: the creation of a divine ruler, the vehicle for light created and given by God, who, as source of all, is the only holder of "sole Dominion":

> Thou Sun, of this great World both Eye and Soul,
> Acknowledge him thy Greater, sound his praise
> In thy eternal course, both when thou climb'st,
> And when high Noon hast gain'd, and when thou fall'st.
>   . . . resound
> His praise, who out of Darkness call'd up Light.   (5.171–79)

In this passage Adam's words "Acknowledge him thy Greater . . . when thou climb'st" as well as "when thou fall'st" may be read as the poem's actual political admonition, based on a true analogy between the sun and a human ruler. It is a comparison that fundamentally undermines, as the censor feared, the Stuart claim to rule by denying the validity of the doctrine of the divine right of kings.

Turning from metaphor to characterization, we may inquire what Milton saw in the makeup of a ruler that leads the ruler to claim the right to absolute power. In the portraits of both Charles and Satan, we may discover behind the false idea of a governor a corrupted idea of heroism. The power gotten by such a hero, who seeks personal glory rather than service to God, is employed, once it has been gained, in a wrong sort of rule over others. Four prose passages in which Milton exposes the false heroism of King Charles serve as commentary on this issue in *Paradise Lost*, where Satan's false heroism, rightly understood, is, like Charles's, criminality. What gives the appearance of courage is really a "hardened heart"; it is the despair resulting from a total commitment to ambition, from a perversion of God-given strength to self-service. Although deeds of great daring are undertaken, ambition and then despair, never courage, overcome the fear attending risk. The resulting appearance of heroism, however, can easily deceive an unwary judge of character, as in book 1 of *Paradise Lost*.

There, recognizing that Satan after his fall from heaven is in a state of spiritual death (see Milton's definition in the *Christian Doctrine*, *CPW* 4:393–98, of the first two degrees of death), we can sharpen our awareness of Satan's spiritual state by comparing his rousing of his troops, often admired by readers of *Paradise Lost*, with the following discussion of Charles's behavior, also admired, at his trial and execution. For both Satan and Charles, when they faced judgment and death at the hands of their enemies, a true courage should result in confession and repentance. What Milton portrays in each, however, is a false courage which results in the donning of a self-righteous dramatic mask. Milton interprets the psychology of the king's fake courage in this passage from *A Defence*: "Do not pay too much heed to that presence of mind so often manifested by the commonest criminals at their death; frequently desperation or a hardened heart gives, like a mask, an appearance of courage, as dullness does of peace. In death as in life, even the worst of men wish to seem good, fearless, innocent, or even holy, and, in the very hour of execution for their crimes, they will, for the last time, display as showily as possible their fraudulent pretense, and, like the most tasteless of writers or actors, strive madly for applause as the curtain falls" (*CPW* 4, pt. 1:508).[7]

Like this disguised desperation at judgment, such criminals' heroic mask in battle has been projected not by a true courage ready for self-sacrifice but by ambition's deluded hopes for personal glory. With this distinction between the appearance and the reality in mind, recall the "acts of oblivion" of God in the war in heaven by which feats of war performed by the rebel angels were not recorded; then consider the explanation that such acts were done "to give the World an example, that glorious deeds don to ambitious ends, find reward answerable, not to their outward seeming, but to thir inward ambition." The latter judgment refers actually to the case of the Hothams (father and son), who, under great risk, betrayed the parliamentary cause to the king and were caught and executed by Parliament for treason (*Eikonoklastes, CPW* 3:429–30). But it applies readily to the ambitious angels; and in fact the issue comes full circle as the poem, speaking of Satan's bravery, refers us back to the world of men:

> for neither do the Spirits damn'd
> Lose all thir virtue; lest bad men should boast
> Their specious deeds on earth, which glory excites,
> Or close ambition varnisht o'er with zeal.   (2.482–85)

The sin-based courage that supplies the strength for the aspiring tyrant's "specious deeds" in battle has a counterpart in his behavior in defeat. The coin of false heroism that has on the one side the indomitable warrior has on its other side the equally dangerous power-seeking image of the great sufferer. "The mind and spirit remains / Invincible" (1.139–40) was Beelzebub's response to Satan's vaunt "What though the field be lost? / All is not lost: the unconquerable Will, / And study of revenge, immortal hate,/ And courage never to submit or yield" (1.105–08). The same had been boasted by the English royalists of their leader: "*he had a soule invincible.*" Milton retorted: "*But he had a soule invincible.* What praise is that? The stomach of a Child is ofttimes invincible to all correction. The unteachable man hath a soule to all reason and good advice invincible; and he who is intractable, he whom nothing can perswade, may boast himself invincible; whenas in some things to be overcome is more honest and laudable then to conquer" (*Eikonoklastes, CPW* 3:434). Charles was, according to Milton's portrait, the "unteachable man" and Satan the unteachable angel (see *Paradise Lost* 2.9). And when the king's defenders resorted to the other side of their hero's image to claim tragic stature for him, saying, "*A glorious King he would* be, though *by his sufferings*" (*Eikonoklastes, CPW* 3:435), Milton offered a counterinterpretation of Charles's sufferings, which applies equally to Satan, who claims his right to rule by his willingness to endure the "Greatest share / Of endless pain" (2.29–30) and who must win "the high repute" "through hazard huge" (2.472–73). The genuine glory of a tragic sacrifice, Milton argued against such claims, "can never be put to him whose sufferings are his own doings" (*Eikonoklastes, CPW* 3:435).

The point becomes even clearer when we see how each tyrant tries to use his own suffering, the very punishment for his crimes, as proof not only of greatness but of innocence. When Charles disclaimed guilt for the devastation wrought by the Irish rebellion "because *he hath the greatest share of loss and dishonour by what is committed*," Milton treated that fact as an irony of the plot. Far from proving Charles's innocence, it proved only this about the nature of evil—that it cannot stop, though it knows it will suffer: "Who is there that offends God or his Neighbour, on whom the greatest share of loss and dishonour lights not in the end? But in the act of doing evil, men use not to consider the event of thir evil doing: or if they doe, have then no power to curb the sway of thir own wickedness. So that the greatest share of loss and dishonour to happ'n upon themselves, is no argument that they were not guilty" (*Eikonoklastes, CPW* 3:478). The same evaluation of the criminal's suffering underlies Gabriel's answer to Satan at the end of book 4, when the fallen angel, flaunting his suffering in an effort to belittle the "inexperience" of the loyal host, claims by having hazarded all, through ways of danger, to have been "a faithful leader":

> O sacred name of faithfulness profan'd!
> Faithful to whom? to thy rebellious crew?
> Army of Fiends, fit body to fit head;
> Was this your discipline and faith ingag'd,
> Your military obedience, to dissolve
> Allegiance to th' acknowledg'd Power supreme?   (4.951–56)

For a historical case parallel to Charles's, Milton chose that, which he and other revolutionaries often repeated, of Pharoah, who for the purported welfare of his people persecuted the Israelites, but in the end incurred for his people and himself the greatest suffering (*Eikonoklastes, CPW* 3:516). In the language of Scripture, Milton explained the psychology of sin: "But whom God hard'ns, them also he blinds." That Satan, like Charles, calls down on himself his own suffering is implied by the simile in book 1 describing the fallen legions scattered on the burning lake, like sedge

> Afloat, when with fierce Winds *Orion* arm'd
> Hath vext the Red-Sea Coast, whose waves o'erthrew

> *Busiris* and his *Memphian* Chivalry,
> While with perfidious hatred they pursu'd
> The Sojourners of *Goshen*, who beheld
> From the safe shore thir floating Carcasses
> And broken Chariot Wheels; so thick bestrown
> Abject and lost lay these. (1.305–12)

Seen with the eyes of truth, Satan and the fallen angels are abject and lost; but, guided by perfidious hatred of that truth, they seek in hell and the newly created world the mastery they could not gain in heaven.

The false core of both Milton's tyrants' seeming bravery in battle and defeat reveals itself also in the covert means each will use in his quest for power. This is the method of treachery and appears, like false valor in battle, disguised in a heroic mask as a kind of nobility designed to retain the loyalty and submission of the tyrant's followers. Satan and Charles move in their plan of attack "from violence to craft." Satan, after his martial defeat in heaven, has Beelzebub propose the "easier enterprise" of corrupting the "puny habitants" of earth. Charles praised his own action in seeking negotiations after battle as *"retiring* from bestial force to human reason." But Milton insisted, in interpreting the king's act and self-defense, that "men may Treat like Beasts as well as fight" and that false negotiating "hath no more commendation in it then from fighting to come to under-mining, from violence to craft, and when they can no longer doe as Lions, to doe as Foxes" (*Eikonoklastes, CPW* 3:520–21). Milton created a symbol from the imagery of the historical setting as he went on to point out, after Charles had promised for treaty's sake not to advance farther, "taking the advantage of a thick Mist, which fell that evening, weather that soon invited him to a designe no less treacherous and obscure; he follows at the heels of those Messengers of Peace with a traine of covert Warr" (*Eikon-oklastes, CPW* 3:522). "That perfidious mist" (528), which in Milton's prose invited Charles to a scheme no less treacherous and obscure than its own physical nature, has the same appropriateness in its use for Satan's entry into the Garden of Eden. In book 9 we see him appear from the under-ground river "involv'd in rising Mist" (75) and watch him search for the serpent "through each Thicket Dank or Dry, / Like a black mist low creeping" (179–80). Mist in the poem is a symbolic and literal cover for hypocrisy, as Satan tries to hide from the guardian angels:

> Of these the vigilance
> I dread, and to elude, thus wrapt in mist
> Of midnight vapor glide obscure. (157–59)

Perhaps he, like Charles, "thought that mist could hide him from the eye of Heav'n as well as of Man" (*Eikonoklastes, CPW* 4:528).

Milton has the two tyrants further reveal the baseness and intensity of their real motive for seeking power as they willingly degrade themselves in order to defend their purported glory. Of Charles's abortive and humiliating attempt to surprise and arrest five members of the House of Commons, Milton explains, "it discover'd in him an excessive eagerness to be aveng'd on them that cross'd him; and that to have his will, he stood not to doe things never so much below him" (*Eikonoklastes, CPW* 3:379). Satan understands this aspect of his own psychology when he acknowledges the baseness of his attack on Adam and Eve: "But what will not Ambition and Revenge / Descend to?" (9.168–69).

Of very great importance to both of Milton's character portraits is the conclusion, in which the false core of all the bravery and eloquence of each of his subjects is revealed unequivocally to his audience as being not only terrible but laughable. In a concerted effort to counteract the martyr image of Charles projected by the *Eikon*, Milton urged that it could hardly "be thought upon (though how sad a thing) without som kind of laughter . . . that he who had trampl'd over us so stately and so tragically should leave the world at last so ridiculously in his exit, as to bequeath among his Deifying friends that stood about him such a pretious peece of mockery to be publisht by them, as must needs cover both his and their heads with shame and confusion" (*Eikonoklastes, CPW* 3:364). This is a reference to the plagiarized "Pamela prayer" of *Eikon Basilike* and reveals why Milton wanted to make such an issue of it.[8] Evil in a character must eventually expose itself to ridicule, so that we finally see it for what it is and distance ourselves from its influence. But does not this passage sound like a paraphrase of the passage in book 10 of *Paradise Lost* where Satan returns victorious from a fallen Eden to his "Deifying friends" in hell? There the fallen angels gather with a great hunger for words of glory and fulfillment and are offered instead "Fruitage fair to sight, like that which grew / Near that bituminous Lake where *Sodom* flam'd" (561–62). The fruit replaces Satan's words, now hisses ("shame / Cast on themselves from thir own mouths" [546–47]), with their material equivalent: fruit beautiful in form, but rotten in substance. So too Milton describes Charles's fair-sounding words as resembling the apples of Sodom: "These pious flourishes and colours examin'd thoroughly, are like the Apples of *Asphaltis*, appearing goodly to the sudden eye, but look well upon them, or at least but touch them, and they turne into Cinders" (*Eikonoklastes, CPW* 3:552).[9]

Such resemblances in metaphor and characterization between Milton's portrayal of Charles and his portrayal of Satan suggest that the two characters' beliefs about the governing power they seek should be compared. What does Milton reveal to be the philosophical fault underlying this image of the invincible, suffering hero? "To be weak is miserable / Doing or Suffering," Satan asserts; and the strength of the hero, "doing or suffering," is what both sides of the false heroic image offer for admiration, even though, as Milton argues in his own voice, "in some things to be overcome is more honest and laudable then to conquer." The rebel angels' strength-worship is pointed out by Christ when, entering the battle in heaven, he tells the loyal angels that though they have proved their moral virtue in battle, the Father has assigned the rebels' doom to him:

> That they may have thir wish, to try with mee
> In Battle which the stronger proves, they all,
> Or I alone against them, since by strength
> They measure all, of other excellence
> Not emulous, nor care who them excels.   (6.818–22)

With this reference to an unnatural separation of "strength" from "other excellence" we are at what Milton reveals to be the heart of both rebellions against the power of God.

Milton held the divine right argument to be false not only when it compared rulers' natural rights to govern but also when it compared the way an absolute monarch may govern with the way God governs—which is not absolutely, by arbitrary will, but justly, by subjecting both himself and the governed to law. The royalists urged philosophical acceptance of a paradox whereby all men are created in God's image and yet one man with absolute power is set by God over the others as a king whose service, like God's, is "perfect freedom."[10] Milton believed, however, that such a "paradox" was simple injustice, impossible to believe of the Christian God, and was in fact to be resolved as follows: The mistake in the royalists' belief in the king's absolute power lay in assuming God's omnipotence to be his primary attribute, to which his justice must be mysteriously reconciled. Milton claimed, on the contrary, that God's primary attribute is goodness, which demands that all other attributes, including strength, be reconciled to it. Arguments from "divine" right in support of human tyranny, he said, revealed no Christian faith at their base, but a "barbarism" which worships "as gods malevolent demons whom they cannot exorcise" (*Second Defence*, *CPW*, 4, pt. 1:551). Such demonic powers would be fearful, but they would not be worthy of either obedience or emulation; and the superstitious acceptance by Charles's followers of God as such a deity is what enables them to make an idol in this world—as a third of heaven did once—of a being that seems to share the prized attribute of power. If people worship a God because of his omnipotence, they have no defense against human tyranny. If they worship God because of his justice, however, they have no excuse for accepting human tyranny.

In *Paradise Lost* we witness the original of this mistaken faith in sheer, undefined strength, first tested in Satan's fatal effort "to set himself in Glory above his Peers." The false premises of Satan's strength-worship have misled critics of the poem in two ways. On the one hand, it has been said in attempted defense of Satan's morality that Milton showed him to have been right in attempting revolution because, until the war in heaven, God had unfairly kept his power hid: "till then as one secure / Sat on his Throne . . . but still his strength conceal'd, / Which tempted our attempt" (1.638–42). Others, reasoning that Satan must have known of God's om-nipotence even without having seen it, have found Satan's original moti-vation to revolt implausible.

Although it is true that God had never, before Satan's revolt, revealed to the angels his power to destroy, it is not true that the angels had no evidence of God's greatest power, that which distinguishes him from any human or angelic ruler, the power to create. Satan himself, the angels, and heaven are all evidence of creation; and the rebels are trying to defend their moral as well as their military position when, during the course of their rebellion, they claim that they are "self-begot" (5.860) and that they will reascend "self-rais'd" (1.634) to heaven. Because they do not, however, feel the creative force within them, they find themselves positing an external, more powerful force at work, some "fatal course" (5.861), "Chance," "Fate," or even "Space" or the "Pit."[11] But while the true creator is "stronger" than Satan, the point is not the sheer greatness, which he does not employ against the rebels, but the different quality of his strength. When Christ enters the war in heaven, there is no battle to provide a test of physical strength. The Creator, the source of their own strength and being, simply appears before the rebel angels, who "astonisht all resistance lost, / All courage; down thir idle weapons dropp'd" (6.838–39). A vision of divinity "wither'd all thir strength, / And of thir wonted vigor left them drain'd, / Exhausted, spiritless, afflicted, fall'n" (6.850–52). Though later in the poem, older in their spiritual decline, the angels slip back into admit-ting God as their creator, the hardness of their hearts blinds them more than before to the significance of that reality.[12] It would be impossible for them to admit that they were at war with the one above them in the chain of being and still remain in revolt; they must cling to the belief that their difference from their adversary is merely one of strength, that to be "weak," not wrong, is miserable.

Since rightness, justice, is the essence of God's ordering power manifested in creation, only a betrayal of the laws of creation, a denial of the
natural order, can justify revolution in heaven or on earth. It would
follow that, if the governor of heaven were not the creator, were an
impostor tyrant, or if the creator himself had abrogated his natural right
to rule by abusing the law of creation, then, indeed, Satan should, like
Milton, have fought whether he had the strength to win or not. A
rational being should not worship a demon, however powerful. But if,
on the contrary, Satan rebels against the creator out of jealousy and
ambition, then the psychological truth for Milton is that he *would* rebel
regardless of God's power; for "in the act of doing evil, men [or angels]
use not to consider the event of thir evil doing: or if they doe, have
then no power to curb the sway of thir own wickedness." He would
find a way to justify his rebellion.

Though it is not until book 5 that we are given Satan's arguments for
rebellion as they were first presented, we may discern his original and
continuing motivation in his self-justification after the Fall in book 1. "To
bow and sue for grace / With suppliant knee, and deify his power / . . . that
were low indeed." These words might have come on the eve of the Stuart
restoration from Milton himself, who would not deify anyone's sheer
power. However, when we include the omitted phrase that modifies "his
power"—"Who from the terror of this Arm so late / Doubted his Empire"
(1.III–14)—Satan's intent is seen to be exactly opposite to Milton's. Satan's
question is, "Whose power shall we deify, that of his arm or mine?" Its
presupposition is, "The greatest strength merits worship." On Satan's
advice, the fallen angels accept their residence in hell by reasoning from the
premise that strength can determine the use to which morality is put, that
might makes right: "since he / Who now is Sovran can dispose and bid /
What shall be right" (1.245–47).

This is the argument for the divine right of kings: that a king or tyrant,
whoever currently holds power over a people, whether just or unjust
according to any heretofore accepted national or natural law, can rightly
by virtue of his strength control his subjects' behavior. This royalist belief
presupposes such a God as Satan here describes. While the ambition of
both Satan and Charles, in Milton's view, leads them to presuppose the
same idea of God's nature, Satan, unlike Charles, openly rebels against that
God. But that is a small difference. Charles, in Milton's depiction, holds
that if God rules thus in his absolute power over all creation, he, being
great in power, can rule thus over England. Satan holds first that if God
can rule heaven thus, he, if he gathers enough strength, can rule heaven
thus. This belief changes only in scope after the war in heaven. Satan holds

that if God can rule heaven thus, he, being only slightly weaker than God and yet stronger than his followers and humans, can rule hell and the new world thus—can break the chain of being and hold divided empire.

> What matter where, if I be still the same,
> And what I should be, all but less than hee
> Whom Thunder hath made greater? Here at least
> We shall be free.   (1.256–59)

THAT Satan's rebellion against fundamental law entails the corruption and extinction of true liberty in himself and his followers has been recognized by many critics of *Paradise Lost*. There remains, however, a lively movement among contemporary critics for contrary readings; and the basis for such readings can be traced to a mistaken impression of Milton's own historical role as a revolutionary. A study of the relation between law and liberty, which Milton argued in his prose works and to which he gave dramatic focus in his accounts of Charles and Satan and their followers, not only corrects misleading historical assumptions but also sharpens our awareness of the political dynamics of the poem, among the fallen angels and within the mind of Satan. The meaning of freedom embodied in Milton's account of Charles and his followers, particularly in the *Defences*, directly informs the poet's picture of Satan's career and is there given the dramatic scope that could not be fully worked out within the constraints of the political debate.

When Satan reasons that the fallen angels will finally be "free" in hell simply because "th' Almighty . . . will not drive us thence" (1.259–60), he is shown to be deceiving himself both about the angels' civil liberties and about the philosophical basis of political liberty in general. For while the rebels' claim to have "endanger'd Heav'n's perpetual King" is literally untrue and they reside in hell at God's sufferance, their more important claim to have sought liberty by putting "to proof his high Supremacy, / Whether upheld by strength, or Chance, or Fate" (1.131–33) is a more fundamental falsehood because it reveals that their revolution was not a valid test of God's supremacy and hence had no justification. A true revolution, like that against Charles I in England, challenges, not the force that upholds the ruling power, but the right. Valid revolution tests whether supremacy is accountable to law, which alone has the power to liberate and which Satan's rebellion defies. Like King Charles, Satan has become fatally confused about the nature of liberty. "As for the Philosophical Libertie which in vaine he talks of," as Milton said of

Charles in *Eikonoklastes* (*CPW* 3:501), "we may conclude him very ill train'd up in those free notions, who to civil Libertie was so injurious."

Milton's analysis of Charles's claim in the *Eikon* that he had been a defender of the people's liberties is paralleled in his portrayal of Satan's claim that he revolted against God in order to gain freedom for his angel followers, and it shows the relation between civil and philosophical liberty. Evidence in Charles's case had been his calling the Long Parliament. But far from seeking the welfare of the people whom Parliament represented, Milton pointed out, Charles had wanted only to use the people's resources for his own cause; he needed tax money to carry out his war to subjugate Scotland. When civil war began in the wake of Parliament's refusal, it was the English king, Milton claimed, who was in rebellion against Parliament, and not the other way around. The king had found the laws enforced by Parliament in behalf of the people hindrances to his own ambitions (see *Eikonoklastes*, *CPW* 3:350–60). So Parliament justly opposed the king as "a rebell to Law, and enemie to the State" (*Tenure of Kings and Magistrates*, *CPW*, 3:230; cf. *Eikonoklastes*, *CPW* 3:529).

The same is Christ's judgment upon Satan, "Rebel to all Law" (10.83). Satan too at the beginning of his bid for power calls an assembly of the angels who are his subjects under God as England was Charles's subject. At each assembly, historical and poetical, two wrongs are committed by each ruler. The first in each case involves merely a factual lie: Charles argued falsely to Parliament that his Scottish war was the most pressing threat to the nation, and Satan falsely informs the angels that Christ has commanded them to prepare an unjustified tribute. But the second wrong is the attempt by each to use the factual lies to do away entirely with the existing order of things, which is the only legitimate source of all particular laws and which stands in the way of his ambition. The great importance of Charles's coronation oath lay, for Milton, in its protection against this ultimate abuse of liberty. Charles had sworn, as had every English monarch, to "grant those just laws which the people shall choose" (*A Defence*, *CPW*, 4, pt. 1:482; cf. *Eikonoklastes*, *CPW* 3:530, 592–93). When Parliament's laws on such matters as just taxation did not fulfill his wishes, he tried to reinterpret his oath so that it would fit into his idea of his divine right to rule "above" those laws he did not like. "Which is the greater criminal," Milton demanded in the face of this abuse, "he who sins against the law or he who attempts to make the law itself his accomplice in crime, and even does away with the law to avoid the appearance of crime?" (*A Defence*, *CPW* 4, pt. 1:529). The tyrant, who denies the law, is far worse than the criminal who simply breaks the law.

Satan, like Charles, seeks to do "away with the law to avoid the appearance of crime." The obvious falsehood in his speech before the assembled host is that God intends to "introduce / Law and Edict on us"; but the falsehood that Abdiel identifies as "blasphemous" is contained in the words "on us, who without law / Err not" (5.797–99), which deny that there ever was a law. Before the fall of Lucifer, there had been of course no need for a "positive" law such as church and state had afterward on earth; but the reason that there was none was that all prelapsarian life was a natural enactment of the law of unfallen reason. This is why Milton could define fallen human law as "reason abstracted as much as might be from personal errors" (*Tenure of Kings and Magistrates, CPW*, 3:200) and why, when Charles tried to claim legal precedents for his "breaking" parliaments, Milton insisted that such trumped up laws could not uphold an indefensible practice: "I hold reason to be the best Arbitrator, and the Law of Law it self" (*Eikonoklastes, CPW* 3:403). That, he repeated in his *Defence*, is the "basic precept of our law . . . by which nothing contrary to the laws of God or to reason can be considered law, any more than a tyrant can be considered a king, or a servant of the Devil a servant of God" (*CPW*, 4, pt. 1:492).

The tyrant's goal is to replace government by rational law with government by arbitrary power, and, unlike the ordinary criminal, the tyrant seeks not obscurity, which could hide his crime, but fame. A successful tyrant must therefore, Milton knew, be a master of rhetoric; for rhetoric is the tool he can employ against the reason of the law to disguise his crime. When Charles wrote in the *Eikon Basilike* of "*the rationall soverantie of his soule, and liberty of his will*," Milton warned the people against such rhetoric, "Which words, of themselves, as farr as they are sense, good and Philosophical, yet in the mouth of him who to engross this common libertie to himself, would tred down all other men into the condition of Slaves and beasts, they quite loose their commendation" (*Eikonoklastes, CPW* 3:412). Furthermore, there is often in such language the appearance rather than the substance of right reason, as when the king "insists upon the old Plea of his *Conscience, honour and Reason*; using the plausibility of large and indefinite words, to defend himself at such a distance as may hinder the eye of common judgment from all distinct view & examination of his reasoning" (*Eikonoklastes, CPW* 3:456–57).

Like the angels Abdiel and Gabriel, a reader of *Paradise Lost* should approach the rhetoric of Satan with "all distinct view and examination of his reasoning." We should examine Satan's reasoning about what he offers the angels in place of law as the basis for their freedom: "those Imperial Titles which assert / Our being ordain'd to govern, not to serve" (5.801–02). We must demand, like Gabriel: "ordain'd by whom? to govern whom? serve whom?" But the answers are implicit in the questions once they are raised: ordain'd by the law of their creator, God, to govern by the law themselves and their fellow angels, to serve God and fellow angels by the same law. Obedience to the law of right reason is the condition for holding the titles that God decreed.

When we see the angels accept Satan's irrational argument that "Titles," rather than laws, assert their right to govern, we are witnessing the first and archetypal instance of the necessary separation, by law, of power from the persons who hold it. That "Majesty is inseparable from the person,"[13] that a "title" asserts not an office but a being, was at the heart of the royalist argument for divine right. It was the position held by Charles in the *Eikon* where, in refusing to obey the laws of Parliament, he argues that he will not *"part with . . . his honour as a King."* Milton exposes the conflict between Charles's rhetorical use of a royal title and his actual abuse of a royal oath to uphold the law, explaining that "when a King setts himself . . . against the . . . residence of all his Regal power, he then, in the single person of a Man, fights against his own Majesty and Kingship, and then indeed sets the first hand to his own deposing" (*Eikonoklastes, CPW* 3:524– 25). Likewise, the "residence" of all the rebel angels' "Regal power" is in the law of God, which they have denied.

Satan's argument for the angels' right from title and against law resulted, as did the historical argument for the divine right of kings, in a vast false analogy between the government of heaven and that of a fallen world. Satan's rival kingdom in hell, which parodies God's kingdom, is the archetypal acting out of the royalists' false analogy. We meet the parody again in book 12 as the tyranny of Nimrod "from Heav'n claiming second Sovranty" (35), or divine right.

Though a tyrant will try to look like a true king, Milton said in answer to Salmasius, we must distinguish the person from his title; for "a tyrant, like a king upon the stage, is but a ghost or mask of a king, and not a true king" (*A Defence, CPW* 4, pt. 1:310). The glory of the true King, Christ, as he appears before the angels, is an external manifestation of the spiritual essence of the Father, who is too radiant for angels' eyes to behold; the purpose of the Son's "great Vice-gerent Reign" (5.609) is to make the unapproachable radiance of divinity more accessible to finite creatures: "in him all his Father shone / Substantially express'd" (3.139–40). But Satan, not content with the glory that is rightfully his under the vice-gerency of Christ, turns true glory into mockery. His royal seat in heaven, whose splendor had of itself been sufficient to stand for the greatness of his rule, Satan tries to make hold greater significance than his reality can sustain. The result is to turn a great seat of power into a hollow stage property, "in

imitation of that Mount whereon / *Messiah* was declar'd in sight of Heav'n"
(5.764–65). Though the fallen Satan continues to maintain himself as king
of hell in "God-like imitated State" (2.511), the essence of his ability to rule
is gone, and the title of "king" is empty. When he abandoned the law to
seek power, he gave up forever his ability to preserve his own liberty or
that of his subjects. Like Charles, he set himself "against the . . . residence
of all his Regal power" and fought "against his own Majesty and Kingship."

Having led his followers to defeat in the war in heaven, Satan retains his
tyranny over them by means of his rhetorically effective, but false, reasoning about liberty. Even though he has assumed absolute dictatorship over
them in hell, he convinces his subject angels that they will find their liberty
in turn as possessors of human subjects on earth:

> Thrones, Dominations, Princedoms, Virtues, Powers,
> For in possession such, not only of right,
> I call ye and declare ye now . . .
>   . . . Now possess,
> As Lords, a spacious World, to our native Heaven
> Little inferior, by my adventure hard
> With peril great achiev'd.   (10.460–69)

Humankind, as Satan has his followers view them, are the spoils of a
dynastic war; they are the objects won and ruled. Of course when rational
beings are changed from subjects to objects of government, to "posses-
sions," then they have become slaves. As the idea of a people's slavery is
not an unacceptable means to Satan for achieving his own "right," so it
was also taught in Milton's day as part of the doctrine of divine right to be
acceptable, if the enslavement was to one high enough. Thus it was
Salmasius' argument against a people's right to revolt that a people had
sold themselves to their king as men used to sell themselves as slaves (*A
Defence, CPW* 4, pt. 1:461). Their "freedom" consisted in the king's freedom to exercise his will for them, just as all men's freedom ultimately
consisted in their submission to God's will. Milton's answer to Salmasius
was that even God does not remove his subjects' ability to will their own
actions and obedience, that their freedom consists in their ability to obey
or disobey his law.

Milton's answer went further than the assertion that liberty is impossible
to one enslaved: the devils' belief, like Salmasius', in the liberty of the
enslaver is also a delusion. As Milton admonished even Cromwell, "it has
so been arranged by nature that he who attacks the liberty of others is

himself the first of all to lose his own liberty and learns that he is the first of all to become a slave" (*Second Defence, CPW* 4, pt. 1:673).

That the fallen angels will retain no liberty—neither true liberty based in law nor false liberty based in power—in the exercise of their titular "rights" can be predicted from the illogic of the political argument Satan offers urging rebellion and from the argument he uses to retain his power over them once fallen. The first, as is his later temptation of Eve, is based on a self-contradictory argument for proportion. The angels are, he says,

> not equal all, yet free,
> Equally free; for Orders and Degrees
> Jar not with liberty, but well consist.   (5.791–93)

For orders and degrees to consist well with liberty, however, they must receive their definition in relation to a freedom-giving, absolute source of power; and what the angels' titles measure is the degree of their likeness to God. But, because Satan wants to retain his position of command, he urges the angels to believe that there can be a chain of being that will not fall though it hang from nothing. The basis for his argument is the same lie that denies the Creator.

True proportion forms the basis of the judgment of Satan by Abdiel, the only angel originally under Satan's command to revolt against the incipient tyranny of the archangel, the true Miltonic revolutionary, prototype for "the people [who] with God's approval judge their guilty rulers" (*A Defence, CPW* 4, pt. 1:359). His argument is from the chain of being, the foremost law of both God and Nature:

> This is servitude,
> To serve th' unwise, or him who hath rebell'd
> Against his worthier, as thine now serve thee,
> Thyself not free, but to thyself enthrall'd.   (6.178–81)

The angels who capitulate to Satan's argument, on the other hand, are Milton's poetical archetypes of that effeminacy of a people that he feared and finally came to witness in England: "Unless you expel avarice, ambition, and luxury from your minds . . . you will find at home and within that tyrant who, you believed, was to be sought abroad and in the field— now even more stubborn. In fact, many tyrants, impossible to endure, will from day to day hatch out from your very vitals" (*Second Defence, CPW*, 4, pt. 1:680–81). Nisroch is his example in the war in heaven. He finds newly experienced pain "hard / For Gods" who follow Satan's ambition for freedom to enjoy their divine rights. Pain, once Nisroch discovers it, becomes "the worst / Of evils"—worse even than the tyranny that Satan had convinced him was held by God (6:451–68).

Book 6 reveals a less attractive view of the fallen angels, which is withheld from readers of the poem until well after the powerful opening books have had their effect. However, the description even in books 1 and 2, if we read them as critically as a militant Gabriel would, "argues no Leader, but a Liar trac't / Satan." Gabriel's argument had been that once Satan had broken his loyalty to God, he had simultaneously broken faith with his subjects; and that they, by allowing themselves to be used in the rebellion, became nothing more than an "Army of Fiends." And, indeed, the emotions the rebel angels show toward one another involve not respect but, on the one side, pride and, on the other, fear.

The first reaction of the angels to their commander after their fall is a fear that elicits unquestioning obedience. When Satan summoned them from the burning lake,

> They heard, and were abasht, and up they sprung
> Upon the wing; as when men wont to watch
> On duty, sleeping found by whom they dread,
> Rouse and bestir themselves ere well awake.   (1.331–34)

They are a defeated army. That they have been led not to victory but to great suffering should raise doubt in their minds about the tenability of their original cause for following Satan in rebellion. Satan had argued that God's apparent power would not prove superior to their own and that it merited challenging. This promise has proved false. At this point the remainder of Satan's earlier arguments for revolution, lodged in the memories of the angels he led to war, should reasonably be turned against him. "Who," he had challenged, "can in reason then or right assume / Monarchy over such as live by right / His equals, if in power and splendor less, / In freedom equal?" (5.794–97). Though Satan's challenge to Christ's monarchical power could not apply to the rule of unfallen heaven, its message is very true in a fallen context where the only difference between the fallen angels is in "power and splendor." In book 11 in fact, after the fall of man, the archangel Michael repeats the essence of Satan's egalitarian statement to Adam. Echoing Raphael's hint in book 5 that God might gradually have raised humans, "found obedient," to a higher state, he explains the postlapsarian impossibility of a "patriarchal" government by divine right:

> Eden . . . had been
> Perhaps thy Capital Seat, from whence had spread
> All generations, and had hither come
> From all ends of th' Earth, to celebrate
> And reverence thee thir great Progenitor.
> But this preeminence thou hast lost, brought down
> To dwell on even ground now with thy Sons.   (11.341–47)

That preeminence was lost by Satan in his fall as well. Yet now, as the fallen angels are led into another audience before Satan, they have not the freedom of mind to conquer their mental and emotional torment—"anguish and doubt and fear"—by facing its cause. Instead they succumb to the effects of the Dorian war music offered them, which

> instead of rage
> Deliberate valor breath'd, firm and unmov'd
> With dread of death to flight or foul retreat,
> Not wanting power to mitigate and swage
> With solemn touches, troubl'd thoughts, and chase
> Anguish and doubt and fear and sorrow and pain
> From mortal or immortal minds.   (1.553–59)

We may read the following description of the assembled hosts from two points of view—that of the tyrant Satan and that of the revolutionary Milton. We look at Satan's face:

> cruel his eye, but cast
> Signs of remorse and passion to behold
> The fellows of his crime, the followers rather
> (Far other once beheld in bliss) condemn'd
> For ever now to have thir lot in pain,
> Millions of Spirits for his fault amerc't
> Of Heav'n, and from Eternal Splendors flung
> For his revolt, *yet faithful how they stood,*
> Thir Glory wither'd.   (1.604–23; emphasis added)

The tone in these lines is, from Satan's point of view, a kind of gratification; from Milton's point of view, it is that scorn in which servility deserves to be held. The angels' governor has led them, "followers," into "crime," for which they now suffer terrible punishment as his fellows. They are now truly "his Peers" (1.618), his equals. If they had been deceived by his arguments for liberty before the Fall, they can be so no longer. Now, in order to prove themselves worthy of any chance for liberty that might remain to them, they must rise in revolution against the leader who has betrayed them: "The people . . . do with God's approval judge their guilty rulers"—"yet faithful how they stood."

The very nature of the appeal to the angels of Satan's speech in which he lays claim to the throne of hell reveals their servility. He gives a factual account of their condition; those facts clearly betray the wrong of their position and his falseness to them; and yet they passively accept Satan and his claim. When he persuaded the angels to rebel, Satan had convinced them that they had been living "without Law"; now he says truthfully that "Mee . . . just right and the fixt Laws of Heav'n / Did first create your Leader" (2.18–19). A subject whose will and reason retained any spark of freedom would have to realize that laws that are right and fixed would now have to banish the individual from the office he betrayed. But they do not question his argument. "Next," Satan reminds them, they followed him out of their own "free choice." This again is true; and this again, after what they have witnessed of his false "merit" "in council or in flight," is the point at which their mistaken consent should be withdrawn. Yet now Satan is right when he announces that they have again "yielded with full consent" to his leadership. We have been watching the process of their final yielding: how "troubled thoughts" were mitigated and swaged into "fixed thought," how "for his fault" "yet faithful . . . they stood." Their consent was fully, but not freely, given; they were already slaves of their own fear and cowardice. Satan assures their continued loyalty by reminding them of what has made them cowards:

> but who here
> Will envy whom the highest place exposes
> Foremost to stand against the Thunderer's aim
> Your bulwark, and condemns to greatest share
> Of Endless pain? (2.26–30)

Now, at the last moment in which a moral decision might be possible, Satan takes care to remove forever the chance of a moral "Faction" by removing the concept of morality. Nisroch's discovery in war that pain was for him the "greatest evil" is solidified into demonic policy. "Good" means not righteousness but pleasure; "evil" is not lawlessness but pain:

where there is then no good
For which to strive, no strife can grow up there
From Faction; for none sure will claim in Hell
Precedence, none, whose portion is so small
Of present pain, that with ambitious mind
Will covet more.   (2.30–35)

In this speech Satan removes at one stroke the possibility for moral or immoral revolution among the angels in hell.

The officers whose advice is allegedly sought are no less slaves than the masses. They are finally manipulated by Satan and his spokesman Beelzebub to agree to Satan's plan, but first, by their own counsel, they reveal their self-enslavement. Moloch and Belial are complex developments of the two royalist types that Salmasius had held up for admiration because of their reaction to Charles's fall. Salmasius' "bravely spirited," who, like Moloch, "burned with such a flame of indignation that they could scarce control themselves," Milton had labeled "madmen" whose threats are easily "put to flight with that true courage which is master of itself." Among Salmasius' second type Milton had included Salmasius himself: "little women of the court . . . or some others yet more effeminate" attempting, like Belial, "to draw the strength from manly hearts" (*A Defence, CPW*, 4, pt. 1:312–13).

Satan in his role in the council displays the tyrant's full awareness of his subjects' servile character. His suspicion that some one of his followers might fake an offer to explore the way to the new world, thus "winning cheap the high repute / Which he through hazard huge must earn" (2.472–73), has a parallel in Milton's explanation of the behavior of the lesser tyrant Charles, who, when accused of fomenting the Irish rebellion, had tried to defend his integrity by stressing that "*he offer'd to goe himself in person upon that expedition* [against the rebels]." The fact was, Milton pointed out, that Charles knew his offer would not be accepted: "But [he] mentions not that by his underdealing . . . he had brought the Parlament into so just a diffidence of him, as that they dust not leave the Public Armes to his disposal, much less an army to his conduct" (*Eikonoklastes, CPW* 3:480–81).

Although Charles was a lesser tyrant than Satan, he shared, in Milton's portrait, that fundamental element of tyranny which is self-enslavement. "Every bad man is a tyrant," Milton said, explaining Charles's position, "each in his own degree." And "to the degree that he is the greatest of all tyrants, to that same degree is he the meanest of all and most a slave." This is because the evil man in public power is a slave not only to his own ambition and despair but to his followers' as well: "Other men willingly serve only their own vices; he is forced, even against his will, to be a slave, not only to his own crimes, but also to the most grievous crimes of his servants and attendants, and he must yield a certain share of his despotism to all his most abandoned followers. Tyrants then are the meanest of slaves; they are slaves even to their own slaves" (*Second Defence, CPW*, 4, pt. 1:562–63). This message is embodied in the confrontation in book 2 between Satan and his allegorical offspring Death, who belies the tyrant's claim to control hell, "where," as Death rightly claims, "I reign King, and to enrage thee more, / Thy King and Lord" (2.698–99). The "execrable shape" must be called "my fair son" and promised food so that its power will bend to Satan's goal.

The poet then dramatizes the same message in Satan's journey to the new world. As Milton had shown Charles giving his followers bishoprics and lands so that to keep their rewards they "knew it thir best cours to have dependence onely upon him" (*Eikonoklastes, CPW* 3:511), so he shows Satan forced to seek in Eden "a spacious World" for his followers to "possess / As Lords" (10.460–67) so that their titles can believably stand for something. But in order for Satan to get possession and for Charles to keep bishoprics, innocent people had to suffer. With Charles this suffering had come in the form of religious persecution: "Thus when both Interests of Tyrannie and Episcopacie were incorprat into each other, the King [was] . . . fatally driv'n on" to "extirpating" innocent protestants (*Eikonoklastes, CPW* 3:511).

Though he did not live to see the effects of his intended extirpation of his religious enemies, Charles took the occasion in *Eikon Basilike* to imagine their suffering and claim that he "*cannot but observe this . . . yet with sorrow and pitty*" (*Eikonoklastes, CPW* 3:567). Satan too at first feels himself to be "loath to this revenge / On you who wrong me not" and to "melt" "at your harmless innocence" (4.386–89). He finds, however, that beyond his own wish for vengeance, his "dread of shame / Among the Spirits beneath" (4.82–83) drives him fatally on. And he lulls to impotence his last spark of genuine freedom of conscience, revealed by his revulsion from his own intended action, with the Dorian war music of his own rhetoric:

> yet public reason just,
> Honor and Empire with revenge enlarg'd,
> By conquering this new World, compels me now
> To do what else though damn'd I should abhor.   (4.389–92)

Satan and Charles, in Milton's two portraits of the tyrant, enslave their followers and themselves in a "mistie cloud" of rhetoric that substitutes "prerogative" for the sunlight of God's law, the only basis for a portrait of genuine royalty. In his version of the story of King Charles, a drama not of Christian martyrdom but of tyrannous rebellion, Milton's left hand worked out, though in fragmentary form, fundamental elements of the character, action, underlying philosophy and influence of this minor tyrant, elements that find full dramatization in his right hand's portrait of Satan's epic struggle for power.

THREE

Milton's God: Creativity and the Law

SATAN'S leadership in rebellion and rule in hell are shown by Milton to be tyrannous because of the Archangel's own inconsistency; his attempt to use some of nature's law and deny the rest leads inevitably to his own and his followers' enslavement. Satan's failings, however, are not God's justification for his rule. There could exist, as has been argued to be the case in *Paradise Lost*, a bad rebellion against a bad ruler.[1] Our standard for evaluating the justice of God's rule of heaven should be the same ideal that we took from Milton's prose to judge his hell: a government that preserves liberty, for both the governor and the governed.

> Thou art my Father, thou my Author, thou
> My being gav'st me; whom should I obey
> But thee, whom follow? (*PL* 2.864–66)

That sovereignty exists in the Creator first of all by virtue of the power to create was assumed by everyone in Milton's world—from Sin, who deifies her Author, Satan, in the lines quoted above, to the patriarchalist Weldon, who shared this premise with his libertarian antagonists: that "the *reasonable Creature* must needs acknowledge the original of his *Power* to be from him, from whom he had the *Original* of his Being."[2] Milton's Satan never denies this principle, but only the fact that God is his Creator. In answer to Satan's claim to be self-begot, Abdiel threatens him with the sheer strength of his Maker:

> Then who created thee lamenting learn,
> When who can uncreate thee thou shalt know. (5.894–95)

Creation, however, employs a power greater than the sheer strength employed for "uncreation." We have remarked the difference in kind between the power of Christ and that of the battling rebel angels, whose weapons fall useless in the very presence of his chariot. But these angels do not meet Christ in battle without warning of the uniqueness of his power as Creator. When Christ in book 6 approaches the war-torn landscape of heaven, the angels witness hills which have been uprooted by angelic strength retire: "Each to his place, they heard his voice and went / . . . / And with fresh Flow'rets Hill and Valley smil'd" (6.781–84). The rebel angels here are given, even at the last moment before their fall, clear signs of God's vast ordering providence and power, of his ability not only by strength to destroy his creation, but, more fundamentally, by creativity to govern it. The angels do not fall from ignorance or from stupidity, but from the only force that can oppose itself to knowledge of such creative power, from the pride that hardens their hearts against admitting its significance:

> But to convince the proud what Signs avail
> Or Wonders move th' obdurate to relent?
> They hard'n'd more by what might most reclaim,
> Grieving to see his Glory, at the sight
> Took envy, and aspiring to his highth,
> Stood reimbattl'd fierce.   (6.789–94)

The obdurate angels' goal is impossible, for the glory that grieves them does not derive from Christ's sheer strength; it is rather the unique glory of the Creator-King, which we witness again in book 7 when heaven's gates open to let forth

> The King of Glory in his powerful Word
> And Spirit coming to create new Worlds.   (208–09)

The angels who sing at this world's creation laud not primarily their King's omnipotence but his great ordering beneficence when they affirm: "to create / Is greater than created to destroy" (7.606–07).

It is the goodness, or justice, of the Creator's rule in *Paradise Lost*, rather than his great strength, that renders him a monarch accountable to law and thus worthy of his subjects' praise: "for strength from Truth divided and from Just, / Illaudable, naught merits but dispraise" (6.381–82). His belief in that goodness had led Milton, in his defense of the English revolutionary effort, to his interpretation of the scriptural statement so often quoted by the royalists: "whatever powers there be are ordained of God." Milton had concluded that "the apostle would be understood to mean here legitimate powers," because, he reasoned, "evil and vice, being disorder, cannot possibly be ordained and continue vicious, for this would imply the presence of two contraries, order and disorder" (*A Defence, CPW* 4, pt. 1:384). And God's own goodness is such that he does not subject his creation to contraries: "he cannot deny himself," Milton quoted from Scripture, he "cannot lie"; thus, "the power of God is not exerted in . . . things which . . . imply a contradiction" (*De Doc., CPW* 6:146).

To claim that God "cannot" do something had simultaneously a theological and a political significance in Milton's day. Fifty years earlier Tudor Disciplinarianism had based its claim to divinely ordained ecclesiastical power on a nominalistic doctrine that denied the possibility of natural law, which it saw as being a limitation on God's omnipotence. To defend the freedom of Elizabethan government to settle upon a humanly devised form of church government, Hooker had made Milton's claim about the relation of God's power to God's goodness: "They err therefore who think that of the will of God to do this or what there is no reason besides his will . . . [for] he worketh all things not only according to his own will, but 'the Counsell of his own will' (Ephes. i. ii)." To answer Disciplinarian concern that if we were to believe that God "transgresseth not His own [natural] law," our interpretation would impose a limitation on God's power, Hooker continued: "Nor is the freedom of the will of God any whit abated, let or hindered, by means of this; because the imposition of this law upon himself is his own free and voluntary act." This, he said, is the meaning of the Scripture: "he cannot deny himself" (61–63; 1.2.5).

In the 1650s the same brand of Calvinism that Hooker had struggled with was being used to advise Cromwell against freedom of faith and expression. It was opposed by John Goodwin, the Puritan revolutionary whose name has rightly been linked with Milton's ever since his *Obstructours of Justice* (1649), which defers at length to Milton's *Tenure of Kings and Magistrates*, was, along with two of Milton's regicide tracts, ordered in 1660 to be burned.[3] Goodwin argued that people must be free to choose their own forms of worship and work out their own religious beliefs. He based commitment to religious freedom on his theological belief in God's own "regulated power." For God to breach his own "principles of wisdome and righteousness . . . was unpossible . . . (according to that of the Apostle, *He CANNOT deny himself*)." Goodwin offered the following example: "Of this regulated power of God the

Evangelist *Mark* also speaketh, where speaking of *Christ* now being in his own country, he saith, *And he COULD* there *DO NO mighty work*, etc. Mark 6.5. The expression implieth not that the Arm of Omnipotency, by which the Lord Christ wrought so many *mighty works* in other places, was either shortned, or any ways weakned or enfeebled." The reason why Christ here "regulated and contracted his power . . . the Evangelist Matthew clearly expresseth": "*And he did not many mighty works there, BECAUSE OF THEIR UNBELIEF*, Mat. 13.58. Christ judged it not a thing reasonable or meet (and consequently, it was impossible for him to do it) to multiply miracles, or mighty works, where the people generally were either blockish, and set not their hearts and minds upon the interpretation and import of them, or otherwise were of malicious and perverse spirits, drawing onely darkness out of light, depraving and blaspheming that glorious power, by which they were effected." [4]

This central theological principle, which both Milton and Goodwin had appropriated from Hooker's tradition to forge a revolution, is embodied in Milton's epic's picture of God's providences to angels and humans. There God's creation reflects his gift of order in all things, from heaven's flowering hills to her "Princes, whom the supreme King / Exalted to such power, and gave to rule, / Each in his Hierarchy, the Orders bright" (1.737). And in *Paradise Lost* the order with which they find their world divinely governed renders God's goodness perceptible to all those who do not draw "onely darkness out of light . . . blaspheming that glorious power by which [the divine works] were effected." "God's own will" is shown in Council (Counsell) by Milton in the dialogue of Father and Son (3.80–343). "While God spake" (135) of these bare doctrinal terms of the law,

> ambrosial fragrance fill'd
> All Heav'n, and in the blessed Spirits elect
> Sense of new joy ineffable diffus'd.   (135–37)

God's implementation of his eternal law, for the angels, is a sweet fragrance, ineffable joy.

William Empson speaks for many critics, nevertheless, when he denies that goodness is perceptible in the God of *Paradise Lost*, whom he calls "the harsh Old Testament figure."[5] The Puritans' identification of their cause with that of the ancient Hebrews makes an assumption that the Puritans' view of God should resemble that of the Jews seem reasonable.

And truly, the God of *Paradise Lost* is for Milton the Old Testament God, the God of judgment; but for him, as for the ancient Jews, God's judgment is the cause for great joy, the revelation of his beneficent goodness. To study Milton's conception of him, we should compare our impressions of *Paradise Lost* with Milton's own readings of the Old Testament psalms during the troubled time in which he was preparing to write his epic.

Consider Milton's translation of the first psalm. This is a poem about judgment, and its stress is on the singer's delight in the Law and the spiritual growth it makes possible in the good man: "Blessed is the man who hath not walk'd astray / In counsel of the wicked. . . . But in the great / *Jehovah's* Law is ever his delight, / And in his Law he studies day and night. / He shall be as a tree which planted grows" (162). That a free man who lives true to the law of his own nature can grow like a tree from a seed, that one's own potential beauty and goodness can be realized in interaction with the rest of the universe is the meaning of God's great gift of love, his creation of human beings in his own image. The moral law in which the good man delights is his means for living actively in harmony with that order which he can contemplate in all creation. Consider the singer's meditation in Psalm 19 on the relationship between God's initial creation and the nature of his continuing governance.[6] While God's power to create displays his omnipotence over all being, his gift of the Law reveals the essence of his goodness. For it is the Law which allows all of nature to operate with the greatest complexity and yet allows each individual being freedom to reach the perfection of its nature. This consistency between the physical and the moral order of God's creation permits the psalmist's thought to pass at verse 7 from the one to the other in perfect continuity without transition:

1 The heavens declare the glory of God; and the firmament sheweth his handywork.
2 Day unto day uttereth speech, and night unto night sheweth knowledge.
3 There is no speech or language where their voice is not heard.
4 Their line is gone out through all the earth, and their words to the end of the world. In them hath he set a tabernacle for the sun.
5 Which is as a bridegroom coming out of his chamber, and rejoiceth as a strong man to run a race.

6   His going forth is from the end of the heaven, and his
    circuit unto the ends of it: and there is nothing hid from the
    heat thereof.
7   The law of the Lord is perfect, converting the soul: the
    testimony of the Lord is sure, making wise the simple.
8   The statutes of the Lord are right, rejoicing the heart: the
    commandment of the Lord is pure, enlightening the eyes.
9   The fear of the Lord is clean, enduring for ever: the judg-
    ments of the Lord are true and righteous altogether.
10 More to be desired are they than gold, yea, than much fine
    gold: sweeter also than honey and the honeycomb.

I quote the psalm at such length because the Hebrew psalmist's experience of his Creator is the same experience Milton gives to the angels and
to the humans in *Paradise Lost*. Old Testament revelation confirms the
validity of natural man's experience that God's observable physical order,
by its very nature, leads a rational creature to its correspondent, the moral
order. "Thy hands have made me and fashioned me," says the psalmist in
119, "give me understanding, that I may learn thy commandments." Adam,
on awakening into being, asks the creatures:

> Tell, if ye saw, how came I thus, how here?
> Not of myself; by some great Maker then,
> In goodness and in power preeminent;
> Tell me, how may I know him, how adore.
> From whom I have that thus I move and live,
> And feel that I am happier than I know.   (8.277–82)

God, when he reveals himself in answer to Adam's natural seeking, repeats
this pattern, telling him first: I made you; and second: there are my
commandments (8.316–30). Adam has to learn from Raphael that anything
but the natural desire to obey is even possible:

> can we want obedience then
> To him, or possibly his love desert
> Who form'd us from the dust, and plac'd us here
> Full to the utmost measure of what bliss
> Human desires can seek or apprehend?   (5.514–18)

The angel Abdiel's response to Satan's unlawful power-move is to recall his
experience of the creator's authority, which is both physical and moral.
The sheer power of the creator comes first to his mind:

> Shalt thou give Law to God, shalt thou dispute
> With him the points of liberty, who made
> Thee what thou art. . . .   (5.822–24)

But he continues immediately to reason that even omnipotence would not be cause for worship were God not also known to be all-good:

> Yet by experience taught we know how good,
> And of our good, and of our dignity
> How provident he is. . . .   (5.826–28)

What is the essence of the natural law that makes it worthy of being, as Milton called it in the *Defence* (*CPW* 4, pt. 1:383), "the highest and ultimate power," more to be desired than much fine gold? How does Milton understand the psalmist of 119, who says "Thy Law is the Truth": "I hate and abhor lying: but thy law do I love." The psalmist's faith in the truth of God's law is a theme of Psalms 1 through 7, which Milton translated in 1653. Psalm 4 speaks with the voice of the Lord:

> Great ones, how long will ye
> My glory have in scorn?
> How long be thus forborne
> Still to love vanity,
> To love, to seek, to prize
> Things false and vain and nothing else but lies?

Psalm 7 asks God to behold the enemy:

> He travails big with vanity,
> Trouble he hath conceiv'd of old
> As in a womb, and from that mold
> Hath at length brought forth a Lie.

Psalm 5 asserts: "them unblest / Thou wilt destroy that speak a lie."

What does it mean to say that God's law is truth and that those who break the moral law are liars? It means first of all that the law is primarily descriptive and only secondarily, or derivatively, prescriptive. It means, as Hooker, Goodwin, and Milton's Adam and Abdiel have joined the psalmist in observing, that the physical and spiritual nature of creation contains within itself the rules of its own operation. If a creature denies those rules of behavior, it is denying reality; it is telling a lie about the way its own nature and the nature of all that exists was created. Reality and morality are two ways of describing what is.

As Milton's understanding of reality's utter consistency was the basis for his view of a human magistrate's responsibility to natural and national law, so it is also the basis for his depiction in *Paradise Lost* of God's own government of both angels and humans. We meet the issue first in the exaltation before the angels in heaven of Christ, whose superior nature makes him worthiest to rule. Christ's "right" to rule is no dynastic legalism; he is "rightful" king (5.814–45) in the same sense that for the psalmist the statutes of the Lord are "right." His kingship tells the truth about him; his rule is the function of his nature. The "face" and the "hand" are aspects of the one Son whom God addresses before sending him into battle:

> Effulgence of my Glory, Son belov'd,
> Son in whose face invisible is beheld
> Visibly, what by Deity I am,
> And in whose hand what by Decree I do.   (6.680–83)

Christ does not fight so that he can merit his kingdom as a reward for valor. Rather, because of his great inherent powers, he has been entrusted with the care of God's kingdom. The Son is the true vice-gerent hero whom Satan cannot imitate, strong enough both doing and suffering to serve his subjects and retain his own liberty by living out the law of his nature.

Christ is servant-king, a ruler whose greatness consists in the creativity and strength necessary to harmonize universal law with situational need. This scriptural exemplum is offered as support for the form of government which Milton proposed courageously at the eleventh hour to combat "the inconveniences and dangers of readmitting Kingship" to England in 1660. Christ's own answer to "the ambitious desire of *Zebede's* two sons, to be exalted above thir brethren in his kingdom" should give guidance: *"the kings of the gentiles,* saith he, *exercise lordship over them . . . but ye shall not be so; but he that is greatest among you, let him be . . . as he that serveth. . . .* And what government coms neerer to this precept of Christ, then a free Commonwealth; wherin they who are greatest, are perpetual servants" (*Ready and Easy Way, CPW* 7:424–25).

MILTON strove for an English government modeled on God's government of his creation—not on the outward signs of a monarch's glory but on the rule of law, of "reason abstracted as much as might be from personal errors." Human rulers must be accountable for their acts before law to the governed, who must judge them: "If they [kings] may refuse to give account," he had argued, and "if the King feare not God . . . we hold then our lives and estates, by the tenure of his meer grace and mercy, as from a God, not a mortal Magistrate" (*TKM, CPW* 3:204). This statement assumes that if the king does fear God, he will keep the law; and likewise that if the king does not fear God, but has absolute power, he will be not like the God of *Paradise Lost* but like a deity pagans conceive, powerful but not good. This political belief is allowed fullest expression in *Paradise Lost* where Milton portrays the true king of heaven and earth as a voluntarily accountable monarch.[7] There God is shown to do things because they in themselves are right; God's actions are not "right" (as both Laudians and Presbyterians had found themselves asserting) simply because he performs them. It is on the basis of natural law that God accounts before heaven for his dangerous gift of freedom:

> Not free, what proof could they have giv'n sincere
> Of true allegiance, constant Faith or Love,
> Where only what they needs must do, appear'd,
> Not what they would? what praise could they receive?
> What pleasure I from such obedience paid,
> When Will and Reason (Reason also is choice)
> Useless and vain, of freedom both despoil'd,
> Made passive both, had serv'd necessity,
> Not Mee.

As Creator, Milton's God explains, he has shared his rational nature truly, in essence. He has not given only the external sign of goodness in obedience, but its essence in reasoned and willed obedience.

> They therefore as to right belong'd,
> So were created. (3.103–112)

God created humans not arbitrarily, but in accordance with "right," with "the truth." Milton's God affirms what the psalmist sings: "The statutes of the Lord are right."

It follows that to maintain his truth God must keep faith with humans in the law, even if humans break the faith. To retain their freedom, both divine and human beings must act in accordance with the laws of their natures:

> Authors to themselves in all
> Both what they judge and what they choose; for so
> I form'd them free, and free they must remain,
> Till they enthrall themselves: *I else must change*
> *Thir nature*, and revoke the high Decree
> Unchangeable, Eternal, which ordain'd
> Thir freedom. (3.122–28; emphasis added)

And so it does follow in *Paradise Lost*, that God pronounces judgment on human beings for their sin:

> Man disobeying,
> Disloyal breaks his fealty . . .
> . . . and so losing all,
> To expiate his Treason hath naught left,
> But to destruction sacred and devote,
> He with his whole posterity must die,
> Die hee or Justice must. (3.203–210)

God announces that if "Justice" dies, so does human nature. Empson speaks for many readers when he says God's pronouncement here is "superstition" and "no part of English justice, because the prerogative of mercy has long been a fundamental power of the Crown."[8] We should now be able to recognize, however, that, for Milton and the revolutionaries, the prerogative of the English Crown had to be, like the divine prerogative, bound absolutely to law if it were not to cloud the sun of royalty.

John Goodwin was still doggedly defending this radical theology, which grounded God's own royal prerogative in law, against attacks from ministers of the Cromwellian establishment two years before the Restoration. Because Goodwin argues that the prerogative and sovereignty assigned to God by Scripture must be understood as being consistent with God's fealty to reason and natural law, a voluntaristic Calvinist opponent, George Kendall, "arraigns me of treason against the *most August* and sacred *Prerogative of the Divine Majesty*. And tells me that *my head hath insolently exalted it self against Heaven*, (i.e.) against Master *Kendals* and his Syndogmatists most unworthy notions and conceits about Heaven, and him that dwelleth therein." Goodwin replies that his opponent's theology is a perversion of genuine divine right, that is, righteousness in law, which constitutes God's royal prerogative. This principle had been explained by Hooker: God's mercies have been "granted, not to turne the edge of justice, or to make voyde at certaine tymes and in certaine men through meere voluntarie grace or benevolence that which continuewallie and universallie should be of force (as some understand it) but in verie truth to practise general lawes accordinge to theire right meaninge" (*Laws* 44; 5.9.3).

Goodwin had explained in his theological magnum opus, published two years after the execution of the king who had claimed a royal prerogative above all law, "That prerogative which God stands upon in the Scriptures, and claims to Himself as a royalty annexed to the crown of heaven and earth, . . . standeth not in any liberty claimed by Him to leave what persons He pleaseth to ruin [or salvation] . . . but to make the terms and conditions, as of life so of death, as of salvation so of condemnation, and these equally respecting all men." Therefore, "in whatsoever God acteth," he insisted, "we are to look . . . for . . . tendency unto ends worthy of Him; and these discernible enough by men to be such, if they were diligent and impartial in the consideration of them."[9]

Keeping in mind the faith of revolutionary humanism that the human relation to God's purpose is to be diligent and impartial in the consideration of God's ends, we may examine the actual experience of Milton's Adam as he lives through the justice of an "accountable" God who does not subject him to "meer grace and mercy" but to Law. Adam, in near despair over his sin, wishes for the promised "death," which he conceives to be mental and physical "dissolution" (10.1049). That he has not met such a death leaves Adam, with his fallen reason, facing an apparent paradox: "How can . . . God exercise / Wrath without end on Man whom Death must end?" he asks.

> Can he make deathless Death? that were to make
> Strange contradiction, which to God himself
> Impossible is held, as Argument
> Of weakness, not of Power. (10.796–801)

Adam holds that God cannot contradict Himself. Humans, he reasons, were made from the dust of the earth, which God regulates, as he does all things, according to the laws of the nature with which he created it. For God to deal falsely with a law of any nature, even physical nature, would be unjust:

> Will he draw out,
> For anger's sake, finite to infinite
> In punisht Man, to satisfy his rigor
> Satisfi'd never; *that were to extend*
> *His Sentence beyond dust and Nature's law*
> By which all Causes else according still
> To the reception of thir matter act,
> Not to th' extent of thir own Sphere.   (10.801–08; emphasis added)

Since matter must remain finite, Adam's thought continues, perhaps death does not mean merely extinction to that part of a person which is matter; perhaps it has a larger meaning:

> But say
> That Death be not one stroke, as I suppos'd
> Bereaving sense, but endless misery
> From this day onward, which I feel begun
> Both in me, and without me, and so last
> To Perpetuity.   (10.808–13)

Death may affect that part of human nature which is not subject to physical laws—that part which as spirit is capable of existence "to perpetuity"—and, therefore, death may be something other than a mere cessation. The acknowledgment that death is primarily a spiritual phenomenon forces Adam to see also the justice of his posterity's condemnation. "Ah, why should all mankind / For one man's fault thus guiltless be condemn'd / If guiltless?" he cries. But he knows that they cannot be guiltless, that since he has himself been false to the law of his nature, the world he has been given to initiate and govern cannot remain unaffected. He will pass to his descendants not only a fallen world "without" but a "Will deprav'd" from which sin and hence judgment will once more inevitably proceed.

> But from me what can proceed,
> But all corrupt, both Mind and Will deprav'd,
> Not to do only, but to will the same
> With me? how can they then acquitted stand
> In sight of God?   (10.822–28)

Here Milton dramatizes the first and archetypal incidence of a sinful human being wrestling with the government of a God who is utterly accountable to a perfect law. Adam has reached the realization that, because of his law, there are things God "cannot do."

When the English Parliament found itself, in John Goodwin's view, in a similar bind as it attempted to effect a just revolution in 1649 in the face of the "unthankfulnesse" revealed by the public's fiercely divided reactions to the king's trial and execution, he advised the Members of Parliament to wrestle with God as Jacob had: "*let him not go*, and he will *blesse* you." "I confes," he admitted, referring to the texts from Mark 6:5 and Matt. 13:58, which we have seen him use in another context: "When I look upon the manifold and grand discouragements, which you still meet with from the unthankfulnesse of that People, with whose liberties, comforts, and well being in every kind your soul daily is *in travail*, I apprehend great cause of fear lest your hands should hang down from the work, considering that the arm of omnipotencie it self contracted an impotencie when time was, from the unworthinesse of those, for whose sake it was otherwise readie to have lift up it self gloriously." And yet, Goodwin reminded Parliament of the very greatest guarantee to be found in the law of Freedom: "If ye shall chuse out the God of *Israel* . . . to serve . . . he will not, *he cannot denie himself* to be yours."[10]

There is, he had reflected in a tract written a year earlier concerning a truth that Milton's Adam is about to experience, "a certain mysteriousnesse in the means, which shall at any time be levied and advanced for the bringing of some great end to passe . . . [such that men's understandings will confess] that according to the rate of their speculations and workings, they should never have come near it."[11] With the hindsight of history, Goodwin reminded Parliament in 1649 that God has shown himself most likely to "act such matters of Grace for the Children of men . . . when he hath Agents at hand," mentioning especially the agency of Moses ("of God / Highly belov'd" [*PL* 12.307]), who was "able and willing too, to bring *water in abundance out of a rock* for the preservation of the lives of such men . . . whom *Moses* himself thought it no wrong, to call Rebels." Goodwin's fervent hope was to convince the Commons "that God hath fitted you . . . to the lifting up of this poor Nation from the gates of death."[12] His approach was to try to impart to his readers an appreciation of God's sheer inventiveness in the means that he finds to govern under law, to maintain the perfection of his creation. That God's ways are accessible to rational understanding, Goodwin had pointed out, does not mean that they are all as predictable as the secondary effects of nature's physical operations. One unpredictable "wonder" is to be experienced at the act which for humans forms the basis of all God's "sundry dispensations," that is, at God's invention of the Incarnation, which brilliantly incorporates "co-eternality and consubstantiation . . . being made flesh," and so on.[13] A God who could imagine the Incarnation, he told Parliament, can use you, under natural law, to accomplish any holy goal, however impossible seeming.

Similarly, Milton shows us that there was a time when "Admiration seiz'd / All heav'n, what this might mean and whither tend / Wond'ring" (PL 3.271–73). Christ's engagement of manhood and death was a "means levied" that "according to the rate of their speculations" even the angels "should never have come near." However, just as Goodwin had insisted was possible for human beings, once Milton's God has revealed his solution, the angels understand it fully, as their song of lines 372–415 confirms, expressing their joy in the operation of God's law, which, encompassing "Mercy and Justice both" (132), is used "by Heav'nly love" wonderously to "outdo Hellish hate" (298).

Milton's newly fallen Adam must work his way toward such an understanding of God's ways. He has asked exactly the right question concerning his posterity: "How can they acquitted stand / In sight of God?" In the drama of the moment its tone is rhetorical, yet the question has in fact been answered by Christ's offer to die for humanity's offense. But Adam rightly knows that he himself has forfeited his own ability to serve (rule) his posterity.

For Adam to be able to determine his own role in experiencing death, he must first come to appreciate that, under natural law, death has its own nature and consequences. It is at the moment that he corrects Eve for suggesting suicide that Milton shows him beginning to see God's solution, to suspect that death may in reality be somehow a liberating force. Eve's "contempt of life and pleasure seems / To argue in [her] something more sublime / And excellent than what [her] mind contemns" (10.1013–15).

The farthest that Adam can now come toward identifying "something more sublime / And excellent" than the pleasures of unfallen earthly life is, first, to recall God's promise of just punishment for Satan and, second, to surmise the possibility of something even "more sublime" from the God who has already shown them the divine mercies of sustaining work and the joy of children. Having come around "diligently and impartially" to remember God as they have actually experienced his rule, Adam and Eve are ready to pray, and so the long way to a full knowledge of the complex workings of God's righteousness, of Providence, is open to them.

As Goodwin tried to instill courage in the Parliament, so Milton offers this central insight to the readers of his poem: death, in truth, is one of God's surprising mercies. The God of justice is not opposed to the God of love: God's infinitely creative fulfillment of the law's terms is what pre-

serves human freedom and hence humanity. That God's law allows punishment for evil—that it does not either allow evil to exist unchecked or
allow simple extinction—is its perfection. So death, we are urged to see
from the point of view of the King of Heaven, becomes man's final
remedy:

> I at first with two fair gifts
> Created him endow'd, with Happiness
> And Immortality; that fondly lost,
> This other serv'd but to eternize woe:
> Till I provided Death; so Death becomes
> His final remedy, and after Life
> Tri'd in sharp tribulation, and refin'd
> By faith and faithful works, to second Life,
> Wak'd in the renovation of the just,
> Resigns him up with Heav'n and Earth renew'd.   (11.57–66)

There is only one ruler who is capable of serving fallen human beings
under the terms of God's justice, who can be an absolute monarch *because*
he will infallibly adhere to law; and he is Christ, whom God exalted to rule
and "whose coming we look for" (*A Defence, CPW*, IV, pt. 1:427). Not
only on earth, but in all creation, the law is between king and subjects; yet
the omnipotent God is not prevented but enabled by the law to perform
his great creative works of love.

WE HAVE seen that the law allows God, regardless of angelic or human sin,
to retain his divine freedom ultimately to do good. Sinful creatures,
however, suffer under the law. From their viewpoint the God of law seems
harsh; yet Milton still believed that the law is God's greatest gift and mercy
to them. "I will walk at liberty," the psalmist vows, "for I seek thy
precepts" (Psalm 119:45). God's precepts free a rational creature, even a
fallen one; for they ensure his or her contining liberty to choose the truth.

Psalm 5, which Milton translated in 1653, develops a commentary on the
relation of the law to the creature's freedom. There the singer prays for
God's punishment of the wicked: "God, find them guilty, let them fall /
By their own counsel quell'd," and concludes, "Then all who trust in thee shall
bring / Their joy . . . For thou Jehovah wilt be found / To bless the just
man still." Compare the theme of Psalm 7: the wicked one "digg'd a pit,
and delv'd it deep / And fell into the pit he made:

His mischief that due course doth keep,
Turns on his head, and his ill trade
Of violence will undelay'd
Fall on his crown with ruin steep.

And compare the conclusion:

Then will I Jehovah's praise
According to his justice raise
And sing the Name and Deity
Of Jehovah the most high.

The speaker in both psalms seems to set the terms under which he will worship Jehovah: God must, by the evidence of his justice, prove himself to be the true God. Only then will the psalmist acknowledge the "Deity / Of Jehovah."

This setting of terms is the most essential exercise of the freedom of a rational creature. A free man cannot worship a false God who would sell him into slavery to evil. And slavery means either the emasculation that is wickedness unpunished or oppression that is goodness punished. Thus the singer of the seventh psalm pleads for judgment, first of all, on himself who is accused of wrongdoing: if I have thought or done wrong, he says, judgment is what God commands and what I desire. And second, on his accusers: if I am found innocent, cause both the wickedness and the power of evil men over myself and over nations to cease:

So th' assemblies of each Nation
Will surround thee, seeking right,
Thence to thy glorious habitation
Return on high and in their sight.
Jehovah judgeth most upright
All people from the world's foundation.

In the heaven of *Paradise Lost* we see one angel of an assembled nation depend similarly on the righteousness of God's judgment when he finds himself falsely accused by his ruler of servility to a declared enemy and disloyalty to his governor and peers. Following the injunction of the Apostle—so constantly quoted by the English revolutionaries—to "try all things and hold fast to that which is good," Abdiel reasons that by the first law of created nature Christ is the angels' superior, and that by the same law they hold their own titles and powers. Neither Satan, he argues, nor all the angels together can rightly claim to be

> Equal to him begotten Son, by whom
> As by his Word the mighty Father made
> All things . . .

The angels' realization, confirmed through Christ's exaltation, that Christ is not an immensely superior angel impossible to measure up to, but a divine being, frees them to achieve angelic greatness in the exercise of their roles as

> Essential Powers, nor by his Reign obscur'd,
> But more illustrious made, since he the Head
> One of our number thus reduc't becomes.

In response to Satan's claim that Christ plans "to bind with laws the free," Abdiel recalls the very definition of freedom:

> His Laws our Laws, all honor to him done
> Returns our own.   (5.835–45)

Satan lies by distorting elements of the truth; the angels have until now been free and have acted without checking their actions against a codified law. That is what it means to be unfallen, to know the good—the law—without knowing ill. The angels have not lived, as Satan tries to claim, without law. Like God, they have lived the law itself—"His Laws our Laws." Those who now fall, fall still under the law. Thus Abdiel is confident that "other Decrees" than "those indulgent Laws"

> Against thee are gone forth without recall;
> That Golden Sceptre which thou didst reject
> Is now an Iron Rod to bruise and break
> Thy disobedience.   (5.884–88)

Abdiel's confidence is that of the psalmist whom Milton translated in 1653. Psalm 2 is a threat to the Gentile nations who "Lay deep their plots together . . . / Against the Lord and his Messiah dear." "Let us break off, say they, by strength of hand / Their bonds"; "the Lord shall scoff them, then severe / Speak to them . . . but I, saith hee, / Anointed have my King (though ye rebel) / On Sion my holi' hill." The psalmist continues in the voice of that King with words that are echoed in God's exaltation of the Son (*Paradise Lost* 5.600–15) as well as in Abdiel's warning:

> the Lord to me hath said,
> Thou art my Son, I have begotten thee
> This day; ask of me, and the grant is made;
> As thy possession I on thee bestow
> Th'Heathen, and as thy conquest to be sway'd
> Earth's utmost bounds: them shalt thou bring full low
> With iron sceptre bruis'd. . . .

God's judgment and reward comes for Abdiel's absolute righteousness more immediately than it can come to righteousness in a fallen world, but the justifications of Abdiel and of the Jewish psalmist and of the English revolutionaries are the same:

> Servant of God, well done, well hast thou fought
> The better fight, who single hast maintain'd
> Against revolted multitudes the Cause
> Of Truth.   (6.29–32)

Satan himself identifies God's justice as the only possible meaning for the word *love*. To have judged him differently, Satan recognizes in his soliloquy in book 4, God would have had to betray the law which defines the freedom of the other angels.

> Hadst thou the same free Will and Power to stand?
> Thou hadst: whom hast thou then or what to accuse,
> But Heav'n's free Love dealt equally to all?
> Be then his Love accurst, since love or hate,
> To me alike, it deals eternal woe.   (4.66–70)

God's wrath is a manifestation of his love; and Satan's woe must last as long as he holds himself outside of the law of his own being.

EVE FALLS before the same argument that Abdiel rejects, even though she has heard Raphael's story of that first Fall. From Raphael, Adam and Eve learn about their own free will, that "freely we serve, / Because we freely love, as in our will / To love or not" (5.538–40). This new insight changes nothing, however, in their relation to God and his law

> nor knew I not
> To be both will and deed created free;
> Yet that we never shall forget to love
> Our maker, and obey him whose command
> Single, is yet so just, my constant thoughts
> Assur'd me and still assure.   (5.548–53)

Before the Fall, Adam and Eve are like the unfallen angels, aware that "His Laws" are "our Laws." When Adam sins, he falls as Abdiel stood, still aware, "not deceiv'd." It is Eve, separated from Adam, who becomes confused by Satan's claims about the relation between God's goodness and his power, about the connections between natural and positive law. "God therefore cannot hurt ye, and be just: / Not just, not God; not fear'd then, nor obey'd" (9.700–01). Satan's aim, as with the angels he has corrupted, is to use the subject's belief that only a just ruler should be obeyed as his means to wrench the subject's loyalty from God, whose justice he impugns.

Eve's response upon seeing that the serpent has led her to "the Tree / Of prohibition" is to rehearse the laws, positive and natural, which she and Adam had discussed at their parting.

> But of this Tree we may not taste nor touch;
> God so commanded, and left that Command
> Sole daughter of his voice; the rest, we live
> Law to ourselves, our Reason is our Law.   (9.651–54)

Satan's plan in light of this faith in reason is—as it was in seducing the angels—to pervert the sense in which humans live "law to themselves" by making a positive command of God, a letter of the law, appear unreasonable and thus to seem to open up a whole new reality with no, or as yet unknown, laws; or, as Adam fears, "by some fair appearing good" to "dictate false, and misinform the Will / To do what God expressly hath forbid" (9.354–56). Satan paints for Eve a vision of a world in which God's revelation is no longer the measure of all things, and Eve allows herself to believe she is "ignorant":

> What fear I then, rather what know to fear
> Under this ignorance of Good and Evil,
> Of God or Death, of Law or Penalty?   (9.773–75)

Eve's ignorance is, of course, an illusion, penetrable by reason. Apart from intuition, knowledge is attained in only two ways: by the intellect contemplatively and by experience actively. Thus, one may know good by experience and by understanding at the same time as one may know evil intellectually: this is the condition of Adam and Eve before their fall. Or one may know evil by experience and then good only intellectually: this is Satan's condition. But the experience of pure good and the experience of evil are mutually exclusive. Evil is the absence of good; and therefore the tree is, as Adam afterward acknowledges, the tree of the knowledge of good lost and evil gained.

At the moment before her fall, given her intellectual confusion, Eve has open to her two morally valid courses of action. She can, with no further thought, dismiss the amazing serpent as mistaken, once he suggests the betrayal of the "sole daughter of God's voice," or she can try to understand how the many twisting confusions that the serpent raises are to be deciphered without betraying the command. A fideistic belief in God's divine right to be obeyed would underlie a choice of the first alternative. But however much latitude Milton's unfaltering commitment to religious freedom allowed his tolerance of the many versions of faith possible to fallen humanity, we should never expect to see fideism in his free Eden, as his Satan is well aware.

Satan defends his "great cause" (9.672) first with echoes of Eden's theology. A command from the governor of the universe, the serpent implies, must be just to be obeyed—"Not just, not God" (9.701). His temptation finally, however, is to atheism—"The Gods are first, and that advantage use / On our belief, that all from them proceeds" (9.718–19)— and *simultaneously* to a fideistic emphasis on God's omnipotence—"What can your knowledge hurt him, or this Tree / Impart against his will if all be his?" (9.727–28). The reasoning of Milton's serpent is so devilishly brilliant that even its conjunction of the blind disbelief of atheism with the blind faith of fideism has not stopped some readers from yielding to a "fideistic" reading of Eve's temptation and fall: Milton must have meant that though she cannot understand why, she should unquestioningly obey the letter of the law. Such blind obedience, though, is not commanded by Milton's God. In the "divine order," as Hooker explains the humanist position, "the prominence of chiefest acceptation is by the best things worthily challenged" (*Laws* 80; 1.7.7). Satan will challenge Eve's "chiefest acceptation," and she is not wrong—in Milton's prelapsarian world—to let her mind engage the serpent's claim to represent "the best thing," however surprising it seems.

"There is not that good which concerneth us, but it hath evidence enough for it selfe, if reason were diligent to search it out. Through neglect thereof, abused wee are with the shew of that which is not,

sometimes the subtilty of Satan inveagling us as it did Eve" (*Laws* 81; 1.7.7).
Eve's failure comes in not reasoning long or hard enough, and in not
calling upon the collaboration of another reasoner.[14] Her rational sin lies
not primarily in her faulty logic, but in her failure to persevere until logic
and evidence yield an understanding of God's consistency: "In doing evill,
we prefer a less good before a greater, the greatness whereof is by reason
investigable, and may be known" (*Laws* 81; 1.7.7).

The tree, as she has known, is a sign of human free will; and free will is
the necessary condition for the existence of goodness and evil in the
experience of a rational being. Now, at the fall, if God *is* just, the vehicle
appointed for the "knowledge of good and evil" must yield what its name
and command promise: that knowledge by experience of evil's relation to
good which is the experience of death.

Had Eve persevered, she would have to have seen that the "wisdom"
which Satan offers brings with it a whole new and unknown world. Once
her reason admits Satan's position as possible, then everything in the old
order should become suspect—including those parts of it which Satan
wants her still to assume (as that she shall be as a god, since the snake has
become as a human, is "but proportion meet") and including the validity,
the "rightness" of her reason. For what reason until now has been right
about is the same truth that every known thing in creation has existed in
proportion to: the absolute fidelity to law of the God who forbids the fruit
of this tree. It is indeed a "rash" hand that, in the face either of moral
wrong or of a reality whose principles are as yet completely unknown,
plucks the fruit.

Satan's new reality, like the destination of Eve's flight in her dream,
does not exist. God is just, he is God, and he must carry out sin's
punishment: "they not obeying, / Incurr'd, what could they less, the
penalty" (10.12–15). Adam himself after the fall considers his judgment in
view of the conditionate terms of God's decrees, which insure their
validity. "Did I request thee, Maker, from my Clay / To mould me Man,
did I solicit thee / From darkness to promote me, or here place," he
demands, crying for the extinction which God will not give him; "inexplicable / Thy Justice seems." Still, he must admit all of the truth that he
knows thus far about justice:

> yet to say truth, too late
> I thus contest, then should have been refus'd
> Those terms whatever, when they were propos'd:
> Thou didst accept them; wilt thou enjoy the good,
> Then cavil the conditions? (10.743–59)

Empson objects that Adam is being unfair to himself here since we saw him enter into no contract. But we have witnessed the "contract" made as it really happens—not, to be sure, between two equals, but between the Creator and his creatures under the law. God first gives humans the good, so that they fully know how desirable it is. When the conditions of the gift are made completely clear, that is, when humans, who naturally want to and do fulfill the conditions, learn that there is a way they might fall, they then reasonably, freely, confirm their previous acceptance. Humans are free to be what they were created to be—good, in harmony with the natural order—or not. They naturally want to be this rather than nothing or evil.

If we, as readers, prefer to consider an ideal ethical "freedom" as consisting of the ability to make an arbitrary choice with no undesirable consequences from any choice made, then we are not alone: the divine model for such choice-making is the voluntaristic deity whom we have met in the theologies of both priest and presbyter. In Milton's reality, however, the divine image in human beings requires that what we believe about God, we also recognize in the human mirror. If we ask: How can Adam and Eve have been initially free to choose if everything in their being inclined them to accept? we are asking a theological question about the relation of God's goodness to his omnipotence. For Milton, this inclination and this acceptance were the only meaning of freedom; and a just judgment, freedom's only preservation.

GOD's government of his unfallen angels is another area in which divine justice is questioned by readers of Milton's epic. John Peter agrees with Satan's decrying of the angels' "servility"; for Empson, the unfallen angels' freedom is a mockery because there is no room in their lives for meaningful responsibility. When Satan taunts Gabriel, who has not experienced evil or pain, as one of those "whose easier business were to serve thir Lord / High up in Heav'n, with songs to hymn his Throne, / And practis'd distances to cringe, not fight" (4.942–45), the boast rings hollow because Gabriel and the other angels have fought, not against God but against Satan himself. Critics of the poem, however, are accusing not the angels but their God, claiming that what valor the angels show in battle and other attempted service is essentially betrayed by a God who sends them on missions he knows they cannot accomplish.[15]

The same claim has been cast in a more positive light by Stanley Fish, who argues that Milton makes his angels' service seem ridiculous—makes them, in Arnold Stein's scriptural formulation, "fools for God"—so that the reader will learn the true meaning of heroism, that is, obedience to God, not only or primarily in the face of violent enemies but even more importantly, in the face of a temptation to despair of God's purposes and favor. Thus, "Abdiel is a hero because he keeps loyalty even when his objective eludes him [his warning of the good angels turns out to be unnecessary] and his assumptions fail the test of experience [he is unable to defeat Satan in arms] . . . [He] does not abandon his post or question the ways of God when his sense of justice is disappointed; and his stead-fastness is all the more remarkable because it is in no sense necessary."[16]

Boyd Berry has attempted to cast this observation in more specifically seventeenth-century terms: "Milton's is a Puritan God, above all omnip-otent"; he is "the arch-Puritan in the way he repeatedly sends his creatures on missions which . . . eventuate in no conclusion." For Berry, Milton's artistry does not reflect so much a consummate control of his reader's spiritual experience as an unconscious tension in the artist arising from the "ideological illogical" character of "Puritan optimism": "If God does all . . . how can one reasonably undertake to reform society?" "God will prevail yet his . . . Saints must fight." Berry concludes that the seventeenth-century Puritan saint "could not expect to operate transi-tively and decisively upon the universe about him." Similarly, in Mil-ton's epic, "virtuous angels . . . make gestures of faith which testify to their commitment but do not seriously and transitively alter the world around them."[17] Human and angelic interiority in this reading takes its definition from the impotence of the creatures of an omnipotent God, who does not need them.

Much of what these readings have to say about courageous steadfastness rings true both of poetic angels and of historical saints. Yet, as we might expect from the theological assumption about a "Puritan" God, these readings are seriously incomplete. The problem lies in those Puritans chosen as being appropriate to a reading of Milton. Three months after the execution of Charles I, the Leveller and Puritan William Walwyn, then Cromwell's prisoner in the Tower of London, penned two documents which we might consider in this context. They were major strategic efforts for a Leveller settlement of the commonwealth government by means of a revised "Agreement of the Free People of England," which, the "Mani-festation" of April 1649 declared, would be offered "because we know no better, and indeed no other way or means (but by such an Agreement) . . . to settle the Common-wealth upon the fairest probabilities of a lasting Peace, and contentfull Establishment." The imprisoned Levellers believed that their proposals had considerable popular support, "so we have reall ground to hope" for their adoption "(whatever shall become of us)." In the event, the Agreement was not adopted, the Leveller movement retained no major political identity after 1649, and the Levellers might seem to offer themselves as examples of Berry's description of "intransitive" witness to their loyalty to an omnipotent deity. Walwyn himself said repeatedly in self-justification: "We must notwithstanding discharge our Duties, which being performed, the successe is in God's hand."[18]

However, if we study the autobiographical writing Walwyn has left us, we discover that in fact this radical Puritan disapproved heartily and at length—in his writings and in the many critical discussions he admits to have made his habit—of the teaching and practice of those establishment Puritan preachers who are Berry's models, the Presbyterians and "silk-stocking" Independents. Among the few divine writings that Walwyn confesses he was "hearing and reading continually" so that he "had [them] as it were, without book" were "those peeces annexed to Mr. Hookers *Eclesiasticall pollicy*."[19] What the radical Puritan took away from his reading of Richard Hooker was not a "well-developed sense of the vastness of the gulf between God and man,"[20] but the humanist's very practical commitment to active collaboration with God. He trusted that his labor would have a "transitive" effect on his world as well as a "transcendant" effect on his own personal regeneration. In one of Walwyn's favorite pieces, the "Sermon of the Certainty and Perpetuity of Faith in the Elect," Hooker urges us to consider whether, if their thoughts are vain who think that their watching can preserve the city which God himself is not willing to keep, "are not theirs as vain who think that God will keep the city, for which they themselves are not careful to watch?" "Surely," he urges, "if we look to stand in the faith of the sons of God, we must hourly, continually, be providing and setting ourselves to strive." Though Christ's prayer for us, that we fail not, renders us ultimately invincible, yet "His prayer must not exclude our labour."[21]

John Goodwin tried systematically in voluminous treatises to address the mistaken notion that God does not need our help. Such a notion, he said, is admissible only in a limited theoretical sense, in relation to God's omnipotence; but it is not true in actuality because God's power is in fact "regulated": "meaning, that the Omnipotency of God in all the exertions, motions, and actings of it, submitteth it self willingly and with delight to a prudent and righteous regulation which it receiveth from his infinite wisdome and understandinge." Goodwin studies many scriptural texts for examples of how, as Psalm 90 says, *The Kings strength . . . loveth judgment*. One instructive instance is that reported in Acts 27:31, where the Apostle Paul on a ship in a storm says to the centurion and soldiers accompanying him of the mariners who are about to flee the ship, *"Except these abide in the ship, ye CANNOT be safe."* "Questionless," Goodwin comments, "the power of God, simply considered, did not stand in need of the help or presence of the Mariners, to preserve either the ship, or those that were in it from the danger, unto which both were now exposed; but the regulated power of God did." In this incident, according to Goodwin, God was letting the soldiers know, through Paul, "that unless they took a course to keep the Mariners also in the ship, it would not be in his power to save them." This is true because God's purpose in the saving act was to aid Paul in his ministry: "so the deliverance might be discerned to be given unto them by God for [Paul's] sake." Thus, "it would not be in God's power to save them" means "that it would not be honourable in point of wisdom for him to save them; in which respect he could not do it."[22] Walwyn considered Goodwin too long-winded to be an effective teacher (and he suffered at the hands of some members of his congregation, as did Goodwin himself); but the two radical Puritans shared this fundamental belief about God's regulation of his omnipotence.

It is a theological, psychological, and political mistake to attribute to revolutionaries like Walwyn, Goodwin, and Milton a Calvinistic worry about a "temptation inherent in the desire to serve," as Fish seems to do when he summarizes: "The desire to serve God is a particularly subtle form of pride if in fact it is a desire to feel needed and important."[23] On the contrary, these reformers believed that the desire to feel "needed" is God-given and based in God's real (willed) need. From this faith comes the Miltonic version of the Christian practice of "reading the providences," studying experiences, events, and the outcomes of human effort to understand in them God's meaning and to discern in them God's direction for the next actions.

Milton's response to understanding those events in which we are tempted to say we "were not needed" or "did not succeed" is like that of the famous Puritan preacher John Preston, who was active at Cambridge when Milton came to the University with the intention of becoming such a clergyman. Preston, who was silenced by Laud for preaching to the King about the danger of ignoring God's providential warnings, advised the godly not to be simpleminded in reading God's providences, and particularly to consider that no event has a single automatic and generally applicable interpretation, whether the event brings pleasure or pain. Not events, but "God only is able to do good or hurt to a person"; thus no event can be in itself understood as being either good or bad, "successful" or "unsuccessful," except in reference to the state of the souls involved. All people or groups must judge a particular event's meaning for them both "according to the uprightness of [their] heart" *and* "according to [their] works," to the vigor of their commitment to put a plan into action in God's service.[24] Milton claimed in 1654 about the Puritans' success what Preston in the 1620s had urged in the face of their apparent failure. Only Papists, Preston had said, argue that their temporal success proves the justice of their cause. "A cause is neither proved good by success nor shown to be evil," according to Milton. "We insist, not that our cause be judged by the outcome, but that the outcome be judged by the cause" (*Second Defence, CPW* 4, pt. 1:652).

"Use the meanes [that seem best to you] and depend and trust in God for the bringing it to passe," Preston urged. We must be prepared—as Walwyn and Milton were twenty years later—to accept any momentary outcomes of our efforts, reasoning that when we work and pray in God's own cause for an outcome that does not occur, "it may be that God hears [us], but it crosseth some other secret passage of his Providence. There are many things that God, the great Governour of the World, must bring together." We should be prepared, with Goodwin, to admit that though we know the general laws under which God is operating, our speculations *in medias res* will likely not approach the creative brilliance of God's actual solution. "A man cannot see round about all the corners of God's Providence," Preston observed pragmatically.[25] "Suppose we pray, that such a great Prince should raise the Churches, that such a warre, that such an enterprise and project may doe it; put the case the Lord will not do it so, are wee then presently undone? And is there no help, because such a battaile is overthrown, because such a King did not succeed, because such a Generall had not success according to our expectation? It may be that is not the way."[26]

This view of providential history, unlike one that grows from a belief in a voluntaristic deity and a nominalistic universe, looks at events not as discrete manifestations of God's intervention in human affairs, but as a complex, ultimately unified, network of passages comprising God's universal government. The individual faithful participant cannot reasonably doubt that his service is needed. Whether an individual's actions have been accepted as "well done" will be known to the individual, "according to the uprightness of his heart."

This view of providence also is at the base of the Miltonic insistence on the importance of diligently sorting out the individual responsibilities of participants in a cause. Because God's government is rationally accessible, we can expect after an event to understand its justice as concerns us, to judge our own and our peers' roles in it. Such judging—a part of reading the providences—is vital because each event forms part of the context for a next decision and course of action. It is our means of staying actively on course.

This recognition underlay Walwyn's autobiographical writing. Charged with seeking to divide the Army by his insistence on reforms, his *Just Defence* (1649) is concerned to straighten out the issues. What has divided the Army (who now has the responsibility for settling a government) is not Walwyn's idealistic activism but the generals' self-serving willingness to compromise the revolutionary cause: "for my part, I ever most earnestly desired their union, so it were in good, and for that Freedom and good to the Nation, for which, I believe, most of them have fought; and if they divide for want of it, they divide them that keep them from it, and not I, that wish with all my heart that cause of division were not." Though in the event, the Army did divide, it was not "a fault in those that separated themselves for good, but blameworthy in those that would not unite except for evil: So that to unite or divide is not the thing; but whether in good, or evil, is the main of all; and by which my Adversaries and I shall one day be judged" (357–58).

Unlike Walwyn, Milton in 1649 chose to support the settlement arrived at by Cromwell, but consistent with his libertarian belief, he also chose not to attack the Levellers, even though their opposition, as the Council of State recognized, was tactically dangerous to the cause. In 1652 he used his base as a loyal and effective secretary to the Commonwealth, in his most public voice and while defending the Cause, to warn Cromwell against betraying the heart of the revolution (*A Second Defence, CPW* 4, pt. 1:673). The Leveller John Lilburne was quick to point out this fact by translating this section of the *Defence's* Latin into plain English and commending "unto the serious and hearty consideration of the Lord Generall and his Confederates the advice of their valiant and learned Champion Mr. Milton."[27] In 1660 Milton himself implored his readers to judge individual roles in the cause's prosecution and base the next urgently required right action upon that judgment. The revolution, he claimed, had consisted of "just and religious deeds, though don by som to covetous and ambitious ends, yet not therefor to be staind with their infamie, or they to asperse the integritie of others" (*Ready and Easy Way, CPW* 7:422).

This public sorting of responsibilities mattered to Walwyn and Milton because what was at stake for them was not only their own personal (interior) steadfastness, their standing fast, but also the efficacy of the roles in which God needed them to act.[28] Walwyn gave expression to this radicalized Christian humanism in the *Letter to Fairfax* (1649); whether a man's interior state be mastered by covetousness or by love, he said, "let the bodies of men act love, humility and righteousness one towards another."[29]

Milton explained the danger in focusing too much on the interior stances of the agents to an event when we are figuring out the next step in a course of action. A crucial case in point, in 1660, was the behavior of the parliaments under Cromwell's purgings. The members who remained "knew the people of *England* to be a free people, themselves the representers of that freedom." In spite of the motives of the purgers and in spite of the possible virtue of some of those expelled, "if others were excluded . . . [those who remained] were not therefore to leave the helm of government in no hands, to discontinue thir care of the public peace and safetie." Further, even if corrupt members remained with them, they did not "measure votes or counsels by the intentions of them that voted; knowing that intentions either are but guessed at, or not soon anough known; and although good, can neither make the deed such, nor prevent the consequence from being bad." For Milton, it was necessary, but not enough, to be pure in heart; one had also to work hard to figure out a way in each circumstance to act efficaciously: "who had not rather follow *Iscariot* or *Simon* the magician, though to covetous ends, preaching, then *Saul*, though in the uprightness of his heart persecuting the gospell?" (*Ready and Easy Way, CPW* 7:411–15).

Furthermore, a failed effort is never the end of the story, but is another "providence" to be judged and incorporated into the plans for a next step. In 1660 Milton assented to criticism, "Tis true indeed, when monarchie was dissolvd, the form of a Commonwealth should have forthwith bin fram'd; and the practice therof immediatly begun. . . . this care . . . too much neglected . . . hath bin our mischief. Yet . . . Now is the opportunitie, now the very season wherein we may obtain . . . and establish it" (*CPW* 7:430). Milton's prose writings give no evidence to suggest that he ever abandoned this radical (Puritan) humanism with its faith in the importance of what Berry calls acting "transitively," with its readiness to work out the next step most likely to succeed. Neither do the angels in *Paradise Lost*.

If, for instance, we are concerned that Abdiel is not rewarded by success for his efforts, we should be focusing not primarily on his role in the physical war, but on the failure of his first grand effort to serve God by persuading Satan to repent. When he demands, "fervent," after giving all his reasons, that Satan "hast'n to appease / Th' incensed Father, and th' incensed Son, / While Pardon may be found in time besought" (5.845–47), and when Satan, twisting Abdiel's reasons for his own propaganda purposes, turns him into his challenge-bearing messenger, this should be read as the greatest moment of humiliation for Abdiel. Because Satan's evil is so obviously powerful, however, and perhaps because of a twentieth-century proclivity for existential statement, many readers do not even imagine Abdiel's surprise here but imagine instead that his defiance of Satan is simply a courageous (intransitive) gesture of witnessing. In fact, he has intended a transitive effect, Satan's conversion.

What is Abdiel's response to his failed effort? "O . . . I see thy fall / Determin'd" (877–79)—I see that you have passed the point where the plan I was trying could work. For Abdiel here, as for the regicides in 1649, came the realization that the time for words, for "treating," with the rebellious ruler was past. Many of the Puritans at this point had found themselves stymied, unable to accede to the Army's astounding next step, the judgment and execution of the king, and unable to form a new plan themselves. In the poem Abdiel immediately formulates a next plan, which is, simply, to separate. This is a decision for a transcendant, not a transitive, act. We learn in 6.20–21 that Abdiel has intended to share with the other angels the news of Satan's rebellion, the news—as he thinks—that God is about to crush the rebels. His "failure" to be the bearer of news cannot be viewed as much of a challenge to his faith; the message was not part of a plan of action, just a minor expectation. Abdiel is aware that God has full knowledge of Satan's rebellion, as he has told the rebels. But when he sees that the angels not only also know, but are armed, then he learns a new "providence"—that he and some of the other angels will have an active part in God's subduing of Satan. He learns that his service is to be "transitive" again; he is to join the army.

When he encounters Satan's forces, again Abdiel has a new "providence" to read concerning his individual role in the army. He finds himself jolted by the appearance of beauty in Satan and his troops; by his discovery that beauty, for the first time in his experience, is not truth. Here he "ponders" (6.127) a puzzle handed him by Providence. He knows, however, that there is a conditionate term for the "law" that truth is beautiful, that is, that falsehood is not strength; therefore, he resolves that he will put truth to the test in a free and open encounter. The "transitive" outcome he aims for is his own physical defeat of Satan.

What exactly does he think he is doing? In the language of the seventeenth-century revolutionaries, he intends to "Try all things, and hold fast that which is good" (I Thess. 5.21).[30] For Milton, Goodwin, and Walwyn, Paul's words enjoined a personal search for spiritual truth and a corresponding collective defense of religious and civil liberty. Abdiel has tried Satan's moral claims; now he tries his physical claims. His goal is victory in battle; he trusts that he will win because reason must win. He steps forth and defies his former governor: "Proud, art thou met?" (6.131).

Does his action have serious transitive effects? Satan staggers, his troops are furious with rage; the loyal angels are given a "providence," which they interpret as a presage of victory, and they feel a fierce desire for battle. We do not hear that Abdiel expects to end the impending war in one stroke. He expects that he will "win in Arms." He is not disappointed but rewarded with the accomplishment of initiating the battle. This is a task that needs to be done. Satan, as we read and Abdiel here realizes (6.131–35), may well have planned no verbal exchange to begin the battle. The loyal angels are helped by hearing from Satan himself the evil that they otherwise would have had to fight on God's authority alone. They have been prepared to obey by faith; but, it turns out, Abdiel does the very significant service of helping them know their foe's evil (that is, the justice and necessity of their own cause) directly, experientially. His challenge dramatically reinforces the freedom of his fellow soldiers. And beyond this moment, his act performs the same service, through Raphael's telling, to Adam and Eve; and through Milton's telling, to us. It is an act with mighty transitive consequences. Abdiel does not need to know them all; his basic philosophy assumes their existence: God takes his faithful, rational acts—those done in accordance with the law of "God and Nature" (6.176)—and uses them in the government of his creation by natural law.

The Archangel Michael, as head of all the loyal armies, begins the actual fighting by obeying a direct, unambiguous injunction from God to blow the trumpet and initiate the charge. While Michael heads the fight, his heroic leadership, which Raphael calls a "warlike toil" (6.257), is not unlike the work of humans in Paradise in that it consists of directing perfection since "Leader seem'd / Each warrior single as in Chief, expert [and] . . . each on himself reli'd, / As only in his arm the moment lay / Of victory" (6.232–40). This account fits Berry's description of the kind of tasks "Puritans" would positively "enjoy"; it is the military version of Eden's "flowered treadmill."[31]

We may notice, however, that Michael at Satan's approach is "glad" rather at the providence that has shown him cause to "surcease" this toil. He hopes that Satan's singling him out means that this is the moment for the usurper's defeat and the end of the rebellion. The end will come, he reasons, either through an extended but more focused battle begun now by his own "avenging Sword" or immediately by "some more sudden vengeance wing'd from God" (278–79). In either case, this is a providence easy for him to interpret and act upon; since he can leave the second alternative to God, he proceeds immediately to carry out the first. In the event, both of Michael's expected courses happen. Immediately, the Archangel defeats Satan and "begins [his] doom" (6.278) by tumbling him with a physical "rebuke" (6.342) that corresponds to Abdiel's verbal one. The rebuke is a providence to both sides—a revelation of Satan's weakness to be read and acted upon. In response to it, both sides continue the battle, the one in defiance of, the other in obedience to this providence.

Milton offers us Michael's and Abdiel's unfallen insight that each event, or outcome, is a providence to be read in preparation for the next effort, which will then result in an "event" or outcome. The story has many climaxes, larger and smaller; it begins here and will continue until time ends and God is all in all. The angels carry on, responding to the invention of artillery with their own invention of the ultimate natural weapon, the mountains. They do faithfully "what war can do." Now "war"—but not one of the loyal angels—is "wearied" at the end of the second day's battle. Raphael, the providential historian, reports God's account of how he is working through natural law: God leaves the war to itself until it has enacted its natural potential fully. Once the angels have experienced the full operation of this natural law, he reveals to their experience what they have already accepted on faith—a related but higher law—the different power "above compare" of Christ's "Virtue and Grace / Immense" (6.702–05).

How do the angels receive this next providence? They are "surpris'd"; Christ's arrival is "unexpected" (6.774). They have been prepared to continue their "warlike toil," "unwearied," confident that eventually Satan's forces will fall. While the angels have felt no pain or weariness, however, Raphael shares with Adam the strain that they *have* experienced in this second day's battle: they have had to enter a new world, "under ground . . . in dismal shade: / Infernal noise"; the war has seemed to take them out of Heaven, their home, and into Chaos, "horrid confusion heap't / Upon confusion" (6.666–69). But it is a civil war and this "ruin overspread" is their own Heaven. Out of their own resources, they can battle the new artillery, but they cannot recreate Heaven, their home, with "the pleasure situate in Hill and Dale." It seems only likely that "now all Heav'n / [will go] to wrack" (6.669–70). Michael does not doubt that—the battle continuing—eventually his forces will be able to drive Satan's out. In fact, Raphael reveals, Michael is right. God chooses, however, not to allow the battle to go on for as long as would be necessary under the secondary effects of the operation of natural law, for the sin-caused impairment of the rebels to work "sensibly" (6.690–91) to their weakening and defeat. The war in heaven, a magnified, telescoped version of all that war can do, is therefore very short.

It is over very suddenly. The coming of God's twenty thousand chariots, millions of warriors, and the panoplied Messiah on his cherub-borne sapphire throne must have been for the loyal angels a providence too astounding to interpret in an operational sense: who can guess what Christ's orders will be now? But what to *do* with this providence is clear. Michael's "joyful" response is to "reduce" his army, to "circumfuse" its identity into the larger body of all the angels under Christ. Christ's first act, which makes so much rational sense to the loyal angels after the fact, is to recreate their homeland—a providential evidence, as Raphael identifies it, of his creative power. The final providence of the war—the advance of Christ's chariot—is met first with the "silence" of the angelic "Eye-witness" necessary to understand it and then with the "Jubilee" attendant to their celebration of their great happiness in the rightness of their ruler and their world. This victory of their King is God's greatest providence to them, and the touchstone by which all providences to angels and humans will be "read" and acted upon.

Has God needed their services? Christ tells them that *"this day"* (6.802) he does not. But for two momentous days he has very much needed just what they have "done" (6.805)—in exactly the same sense that Goodwin describes—not with regard to his abstract omnipotence, but with regard to his real chosen providence by which rational creatures can freely will their own righteousness. He had chosen the angels as his fit instruments; any of them could have refused to serve, as Satan did. To fulfill his will, God must have free-willed workers. Since God's will is for a universe governed by natural law, the moral part of which requires free agents, he needs their service.

The virtue of Fish's reading is that it stresses the value to the angels themselves of their own inner discipline regardless of the outcome of their external efforts, making the crucial observation that they could at any moment choose not to obey. Its limitation is that it tends to prevent the reader's full exercise of an experience Milton offers: that sorting of individual responsibilities in the reading of any providence which Milton found to be crucial to the maintenance of a revolutionary faith.

In answer to the very human objection that Gabriel's assignment to guard Eden against Satan's entrance is unfair because of God's foreknowledge that it would fail, Milton lets us hear God acknowledge that Gabriel and his troops did not fail to fulfill their task of guarding the garden and of turning back Satan with full warning, that it is with justice that they are "easily approv'd." The radical Christian humanist must understand that it is Satan's failing, not Gabriel's or God's, that Satan enters Eden fully warned. So too Uriel, standing watch from the sun, does not fail to act rightly in instructing the supposed stripling cherub who comes seeking the new world, and in reporting to Gabriel what he later sees on Mount Niphates. Only God can detect hypocrisy, and hypocrisy is the only evil which humans and angels cannot discern. To speak right and yet plot wrong is naturally within the power of a creature whose reason can discern the difference between good and evil. Yet this ability in no way hinders another rational creature from recognizing and rejecting the plotted wrong once it is revealed in word or deed. If Satan in the guise of the innocent serpent had spoken to Eve innocent words such as he spoke to Uriel in the guise of the cherub, her reason would, like that of Uriel, have been right in accepting them. "Who had not rather follow *Iscariot* preaching . . . then *Saul* . . . persecuting the gospell": the inner motivation of another agent cannot determine one's own moral decision or courage.

Satan's entry into the world is not the cause of human sin; its cause lies in the failure of Eve and Adam to act rightly in response to the providences of the risen serpent and fallen wife. If, at her temptation, Eve had weighed the serpent's words as rightly as Abdiel and Uriel do the angel's words, she would have remained blameless. Eve's right response would have been Abdiel's; reasoning thoroughly with the serpent and finding him ultimately intransigent, she should have separated and waited for another providence, for God to do something to the serpent. At his temptation, Adam has the possibility of resolutely sorting his own responsibility from the failed responsibility of his helpmeet. Adam's right response, without abandoning his corrupted co-worker, is to do his best to formulate a new "way to establish a free commonwealth" in Eden and trust that God will use his service for that goal, "whatever may become of him."

Had they read and acted faithfully on the providences, the first humans would have been as the angels are, their own actions, while freely willed, so closely in harmony with their ruler's will as to be thought of as part of him, like Uriel and the others of the seven who "are his Eyes" (3.650). They would doubtless, like the angels, have been able to show their posterity rewards for their service, for their "acts of Zeal and Love" in "Holy

Memorials" (5.592–94).[32] They and their descendants would have been able to experience, like the angels, that natural fulfillment in each others' society which their fall made impossible; and the invention of a state would have been unnecessary. Satan is indignant that humans should be served by angels:

> Man he made, and for him built
> Magnificent this World, and Earth his seat,
> Him Lord pronounc'd, and O indignity!
> Subjected to his service Angel wings,
> And flaming Ministers to watch and tend
> Thir earthly Charge.   (9.152–57)

But this service is simply an extension to the new world of the true meaning of that hierarchy ordained by "just right and the fixt Laws of Heav'n." By the same functioning of "Orders and Degrees," Uriel is of service to the "stripling Cherub," who bows before him in thanks, and Adam "with reverence, / As to a superior Nature, bowing low," is served by Raphael. The source and model for all the creatures' service is their king, who reigns in order to perform the hardest service for both angels and humans. Finally, they might have joined in the intricate harmony of heavenly songs that is possible because their form is a reflection of the vastly complex and yet absolutely unified providential content they express.

Thus to praise the heavenly king had in his youth been Milton's own life's purpose; and it had stayed with him throughout his years of service to the state to find fruition in the great poem of which the angels' song is a part. At the beginning of his involvement in the English reformation praise had seemed a relatively straightforward matter: "to sing and celebrate thy *divine Mercies*, and *marvelous Judgments* in this Land throughout all Ages; whereby this great and Warlike Nation instructed and inur'd to the fervent and continuall practice of *Truth* and *Righteousnesse*" may "be found the *soberest*, *wisest*, and *most Christian People*" on the day of judgment (*Of Reformation, CPW* 1:616). As the limits of his own divinely chosen, but divided nation became familiar to him over the years, he came to deepen his belief that in the course of history, "a man cannot see round about all the corners of God's providence," and that the praise itself of God's rule of this world must call upon all the faculties of angelic natures to mirror the perfect governance of such complexity. The closest Milton can bring us in *Paradise Lost* to sharing the angels' experience is to listen with Adam as Raphael describes their celebration of "solemn days":

> In song and dance about the sacred Hill,
> Mystical dance, which yonder starry Sphere
> Of Planets and of Fixt in all her Wheels
> Resembles nearest, mazes intricate,
> Eccentric, intervolv'd, yet regular
> Then most, when most irregular they seem:
> And in their motions harmony Divine
> So smooths her charming tones, that God's own ear
> Listens delighted.   (5.619–27)

This is the Heaven of "At a Solemn Musick" (ca. 1633),

> Where the bright Seraphim in burning row
> Their loud uplifted Angel-trumpets blow,
> And the Cherubic host in thousand choirs
> Touch their immortal Harps of golden wires.   (10–13)

But the poet's understanding of what God's "regulation," his use of the law to rule, must overcome before humankind may "again renew that Song" has become very much deepened through his years of seeking to bring the government and worship of England "in tune with Heav'n."

FOUR

Milton's Antinomianism and the Separation Scene in *Paradise Lost*

ONE OF Milton's additions to the Biblical story of the Fall is a dramatic episode of two hundred lines in book 9 during which Adam and Eve decide to work separately in the garden for a morning. The scene allows Satan to find Eve alone. But the interlude is too fully developed to be merely a device for getting Adam offstage; something central to Milton's vision of the human Fall is being dramatized. Why do Adam and Eve quarrel?

Fifty years ago Basil Willey suggested that Milton had "to attribute to Adam and Eve some of the frailties of fallen humanity" in order to make prelapsarian perfection "humanly convincing."[1] This line of thinking finds its extreme statement in the claim that Milton's Adam and Eve were created already fallen, that is, possessing vanity, curiosity, and other passions that a perfect creature would not feel.[2] A more recent interpretation of prelapsarian behavior recognizes that Milton, in the Puritan mode, viewed human perfection as a growing, dynamic—rather than static—state of being; that the emotional forces revealed by Eve's attraction to her own reflection, by her dream, by her disagreement with Adam—and by Adam's curiosity and his passion for his wife—are no more "fallen" or evil than is the vitality of the plants in Eden that "tend to wild."[3] They are the life energies of creation, as Milton claims in *Areopagitica* when he asks: "Wherefore did [God] create passions within us, pleasures round about us, but that these rightly temper'd are the very ingredients of vertu?" (*CPW* 2:527).

Readers today are still troubled by the way Milton depicts the life energies and their tempering in this psychologically challenging scene. In the 1950s Tillyard could claim that Eve is being coquettish, that she wants Adam to assert his masculinity and insist that she stay—coax her, tell her how much he loves her, and then put his foot down. In 1969 Fredson Bowers argued more schematically that Adam, as the embodiment of reason, should have commanded Eve, the embodiment of passion, not to go.[4] Others, however, have claimed that when Bowers, following what is implicit in a long line of arguments by male critics, maintains that Milton's Eve is not independently rational as well as sensual, he improperly denies Eve the full human dignity that Milton gives her in the poem; he denies that she is sufficient to stand, though free to fall. All these readings conclude that Adam had to let Eve go in order to preserve her liberty.[5]

I agree that the crux of the scene is in that one word "Go" and believe that what is at stake in this scene, as in the whole epic, is the meaning of human liberty. Because *Paradise Lost* shows us the first marriage, with all its psychological complexity, readers have assumed that Adam and Eve represent private human experience, that only "as a result of the fall" do they "become political beings."[6] But Milton offers us unfallen as well as fallen pictures of political life, in humans as in angels. The assumption that we are witnessing "the domestic drama"[7] of a "bourgeois couple"[8] must be balanced by an awareness that the portrayal of Adam and Eve—instead of simply exemplifying "the progressive privatization and sentimentalization of the domestic sphere"[9]—contains a treatment of "collective agency"[10] sought by politically concerned readers in Milton's day as in our own. The divorce tracts have rightly been taken as a contextual gloss on *Paradise Lost*. However, while it is true in one sense that these tracts emphasize "the satisfaction of psychological needs as the very 'end' for which marriage was ordained,"[11] it is important to remember that Milton's own struggle with a failed marriage was carried on in the midst of his campaign for "true Reformation in the state" (*DDD, CPW* 2:230). This "state," which requires continual reform, is a postlapsarian necessity; but society itself, in the Christian humanist view, was instituted by God at the creation of human beings (see chapter 1). Milton's tracts argue that to view procreation as the end of marriage is to ignore that institution's true ("very") end, which is to turn the private into a public self, to bind "the maried couple to all society of life, and communion [community, collectivity] in divine and humane things; and so associated" keep them (*The Judgment of Martin Bucer, CPW* 2:448). The "God-forbidd'n loneliness" that marriage is meant to allay is "dangerous to the Commonwealth," for it is "the household estate, out of which must flourish forth the vigor and spirit of all publick enterprizes" (*DDD, CPW* 2:247).

In his books *The World Turned Upside Down* (1972), *Milton and the*

English Revolution (1977), and *The Experience of Defeat* (1984) Christopher Hill points out the wide range of beliefs about those "publick enterprizes" that proliferated and received attention in England once parliamentary victories in the civil war had removed royal censorship. He raises important questions about Milton's belief in Christian liberty by showing the startling spectrum of contemporaries who, like the poet, believed the antinomian version of this doctrine. Many of Hill's readers have been distressed to find Milton's views combined with those of such strange characters as the Ranters, New Model Army preachers, New England heretics, and radical schismatics like James Nayler, the early Quaker who rode into Bristol on a donkey in imitation of Christ, who dwelt within him. Hill lists dozens more, including sects that taught that there is no sin in robbery, murder, adultery, or any other act committed while in a state of grace and that based their teaching on that Pauline corollary to the doctrine of Christian liberty cited by Milton himself, quoting Titus 1.15: "To the pure all things are pure" (*Areopagitica, CPW* 2:512). Religious models for binding private to public lives in political reformation abound.

Some have objected to the idea of Milton in the "tavern" associating with the radical fringes of society. Yet since Milton's own personal synthesis of ideas incorporated many of the same heresies as those of the religious radicals, he must have been interested to study their various attempts to apply those ideas in their lives once they were freed from the requirements of the state church. Some antinomians—the Ranting sort—he condemned, as in his sonnet 12: "License they mean when they cry liberty." But what of those many others who suffered bravely and terribly for their beliefs, even at the hands of the Independents, Milton's own party, and whose right to their beliefs he publicly championed from the beginning until the end of his long political career?[12]

In their defense Milton insisted, "No man can know at all times [the divine illumination] to be in himself, much less to be at any time for certain in any other" (*A Treatise of Civil Power, CPW* 7:246). This truth about spiritual life made for an important difference between Milton's polemical prose and his poetry. It was one sort of intellectual activity to trace, as he had in his regicide pamphlets, the ways in which inward slavery in a bishop or royalist developed from conformity to a corrupted church and state. But it was another thing to have to judge one's allies, in some of whom right ideas, freely and sincerely held, nevertheless resulted eventually in corrupt practices, inward slavery. Why, we must ask, and how do genuinely righteous persons fall? Although Milton's role as writer of diplomatic material for the revolutionary cause did not afford him the opportunity to explore this question in pamphlet form, he tackled its dramatic, existential implications in all his great poems. One crux is this scene from book 9.

The antinomian idea of righteousness was idealism of the highest sort, holding that all the Mosaic law, moral as well as ceremonial, had been abrogated for Christians by the coming of Christ, whose spirit now dwelt in the heart of the believer and replaced the codified law as a moral guide (*De Doctrina, CPW* 6:521–41). For Milton, as for the most radical sectary, no law had to be obeyed by a Christian simply because it was a law: as Christ could break the Sabbath to heal the sick, so Christians could break any of the commandments in the spirit of Christ. The new morality did not mean license, of course. Yet, in the face of this doctrine's apparent abuse, there remained the problem of defining a "more perfect" morality than that of the Ten Commandments or of any system of positive law.

The vital question for deeply righteous radical thinkers like Milton and such contemporaries as John Saltmarsh, William Dell, John Goodwin, and others was this: In the absence of intrinsically authoritative external laws, how can one know when one's decision to act is based on the direction of God's spirit dwelling in one's heart and when it is based on personal desire? I believe that in Milton's view the first persons who had to deal with this dilemma of total spiritual liberty were unfallen man and woman, that the separation scene concerns not only relations between the sexes but the basic nature of human government, and that we will be rewarded by reading the quarrel between Adam and Eve in the light of Milton's answer to the epistemological question that faced ethical and political antinomianism.

WE CAN best study that answer by viewing Milton, as Christopher Hill suggests, within the milieu of his radical contemporaries. We should try to understand how radical theology came into being, how it related to political experience, and why Milton wished to embody this dimension of human experience in his epic. Let us consider the Army preachers John Saltmarsh and William Dell, the Ranters, and the Independent minister John Goodwin. These radical thinkers provide a spectrum within which we can grasp the ethical and political implications of Milton's belief in antinomianism.[13] First, however, we must address the problem of what terminology should be used to refer to the various manifestations of radical theology. Because Ranters, Army preachers, a maverick Congregationalist, and the poet Milton are so overwhelmingly different from one another, I am reluctant to follow Hill in simply adopting the seventeenth-century practice of labeling as antinomian all who believed in the abrogation of the whole law, regardless of what else they taught and practiced. Between the seventeenth and the twentieth centuries, the term "antinomian" has undergone a restriction and a pejoration in meaning. Even in the seventeenth century, since the label was used most vigorously by the doctrine's attackers as a term of abuse, those who wanted to preach antinomianism acknowledged a need to define the sense in which they were "antinomian" in order to deny explicitly that their theology gave room for license.[14]

We might consider using the terminology the theologians themselves preferred. Instead of describing their doctrine as the negative *anti*nomianism, many gave it a positive formulation as "free grace." Calling these writers Free-Gratians, however, is no more helpful; it is in fact less precise than calling them antinomians since most churchmen claimed to believe in free grace and argued that the antinomians were perverting an orthodox term. "Free grace" crosses even more categories of believers than does "antinomianism," which, in its root meaning, at least has a distinct doctrinal characteristic.

The only alternative to the use of "antinomianism" appears to be inventing some labels of our own. In doing so, we should notice that all manifestations of antinomian belief, however much they differed, did share two points: a common belief in the abrogation of the whole law, and a common underlying motivation for this belief in a reaction against the frightening, inscrutable picture of the deity preached by powerful branches of seventeenth-century Scottish and English Calvinism. Because of these shared characteristics, it is not misleading to use "antinomian" as an encompassing term that genuinely characterizes a variety of people in the radical wing of the revolutionaries.

Once we recognize the surprising point of similarity, we should seek a historical understanding of the differences among the antinomians. The enormous spiritual power that received a theological formulation as "antinomianism" was what impelled the English revolution during the civil war, Commonwealth, and protectorate: the sectarian and individual differences among the antinomians made the revolutionary effort impossible to sustain beyond 1659. The dynamics of this libertarian idealism inform Milton's interest in Eden.

I should like to identify two different strains of seventeenth-century English antinomianism. I suggest, first, the term "voluntarist antinomianism" to describe that branch to which the Calvinists Saltmarsh and Dell belong; Ranterism was an aberrational offshoot of this branch. The second term, "humanist antinomianism," I use to characterize John Goodwin and John Milton and to indicate that these thinkers descend in the Christian humanist line that reaches from Saint Thomas Aquinas through Richard Hooker into the seventeenth century where, with these thinkers, the traditional beliefs were radicalized.[15] Both strains of antinomianism developed to the point of unorthodoxy an aspect of an originally orthodox theological formulation. These developments occurred in response to the pressures of living with that theology in a revolutionary political and social setting.

Let us begin with a look at the voluntarist strain. Because our primary interest is in watching the doctrine evolve its ethical and political dimensions, I do not refer to the earliest English antinomian theologians.[16] We need to recognize, however, the process of reversal by which Saltmarsh's antinomianism developed out of the deeply pious—and philosophically nominalist—Christianity of English Calvinism. In the nominalist view, God's will for human beings and for all of creation is ultimately secret, inscrutable; it is so because it operates by reinventing itself moment by moment in time. Against the scholastic notion of a transcendent, universal "law of nature" to which God submits his control of the universe, Calvin insisted that "no wind ever rises or blows, but by the special command of God,"[17] and that, likewise, no soul is saved but by its special election. Mainstream Calvinists did not become antinomian; in England the Presbyterians became the movement's most ardent persecutors. The antinomianism they attacked, however, was, in the view of John Goodwin, "nothing else but a system of the due and lawful consequences of their opinions who most fiercely opposed it."[18] Let me offer some account of the way voluntarist antinomianism took shape.

One widespread emotional consequence of the belief in individual predestination was an anxiety produced in the would-be believer who searched his or her own behavior and conscience for signs of sanctification, of an ability to keep the moral laws or at least of a genuine wish to keep them. If evidence of sanctification could be found, one could presume oneself to belong to the elect. Orthodox preachers of the Covenant urged hearers who had not yet discovered a genuine holiness within to try harder to find it. The spiritual biographies contain victorious accounts of those who eventually succeeded. There are also some tragic accounts, ranging from depression to suicide, presented by teachers like Saltmarsh who opposed the Covenant theologians, arguing instead for free grace, or antinomianism.[19]

The "high" Presbyterians implied an answer of their own to the problem of anxiety: one important sign of election would be obedience to a legally constituted Presbyterian state church. In the view of the Free-Gratian Saltmarsh, this solution offered not liberation but a continuation in "the shadows of the Law," in "doubts, fears, terrours." At best, he argued, the "legalist" preachers put one in the position of "natural man," who tries to live by a moral law and whose conscience reproves him though it cannot reform him, a position exactly paralleling the state of the Old Testament Jews. At worst, the churches' legal requirements encouraged a person to become the possessor of a "carnal, formally deceiving heart"—as the fear-based persecution of religious sects clearly revealed.

For Saltmarsh and for Milton the only definition of divine grace that could, as Paul promised, perfect the law of nature and the Mosaic law was antinomian. The imperfection of the moral law had consisted not in any falseness of principles but in the impossibility of its fulfillment by fallen beings, who, because they could not keep the law, must by the law's own terms be condemned. Milton had the Archangel Michael explain the law's imperfection to Adam in book 12 of *Paradise Lost*: "So Law appears imperfect, and but giv'n / With purpose to resign them in full time / Up to a better Cov'nant" (295–97). While God's absolute power and absolute justice were revealed both in nature and in the Old Covenant, the "better Cov'nant" of the gospel revealed—in addition to and subsuming these—absolute love.

Possessed by a conviction of God's goodness, Saltmarsh drew on the Calvinist doctrine of predestination to propose an unorthodox view: that since the elect cannot ultimately fall, moral failures along the way should not discourage the faithful from a belief in their election. He urged the following meaning of "free grace": since, as Calvin teaches, justification by Christ's sacrifice is absolutely unmerited and unmeritable, so we may conclude (contrary to the teaching of all Presbyterian and most Congregationalist preachers) that justification is given without the requirement by God of "legal" evidence of sanctification. A Christian need feel no anxiety about his or her own legal failing, for the simple wish for salvation is sufficient sign that one is saved; and salvation, even in orthodox thought, is absolute.

Milton differs importantly from Saltmarsh in that he did not accept the doctrine of predestination or "perseverance." Nevertheless, his politics and his poetry express and explore the belief, shared with Saltmarsh, in a dynamic, antinomian ethic that grew out of confidence in God's absolute goodness, which renders his will for human beings not inscrutable but accessible to individual regenerate persons, filling them with spiritual power. This is the central theme of *Samson Agonistes*, which embodies legalist mentality in the Chorus and dramatizes antinomian liberation in Samson (see chapter 5). The Chorus' spiritual condition is in fact described in Saltmarsh's book *Free-Grace*, under the heading "The fears of weak

Believers": "they think every affliction or trouble that befalls . . . is a punishment for some sin." Saltmarsh admonishes these weak believers to trust that afflictions are not judgments, as Milton's Samson learns, but "onely chastenings; love working by that which is evil in itself" (172–76).

We can find a vigorous expression of voluntarist antinomian moral confidence in the writings of Saltmarsh's fellow Army preacher, William Dell. Dell helps to clarify the way in which an emphasis on good works could have evolved from Calvinism, the way in which people who held a determinist view of their experience—with "no good works and no free will"[20]—could have found in their religion a basis for such an active belief in political liberty as that offered by the Calvinist Saltmarsh in defiance not only of the Anglican enemy but of the Presbyterian and Independent establishments: "The interest of the people in Christ's kingdom is not only an interest of compliancy and obedience and submission, but of consultation, of debating, counseling, prophesying, voting, etc. And let us stand fast in that liberty wherewith Christ hath made us free."[21]

Reading Dell leads us to consider the relation between belief and practice in reverse, to see how a fervent commitment to political and religious reform—to "good works"—can have furthered belief in an antinomian version of the received Calvinist theology. In his vision of things, the failure of people who have the appearance or "form" of godliness, like the Presbyterians or Milton's Chorus in *Samson Agonistes*, is not in their doctrine but in their spiritual strength: "When men by occasion of this form [appearance of godliness] are called forth to do the great works of God, and yet are destitute of the *power* of God, their duties are above their *strength*. . . . And sooner or later, meeting with *difficulties*, they faint and languish as a Snail, their works being too high for their faculties. For *nature* being strained above its power, and offering at that which is beyond its abilities, by degrees grows weary, and returns to its old *temper* again."[22] As Saltmarsh was concerned that his hearers confidently experience the forgiving love of God, so both he and Dell sought to establish their hearers' confidence in the personal power that came with God's goodwill toward them. That power, Dell urges, "makes a man *invincible*. . . . if this power, in a *Christian* should be prevailed against, *God* himself who is that power, should be conquered, which is impossible."[23]

Dell's straightforward conversion of a theology of predestination to an antinomian doctrine of assurance removed for him some of the complexities of the epistemological question with which we began this investigation. During the 1640s, at least, the needs of "right reformation" seemed obvious. When he confronted the Presbyterian challenge, "May a christian then live as he list?" his answer showed that he felt the question itself

revealed the powerless spiritual state of the questioner, who was either
unredeemed or not yet visited by the Spirit. "Those of them that are
godly," he had argued elsewhere, "are better able to judg of the vertues
and influences of the holy Spirit . . . then *they* that are destitute of the
Spirit themselves, and yet will be judging of the operations of it, in
others."[24] But may a Christian then live as he list? "No, by no means," Dell
answered in a sermon preached before Parliament in 1646, "for he hath the
word and the spirit in him, to keep him living as he list." The dialogue
continues:

3 Object.: But would you have no *Law?*

Answ.:   No Laws in Gods kingdom, but Gods Laws . . . and these are
     these three:
     The *Law* of a *new nature.*
     The *Law* of *the spirit of life that is in Christ.*
     The *Law* of *love.*

4 Object.: But would you have no [church] *government?*

Answ.:   Yes, but the government of Christ the *head.* . . .

6 Object.: But would you have *sin* suffered?

Answ.:   No, but more truly and thoroughly destroyed, then any
     power of the world can destroy it.[25]

Dell argues, as does the young Milton, that while anyone who is "out-
wardly wicked" should be kept in order by the magistrate, the regenerate
citizens of a reformed society will make the magistrate's task an easy one
since "the whole Inheritance of God will grow up so straight and blameless, that the Civil Magistrate may with farre lesse toyle and difficulty . . .
steare the tall and Goodly Vessell of the Commonwealth" (*Of Reformation,*
CPW 1:601).

 At this point in the revolution the epistemological question did not
appear to any of the rebels to have a difficult answer. Saltmarsh simply calls
on the known moral laws as useful checkpoints. He asserts that while there
is no human authority that can prescribe what behavior an individual
believer must follow in a particular ethical situation, "if any man sin more
freely because of forgiveness of sins, that man may suspect himself to be
forgiven." The Old Testament moral law, from which believers have been
released, was genuine law in that it had "something of the Image of God
in it." "That law . . . [however] was but a few beams of righteousness, even
ten, but a decalogue of righteousness." In the gospel, "the righteousness of
God is brought forward in more glorious and spiritual Commandments;
and for ten, there are scores." The new image of God offered in the gospel
is not embodied in a list of positive laws: "the Gospel commands us rather
by patern than precept, and by imitation [of Christ] than by command."

We move, Milton says in *Paradise Lost*, from "strict Laws" to "large Grace." "It is not a less perfect life that is required for Christians but, in fact, a more perfect life than was required of those who were under the law" (*De Doctrina, CPW* 6:535).

The liberating psychological effect of this antinomianism has been well demonstrated in the primary audience of Saltmarsh and Dell, the New Model Army, whose soldiers learned not to wait until they had experienced an unambiguous conversion before exercising their faith. "Shew me thy faith by thy works," Saltmarsh typically admonished, "they are the beams of Christ the Sun of righteousness."[26] Antinomian "works," righteous actions, could be performed confidently, as fruits of a divinely given faith, rather than studied cautiously and self-consciously as signs and kept subservient to a divinely approved temporal authority. The result was a courage such as that illustrated by Saltmarsh's own campaign for religious toleration against the Presbyterians' "chaines and fetters to the glorious and free spirit."[27] There were, he believed, no a priori restrictions that a state church could impose on a Christian's belief or religious practice. Every enactment of positive law was subject to interpretation and judgment by the individual Christian spirit. His own interpretation of the required oath to support the Solemn League and Covenant of 1643 was typical: to subscribe to the Scottish model for reformation in England "according to the word of God" meant "so far as we . . . in our consciences conceive the same according to the word of God."[28] Milton argued similarly about regicide. When royalists quoted Rom. 13, "There is no power but of God," he insisted that these words "be understood of . . . just power" (*Tenure of Kings and Magistrates, CPW* 3:209–10).

That saints should act according to their intuited perception of relevant higher law did not mean that no presumed saint's ethical actions, once they had been performed, could be judged morally. Fairfax and his army had been right to wage a war of liberation against the king, but in Saltmarsh's view the generals sinned when they imprisoned the Leveller agitators. Saltmarsh climbed off his deathbed and survived a hard journey to the Army camp at Windsor in December 1647 to tell the generals that "though the Lord had done much for them and by them, yet . . . God would not prosper their consultations, but destroy them by divisions amongst themselves . . . because they had sought to destroy the people of God."[29] Milton too did not hesitate to warn Cromwell that governing justly in peacetime would be harder than winning the war.[30]

Fairfax, Cromwell, and the Grandees did not allow the reforming Levellers to continue. Soon after the Levellers' final defeat at Burford, there came into prominence that extreme left-wing religious movement, the

Ranters. In Ranter theology and/or rhetoric, we find the Army preachers' comparatively mainstream Christian antinomianism transformed into a pantheistic denial of God's personhood and an ethic of absolute individualism. I raise the Ranters for consideration not because they resemble Milton but because they influence our twentieth-century perception of seventeenth-century antinomianism and need to be clearly classified as merely a short-lived offshoot of the voluntarist kind of antinomianism and not a central example of the phenomenon we are studying.

Dell taught that because Christ's spirit "is not idle in us, but continually active" and imparting grace, we are empowered to perform even greater works than the incarnate Christ because, while Christ overcame the devil's whole power of "Law, Sin, Death and Hell," he did so by acting out of a pure nature, whereas we will do the same, but with a nature we had thought hopelessly polluted.[31] Although this sort of claim sounded heretical to the orthodox, it meant nothing like the claim of the Ranter theorist Jacob Bauthumley that because we partake of the divine nature, we are God.[32] Ranterism gave a material, pantheistic interpretation to the meaning of Christ's indwelling spirit. The ethic that accompanied this theology took literally the antinomian assertion that a regenerate Christian cannot fall. It transmuted the doctrine of final perseverance into a notion of immediate perfection so that the believer claimed not that he would inevitably find his sins forgiven in the end but that he "was in that condition that he could not sin."[33] The Calvinist insistence that a person cannot take credit for any virtuous deed performed was turned around to say that a person can take no blame. Bauthumley maintained that "they did no more that crucified Christ, than they that did embrace him."[34]

A. L. Morton convincingly suggests that Ranterism is the language of a politically defeated people who had abandoned the rational hope that had inspired men like Overton and Walwyn to work for social reform. Certainly in Ranterism the epistemological question is buried altogether: every impulse is from God. Lawrence Clarkson in his Ranter phase felt obliged to act out all behavior that had been called sinful: "The ground of this my judgment was, God made all things good, so nothing evil."[35] The Ranter, when asked, "May a christian then live as he list?" answered a loud "Yes!"

Radicals who did not feel themselves cut off from the future of the revolutionary effort, however, did not abandon rationality; they further developed and radicalized the old Christian humanist faith in reason. In the thought of John Goodwin, whom we have met in earlier chapters, that development took the direction of a belief in free will. Twentieth-century readers generally view the Arminian heresy as antithetical to the antinomian heresy. The opposition seems logical since Free-Gratians based their antinomian belief on the claim that the fallen human will is not free and that salvation is predetermined, whereas writers who were labeled by their detractors as Arminian believed that the will is free to accept or refuse a salvation that is offered to all.[36] In the seventeenth century, however, the two heresies were often lumped together and attributed to one person, even while the "heretics" contested one another's formulations. In fact, both psychologically and in terms of practical ethics, Saltmarsh's belief in "free grace" had an effect similar to that of Goodwin's in "free will." Goodwin's impetus toward that belief and away from the Calvinist formulation of the doctrine of predestination was the same as Saltmarsh's impetus toward antinomianism. As Saltmarsh had believed that a good God would not keep his chosen ones in an agony of suspense over their election, so Goodwin believed that a good God would not inflict the agony of reprobation arbitrarily.

Saltmarsh's teaching was more experiential than theological. In the experiential part, where he described what it was like to live life as an antinomian Christian, he often wrote as though the act of believing involved a free choice.[37] When Goodwin began to theologize about the restoration of God's image in redeemed mankind, he made the move over to accept the freedom of the will that Saltmarsh theoretically denied. To defend and develop his views, Goodwin, like Milton, drew on the Christian humanist tradition and, in doing so, radicalized it.

Puritan Arminians claimed to have developed their theology not through the influence of Arminius of the Netherlands but through study of the Scriptures. Their thinking about the will parallels the pattern articulated by Richard Hooker. Although in his day Hooker was a spokesman for Anglicanism, the Disciplinarian movement, whose voluntarist Calvinism he opposed in the 1590s, was the same group that opposed the definition of law and liberty posited by the Independents John Goodwin and John Milton in the 1640s and 1650s. By 1650 of course the political alignment of the theological debate had reversed. Under Elizabeth, the Anglican state church had seen itself as resisting a minority's demand for nationwide imposition of the more rigid Calvinism of some of the Marian exiles. Under the Commonwealth, the Disciplinarians were trying through the Westminster Assembly to establish and maintain a Presbyterian state church. Though they did not finally succeed, they were now the besieged establishment seeking to impose uniformity rather than the radical minority seeking toleration. During the fifty-year interval, the issue of religious freedom had received vigorous testing both in theory and in practice, as men who fought early in the century against a rigid Stuart Anglicanism discovered that the same battle had to be waged against the Presbyterians and then the Independents. This discovery caused many to reexamine their theology. Milton and Goodwin followed a typical Puritan radical's development in their progression from an unexamined Calvinism that had been inspired by the courage of the reforming Presbyterians, to an Independency based initially on a reaction against Presbyterian intolerance, and finally to individually posited heretical views.

The heresy at which John Goodwin arrived had its source in the same concept of the deity that his contemporary Saltmarsh intuited and that Hooker had urged fifty years earlier. Hooker had explained that within God's own nature goodness supersedes and informs will. He cited Ephesians 1.2: "He worketh all things . . . not only according to his owne will, but the *counsell of his owne will*" (*Laws* 60; 1.2.5). This text served as the basis of Goodwin's radical Arminianism, which had for its adherents the same ethical effects as Saltmarsh's antinomianism did. "In whatsoever God acteth," Goodwin says in *Redemption Redeemed*, "we are to look not only for will, but counsel; i.e., wisdom, and tendency of ends worthy of Him; and these discernable . . . by men."[38]

"Of discerning goodness," Hooker had said, "there are but . . . two wayes." He went on in the *Laws* to work at greatest length only with the second of these two ways, but the first way, which underlay his own thought and which illuminates the second, had politically radical implications for those who reconsidered it in the seventeenth century. "And of discerning goodnes there are but these two wayes; the one the knowledge of the causes whereby it is made such, the other the observation of those signes and tokens, which being annexed alwaies unto goodnes, argue that where they are found, there also goodnes is, although we know not the cause by force whereof it is there" (*Laws* 82–83; 1.8.2).

"The former of these is the most sure . . . way, but so hard that all shunne it"; therefore, "considering how the case doth stand with this present age full of tongue and weake of braine . . . into the causes of goodnes we will not make . . . deepe . . . inquirie." It is the inferior, second way that yields Hooker's famous sentence, "The generall and perpetuall voyce of men is as the sentence of God him selfe" (83–84; 1.8.3). Yet even Hooker accompanies that conservative-sounding claim with a qualification: since "the generall perswasion of all men" is a sign of goodness, mere custom (which includes all positive laws) has the power to perpetuate error and evil as well as good: "And therefore," he concludes, "a common received error is never utterly overthrowne, till such time as we goe from signes unto causes" (83; 1.8.3).

Going from signs to their causes, from positive laws to natural law, was the procedure of the revolutionaries fifty years after Hooker wrote these words.[39] The resulting concept of belief was, in the revolutionary context, even more spiritually empowering than Calvinist antinomianism was. People now not only had Christ's spirit dwelling within but could cooperate with their minds as well as their wills. The spirit worked to rectify fallen reason and allow it to sort possibly relevant moral truths into an order genuinely applicable to a particular situation. The positive laws do that task for us well much of the time. When they do not, we are free, the radical Christian humanists claimed, to inquire into root causes and to develop a new procedure for meeting whatever circumstances render the positive law morally ineffective.

In *Right and Might Well Met* (1649) Goodwin justified Pride's purge on antinomian grounds. Though the Army had no warrant in positive law for their action, they were fulfilling the spirit behind their commission "to act in the capacity of soldiers for the peace, liberties, and safety of the kingdom."[40] The Presbyterian objection that many of the ejected members of Parliament "were religious and conscientious men" he met in the same terms that Milton's Samson answers Dalila's theological and moral relativism; Goodwin appeals to the universal law of nature against false political and religious teachings to assert that a true God and nation would not ask to be served by ungodly deeds. All human authorities—Philistine, Hebrew, or English—"all human laws and constitutions are but a like structure and frame with the Ceremonial Laws of old made by God himself, which were all made with knees to bend to the law of nature."[41]

Goodwin's conservative opponents denounced him as, among other things, an antinomian—an appellation he disliked not only because it implied a moral libel but also because he found the doctrine of final perseverance impossible and offensive. However, if we look at his concept of the moral nature of the deity and at his method of ethical reasoning, with its faith in the spiritual power available to the individual believer, we may recognize a kinship with Saltmarsh. Drawing on the Christian humanist faith in the accessibility to right reason of natural law, Goodwin developed a theology that would explain the kind of spiritual power and ethical freedom that Saltmarsh experienced and taught. In the 1640s, for instance, he argued on what we may call antinomian grounds against the legalistic "Covenant" requirement of the conservative Congregationalists. Sounding like Saltmarsh, he asserts, "To me there is no imaginable use or necessity of this your Covenant, because beleevers . . . are bound by greater bonds a thousand fold. . . . Christ himself is the greatest of bands."[42] Sounding much like Hooker on the Disciplinarians, he sees the Covenanters as "destroying all sympathy and agreement between a na-

tional Church and that which you call instituted or particular," as prefer-
ring legalistic ceremonial and doctrinal formulations to fundamental
values.[43]

Ten years later, in the 1650s, Goodwin was battling the legalism not only
of the orthodox Calvinists but also of the many-pronged separatist movement that was dividing the Puritan reformers and thereby weakening the
morale and the moral fiber of the nation. Once again, like Hooker, he
urged voluntary conformity in things indifferent, the spirit of peace over
the letter of dogma.

There was a progression in radical thought from Saltmarsh to Goodwin.
Within the voluntaristic Calvinist tradition, antinomianism provided a
release from religious fear and an impetus for moral courage. The com-
bining of this antinomian sense of God's goodness with the Christian
humanist concept of natural law as the embodiment of that goodness
brought a return to the roots of individual freedom and the source of
social change. This combination was achieved most consciously by John
Milton, who articulated both a belief in "general predestination," that is,
free will, and a belief in the abrogation of the moral law, that is, the ethical
dimension of antinomianism.

One vital aspect of that Miltonic liberty is the believer's freedom to work
confidently in an ethical situation with the divine spirit that dwells in his
or her heart. The voluntarist antinomians, because they believed that a
divine command had to be entirely arbitrary from the human perspective,
lacked a method for addressing the problem that Goodwin warned against
often during the 1650s: "Be . . . admonished . . . that the importunity of an
inward solicitation is no argument that the perswasion unto which you are
solicited cometh from God."[44] But the humanist antinomian had available
the entire law of nature to order the moral vision with which he or she
viewed the elements of a particular situation. Reasoning under the complex circumstances of a particular moment in time from effects to causes,
from positive law and custom to "the condition upon which the decree
depends" (De Doc., CPW 6:155), to the spirit of the law, and creating a
moral balance—this is, as Hooker said, not for the "weake of brain." It is,
however, possible for Milton's "fit audience." Released from all positive
laws, the Christian must build his or her moral judgment, inner authority,
through the discernment of the valid hierarchy of natural laws that apply
in particular ethical situations.[45] The more difficult the situation, the more
effective the exercise gained. For this reason, Milton gives us the dynamic,
challenging moral situations of Satan, Eve, and Adam; the Chorus, Dalila,
and Samson; and the Christ of Paradise Regained. Fitness to be Milton's
readers comes not, as has been suggested, from an infusion of incompre-

hensible, or infallible, grace, but from the strenuous effort of the regenerate moral reason.[46]

IN THE separation scene of *Paradise Lost*, which is a concentrated explora-
tion of the antinomian experience, Milton addresses the question that
confronted Puritan radicals as the revolutionary cause, to which God had
given the victory, wavered, fell into confusion, and suffered defeat: "How
do genuinely righteous persons fall?" Prelapsarian Adam and Eve dramatize his answer. Because they are perfect beings, their moral decisions do
not concern whether to obey God's will as expressed in a code of laws;
such decisions can face only fallen beings, those who have experienced sin
and are bound by law in a covenant with God. Unfallen beings are those
who without positive law err not. They remain true not because, as Satan
implies in book 5 (lines 798–99), they are incapable of error. The task of
prelapsarian obedience is, like that of antinomian morality, even more
complex than the keeping of the law. In Milton's Eden, to obey God's will
means to work in ever new situations toward discerning God's meaning.
As Goodwin had phrased it: "In whatsoever God acteth, we are to look
not only for will, but counsel; i.e., wisdom, and tendency of ends worthy
of Him; and these discernable . . . by men." To the already perfect, obedience means growth through the steady exercise of the inner light within
a dynamic moral context.

In discussing the historical setting of the poem's composition, I distinguished between, on the one hand, voluntaristic antinomians like the
Ranters and, to a lesser extent, the Calvinist Army preachers and Levellers,
who believed that the inner light that supersedes all external authority is
Christ *as* the self, speaking directly to the will of the believer, obviating the
need for reason, and, on the other hand, humanistic antinomians like
Milton and John Goodwin, who believed that the inner light is Christ *in*
the self, rectifying reason (*De Doctrina*, CPW 6:477–84). In Milton's
interpretation right reason is supreme over the codified law; and he believed that the revelations granted by the indwelling spirit are always
consonant with reason.[47] But, as we learn from reading Milton's *Art of
Logic*, reason is not simply ratiocination, not merely logic; reason operates
on different levels to attain knowledge of reality: on the intuitive level of
the angels and sometimes of humans; on the noetic and dianoetic level of
reasoning from axioms alone; and on the level of such elaborate aids to
insight as the syllogism and its extensions—what we call discursive reasoning.

That which right reason can discover or verify by any of these methods is the oneness of truth, the unity of God's nature, or, as it is called in political discussions, the "natural" or "unwritten law" (compare *De Doctrina*, *CPW* 6:516). Although the Mosaic commandments no longer act as external, absolutely prescriptive rules, Milton believed like Saltmarsh that they still express or describe parts of the eternal and absolute truth of things. The greater perfection is the total vision of moral reality, of which the codified laws are extractions. The liberated reason bears the responsibility for perceiving God's order among the moral axioms known to human beings. Milton expressed this idea in *De Doctrina* when he said that decrees of God are made not absolutely but conditionally and that seeming contradictions among the laws must be reconciled into a consistent hierarchy that identifies the right basis for action in any situation (*CPW* 6:155–56).

Thus, while Christians should not unquestioningly obey the law, as codified by Moses, or Archbishop Laud, or the Westminster Assembly, in the blind faith that God will somehow make the whole cohere, they also should not irrationally abandon the positive laws altogether, as the Ranters did. Milton agreed this much with the Ranter Clarkson: there is no single commandment that literally and absolutely must not be broken. (Milton himself advocated, in the regicide tracts, what royalists called murder, in the divorce tracts, what clergy called adultery.) And yet, William Empson was wrong to say, in his brilliantly perverse antinomian judgment of Eve's fall, that, because Eve, in spite of the literal prohibition, believed she was right, she ate the apple in accordance with the spirit of liberty with which Milton believed God had endowed human beings.[48] For a particular law may be justly broken only in deference to a rationally understood higher purpose of the whole law, not simply in deference to anything one sincerely feels at the moment to be right. In any ethical situation right reason strives to balance all applicable laws in a noncontradictory hierarchy consistent with the unified divine purpose, with "natural law," ultimate truth. This rational balancing is a normal activity of the divine spirit within us. As an ethical concept, it is not different from Aristotle's notion, in the *Nichomachean Ethics* 2.6, of perceiving the mean, which Aristotle describes as analogous to the formal cause of a work of art, reminding us that "we often say of good works of art that it is not possible to take away or add anything, implying that excess and defect destroy the goodness of works of art, while the mean preserves it."[49] To be able to create such a balanced picture in one's own moral vision is to have seen the unifying spirit underlying the particular letters of the law.

In his divorce tracts Milton used the Aristotelian mean to reconcile contradictory passages of Scripture on marriage (for example, *CPW* 2:745).

His view of marriage as a rational relationship enabled him in *Paradise Lost* to portray the first marriage as the first ground for developing an ethic based in humanistic antinomian liberty, an ethic that is the base of unfallen politics or government. Rational balancing is what Raphael reminds Adam to do in book 8. Eve likewise is taught, from her beginning beside the pond, to discriminate the greater good and to balance the elements in nature that she governs.

The Edenic couple work in harmony (balance) until the separation scene. At this point we witness two sorts of antinomians, neither able to retain a perfectly balanced spiritual liberty. They do not fall here, they do not sin;[50] but they lose their balance in particularly antinomian ways and render themselves more vulnerable than usual to a push from the enemy. Both, as they have before in Paradise, here experience unsettling passions. Eve feels an urge toward independent action and a greater personal efficiency than is possible, or necessary, or desirable in the prelapsarian balance. Adam, though, finds himself desiring a greater sense of interdependence, a more complete security in his relationship with his beloved, than is possible to rationally free creatures. Both seek to reason their way toward an answer to the proposed separation and toward settling the passions underlying the debate. Adam reasons largely noetically by arranging axioms in their natural hierarchy: efficient work is good, rational (conversant) love is a higher good; and, later, security is good, but freedom is a higher good. Eve, once her initial notion is challenged, resorts to the more tedious method of syllogisms; she makes impressive use, for instance, of the technique of the sorites in her speech beginning at line 322: "If this be our condition, thus to dwell / In narrow circuit strait'n'd by a Foe."[51]

Critics have rightly argued that Eve is no mean reasoner and that her logic is highly sophisticated.[52] In Milton's view, however, she uses the logical methods of those whose reason is not sharp enough to reach an understanding of the issue immediately on having it raised. "This . . . deducing," he wrote in his *Art of Logic*, "has arisen from the weakness of the human intellect, which weakness being unable by an immediate intuition to see in an axiom the truth and falsity of things, turns to the syllogism in which it can judge whether this follow or do not follow" (*CPW* 8:350). Adam's axiomatic reasoning shows his quicker logical ability, closer to that of the angels.

P. Albert Duhamel has argued, however, that the faith that the *Logic* expresses in "immediate intuition" resembles the enthusiasts' notion of an "inner light," too radical a view for Milton, the learned humanist, to have held.[53] We must examine Milton's antinomianism to decide how the claims of the *Logic* operate in the poetry. We must ask several questions concerning this separation scene. What is the "instinctive insight" available to "right" reason? What is the divine inspiration of the indwelling spirit of God? How does it relate to other urges and to the discoveries of discursive reason? How, in the terms of seventeenth-century controversy, can one tell a true prophetic voice from a false one or a divinely approved desire from a personally mistaken one?

When Eve, at the scene's beginning, urges "what to [her] mind first thoughts present," those "first thoughts" are of the sort that distressed orthodox attackers of antinomianism such as the London ministers who insisted, "It is not safe for them to be guided by impulses or pretended impressions of Spirit."[54] Had Eve simply gone off at that point, following her initial impulse, she would have resembled antinomians of the extreme, Ranting sort, who could not believe themselves capable of a mistake— much less of a sin—if God dwelt in them, who said: "Men may live as they list, because God is the same, and all tends to his glory."[55] But Eve is not following impulse; she is seeking counsel. And her counselor immediately understands the correct judgment of her "first thought." Adam reasons that they should not, under the circumstances, separate. The orthodox Anglican and Puritan answer to Eve would be that she should ignore her mistaken thoughts and accept the reasoning and decision of church and state (that is, Adam, in this prelapsarian microcosm), to whom God has given authority over her. Yet Milton's antinomian answer was that Eve's decision must be freely made, not simply accepted from another's authority and not coerced. Most critics believe that it is freely made and that Adam is right to tell her, after all his reasoning to the contrary, "Go, for thy stay, not free, absents thee more." I believe, however, that Milton's understanding of the inner light as right reason means that Adam fails as Eve's governor when he "lets" her go, because by giving his permission when he does, he substitutes his own authority for her truly free decision.

I admit that the first response of most of us is, and is probably meant to be, "What more could he have done, short of forcing her to stay? He gave all the right reasons for staying." This is Adam's fallen response at the end of book 9, spoken when, as Milton tells us, his own "Understanding rul'd not" (line 1127):

> what could I more?
> I warn'd thee, I admonish'd thee, foretold
> The danger, and the lurking Enemy
> That lay in wait; beyond this had been force.
> And force upon free Will hath here no place.   (1170–74)

We, however, can take literally Adam's fallen rhetorical question, "what could I more?" We can examine the several different routes that the reasoning faculty has for arriving at, and for imparting, the truth.

Genuine insights, inspirations, "motions" from God, are, in Milton's view, rational in the sense that they are capable of rational analysis by any logical method, given the axioms of faith to start from. The very alert reason perceives their truth axiomatically. The very slow or impaired reason, which cannot figure them out at all, must be convinced by the testimony of a witness previously found to be a reliable reasoner. But reliance on testimony is not a suitable method in important investigations, because it takes away a person's freedom by circumventing his or her reason. Even divine testimony, Milton says in the *Art of Logic*, while it "makes me believe; it does not prove, it does not teach, it does not make me know or understand why it is so, unless it also adds reasons" (*CPW* 9:319). Most of humanity most of the time is in between: We perceive the validity of familiar axioms and of some newly considered axioms. But very complex truths or those that some personal failing or distraction keeps us from seeing immediately we arrive at by careful, thorough discursive reasoning. The important thing to remember is that the insight arrived at, the propositions affirmed or denied, will be identical, and true, no matter what method is used as long as it is used rightly. This is why most readers are able, with Adam's help, to point out what, given Milton's universe, is wrong with Eve's reasoning, even though it is very "intelligent."

In the separation scene Adam, whose reason leads him to the right answer about the question confronting Eve, that is, the advisability of separation, does not succeed in reasoning rightly about the question facing him as Eve's governor, that is, how to deal with Eve's desire to separate. Because he wants so fervently to be wanted by her, he lets her rest in her mistaken beliefs and act on the basis of his (permissive) authority. He justifies this decision by appealing to the letter of the law of freedom— "thy stay, not free, absents thee more." But he transgresses the spirit of that law: freedom for Eve means not "Do what you want" but rather "Understand and choose the right"—the "right" being that act which completes the perfectly balanced picture, the mean, the unifying spirit behind the particular letters, the situational embodiment of natural law. A balanced picture of the work Eve wants to be good at involves more than gardening; it involves her whole marital (societal) relationship, her prog-eny and humankind's relation to Providence, as Adam shows. So too does the love Adam desires from Eve mean more than her simply feeling that she wants to be with him. It requires her being "for God in him." She must, with Adam's aid, attain within herself and in her sphere the same genuine *imitatio* of the divine nature that he has. He must use the rhetorician's patience as well as the logician's rigor to bring her to the point where, not the authority of his testimony or his permission, but his right reasons enable her right reason to understand the whole picture that her balancing choice will perfect. He needs to find a way out of the command/permission dichotomy that has entered the conversation with his reduction of *ratio* to logical method.

Rhetoric, for Milton, is no mere decoration. Its importance lies in the bond it addresses between the reasoner and the audience or, more appropriately, the "other." If "logic" is not the proper word for the reasoning Milton values in this scene, a better choice might be the Aristotelian "phronesis," that "intellectual virtue" that yields an ethical know-how in which the reasoner's own being and knowledge are interlaced in a continual becoming; what is universal and what is particular are codetermined as the situational Good is recognized; the reasoner is "united by a specific bond with the other, . . . thinks with the other and undergoes the situation with [the other]"; and the knowledge becomes constitutive of the reasoner's *praxis*, practice, action.[56] If we are willing to consider such a definition of reasoning as valuable—more valuable for the creation of individual human freedom and of collective human society than mere logical empiricism—then certain terms in our definition of human worth are affected. Wisdom, for instance, and consequently freedom, do not depend centrally either upon an aptitude for abstract ratiocination or upon uniform methodological processes of logic, but upon the interpreter's ability to keep the dialogue genuinely open. The function of both logic and rhetoric in right reasoning is to keep the dialogue open and moving toward the truth. Thus, Adam should not say, "Go, if you think you should," when he knows Eve's thought is mistaken. He must have the courageous faith of Milton's *Areopagitica* that truth—including the truth of the bond uniting the reasoners—will not be "put to the wors, in a free and open encounter" (*CPW* 2:561). He must not *close the encounter* before both participants have been freed of the passions clouding their reasons. Milton's Adam and Eve are revolutionary Christian interpreters together engaged in understanding the dynamics of God-given human power.

In one sense Milton provides his Adam with a model in Raphael. Surely, Adam's human questionings and reasonings must be as tedious and exasperating for the benevolent angel to bend his intuitive reason to as Eve's imperfect understanding and discursive reasoning are for Adam's quicker, axiomatic mind. But Adam, who experiences a complex human relationship with the "other," which the angel does not share, is not able to follow through with a rationally "contracted brow" like Raphael's. Instead he ends the deliberation by acquiescing, out of his passion for Eve, to their separation. Eve then follows the prompting of her own—at the moment, different—passion to take Adam's permission and carry out the decision *he* has made. Adam lets Eve leave his side holding a dangerously mistaken idea of the nature of her freedom, that held by many voluntarist antinomians who, like an opponent of John Goodwin, were "not able to conceive or comprehend, how the Covenant of Grace, should be . . . absolutely and soveraignly free, in case [there was] . . . required by God . . . a condition, for the obtaining [it]." "He that is not able to understand this," Goodwin asserted, "I can hardly look upon . . . as [having] as yet attained the A.B.C. of Evangelical knowledge."[57] Yet Eve still believes that her complete freedom means she is really free from danger, that she will not fall. Though Adam, like the humanist Goodwin, does not hold this view, Eve has not understood his reasoning; and his literal permission has given a sanction that seems to her a testimony to the rightness of her reasons for wanting to go.

Some of Eve's self-confidence comes from knowing that she was right to react strongly against Adam's protective instinct as a justification for staying (lines 327–31). If he had insisted on his desire to protect her from insult, he would have undermined her freedom; he would have acted as erroneously as the anti-tolerationists, who wanted to protect the nonconformists from contamination by false doctrine. Adam's predicament is complicated by Eve's possible anticipation of his temptation to assert his role as governor legalistically when she addresses him as "all earth's lord" (273). She is right to remind him, if that is what she is doing, that he would deny her spiritual freedom if he relied on his legal authority to determine her decision.

Nevertheless, Eve displays her inferior perception of the reality of their situation when she wants trial alone; in effect, she censors Adam. Readers usually remember only the first half of Eve's line "And what is faith, love, virtue unassayed," recognizing rightly the tone of *Areopagitica*; but the sentence continues: "Alone, without exterior help sustained." What Adam offers, in wanting to accompany her, is the "exterior help" of a fellow thinker, debater, pamphleteer, student—his companionship in the archetypal "mansion house of liberty," "trying all things, assenting to the force of reason and convincement" (*Areopagitica, CPW* 2:554). This strenuous, complex, and collaborative exercise of the inner light in new and demanding circumstances is the shape of prelapsarian collective obedience. Eve's rationalization for declining Adam's collaboration illustrates the process by which the radical antinomian view could veer from its precarious course, surrendering total freedom to an appearance of freedom that actually leads into captivity. Perfect freedom is, in a way that Eve fails to realize, "frail" (340).

Eve does not sin when she decides to leave, because the decision facing her is not a moral one; to go or to stay is itself a morally neutral decision, in seventeenth-century terminology a "thing indifferent." As we know from history, however, controversies over things indifferent were fraught with moral complexity. In this scene Adam could have made Eve face a moral decision if he had refrained from giving her permission to go, regardless of how little warmth she might feel toward him, until she genuinely understood his reasons. By leaving before then, she would have had to break an actual, positive law of Paradise—her cooperation with Adam's governance.

Adam's admonition in the face of Eve's incipient voluntarist antinomianism parallels Milton's to the sectarians of his own day—those, like Nayler, whose freedom he sought all his life to establish, and who, of their own will, even when they were externally free, fell:

> Seek not temptation then, which to avoid
> Were better . . .
> . . . trial will come unsought.
> Wouldst thou approve thy constancy, approve
> First thy obedience.   (364–68)

But the most interesting figure is the humanistic antinomian Adam, who has advised the conservative path of obedience. What is there for Eve to obey in this particular dramatic encounter? The only word Adam utters that sounds like a command, as it turns out three lines later, is "Go," which is what does. In rhetorical effect, he gives a positive command that allows Eve to reduce "obedience" to its merely logical, or legalistic, meaning. Rationalizing from his known responsibility to rule so as to allow Eve a spiritual liberty as total as his own, Adam ends by fragmenting his vision of the ethical picture and letting his reason fall captive to a partial good. Some have argued that Adam as ruler is in the position of God, who explained human freedom in book 3: "Where only what they needs must do, appeared / . . . What pleasure [receive] I from such obedience paid" (105–07). So too Adam desires the pleasure of Eve's freely willed companionship and of her conformity to his advice. But in his desire for this high pleasure, he fails to provide for the spirit that underlies such freedom as God defines it, for the beloved's will to be rightly informed by its own reason. By bending over backward to avoid being authoritarian, he loses balance and ends by reasoning "legalistically" anyway, though on the permissive end of the spectrum. He yields to a partial law as authoritative instead of requiring her to stay until he can reach her essential freedom. The challenge to Adam's diplomacy in this scene is as ponderous and as delicate as the task of implementing an unpopular public policy is to any righteous governor of a free and godly people beset with enemies. His failure is one of the most fascinating moments in the poem, in which Milton gives complex recognition to the necessarily precarious nature of an antinomian liberty of conscience.

His failure here is tactical rather than moral. We may gain an appreciation for the spiritual and political health inhering in the "radical undecidability" of the separation scene if we consider the role of *recta ratio* or phronesis at the moment of Adam's fall into sin. Here Adam experiences psychological pressures similar to those in the separation scene. He is still "united by a specific bond with the other," as phronesis requires, but he fails to attain the "situational Good" and the bond is perverted. In this encounter there is no dialectic. Adam resolves to die with Eve, offers a few conscious rationalizations, and eats (acts). What would a dialectic have sounded like if Adam had managed to keep a dialogue going?

Northrop Frye, recalling Milton's divorce tracts, suggests that this "is the point [in *Paradise Lost*] at which Adam should have 'divorced' Eve; hence," he says, "divorce comes into the very act of the fall itself."[58] This reading is close to my own, but I would point not to the dichotomizing act of divorce, but to a moment in the divorce argument that is held out by Milton as an alternative possibility for one who is in the unfallen Adam's situation. This is the passage where he reconsiders Saint Paul's question concerning the dilemma of the Christian who is married to an infidel: "How knowest thou, o man, whether thou shalt save thy wife?" In *The Doctrine and Discipline of Divorce*, Milton interpreted Paul's answer to support his argument for divorce: One must walk "in his inferior calling of marriage, as not by dangerous subjection to that ordinance [of marriage] to hinder and disturb the higher calling of his Christianity" (*DDD*, *CPW* 2:268). In the *Tetrachordon* he envisions a situation in which the act of staying married to the infidel would fulfill both the calling to marriage and the calling to God. Though the dangers of remaining married to an infidel are great, he says, "if neither the infirmity of the Christian, nor the strength of the unbeleever, be fear'd, but hopes appear that he may be won ... [St. Paul] judges it no breaking of that law [if] the beleever be permitted to forbeare divorce, and can abide, without the peril of seducement, to offer the charity of a salvation to wife or husband, which is the fulfilling, not the transgressing of that law; and well worth the undertaking with much hazard and patience" (*CPW* 2:689). Adam has before him the possibility of such an undertaking: not to acquiesce and not to divorce, but to keep the dialogue open, to become "with much hazard" in but not of the postlapsarian world.

In the human dynamics of the repentance scene at the end of book 10, it is Eve rather than Adam who is the more skilled, or right, reasoner. She is the phronimos (possessor of phronesis) who accomplishes the opening of the dialectic. She remains able to hold in her view vital elements of the universal relevant to the new situation, to let "what is universal and what is particular [be] co-determined," to hold onto "the specific bond with the other," and to assume that knowledge will become praxis. One reader has worried that Milton is showing Eve in this scene as the stereotypical "inferior" female, as a "petitioner, a suppliant," while Adam is shown to "exert his dominant role" by outreasoning her and "taking the lead in executing" action.[59] If phronesis is our model for effective (right) reasoning, however, she "outreasons" him; and it is Eve, as many readers have recognized, who "takes the lead" into praxis, opening the road to post-lapsarian freedom.

FIVE

Liberty under the Law: *Samson Agonistes*

To PORTRAY human interaction in his unfallen Paradise, Milton drew upon his vision of perfect freedom in its original antinomian purity. Antinomian liberty, although "frail," is also dynamic, like the creative power of God himself; its power remains attainable by fallen beings. In Milton's universe, failure is never the end of the story.

Samson Agonistes is a drama of spiritual struggle in the context of revolutionary political commitment and defeat. Some have argued that Milton's tragedy reflects a post-Restoration retreat from the author's earlier Christian humanist belief in a rationally accessible deity and/or that the poem signals his withdrawal from political commitment in a corrupt world. I shall address these issues by considering how the Chorus illuminates the development of a rational faith in Samson; how Samson's role as a public person and revolutionary addresses the question of cultural relativism; and how the play's violent ending relates to the justice of Milton's God.

MODERN criticism of *Samson Agonistes* is divided on the nature of Samson's regeneration. Does the meaning of the action lie in the movement of his spirit from despair toward a kind of fideism, which would see God moving in mysterious ways not accessible to human reason? Or is the faith Samson achieves consonant with the humanistic Christianity that Milton defended with the great argument of *Paradise Lost*? A viable approach to these complex questions lies in understanding the pietistic comments of the Chorus—comments that specifically identify the Chorus and, in so doing, define the nature of Samson's spiritual growth. The tension built on the contrast between the Chorus' and Samson's religious experiences shapes our dramatic experience and philosophical understanding of the play.

In "Structural and Doctrinal Pattern in Milton's Later Poems" Arthur Barker argues that, in Samson's struggle, Milton portrays mimetically what he defines abstractly in the *De Doctrina* as the process of regeneration and its resulting liberty. Since the coming of Christ, this process has been identified as Christian liberty, but Barker shows that Milton believed it to have been continually operative throughout historical dispensations.[1] John Goodwin believed that all people who experience true repentance for sin are saved by faith in Jesus Christ, "whether he be known or not known to them." This was his understanding of Romans 2:4: "The goodness of God leadeth men to repentance." Repentance *means* faith in Christ, Goodwin believed, "in one sense, or in one kinde, or other."[2]

Milton's concept of liberty, Barker points out, is based on faith in a rationally ordered universe, on a deep understanding of God's ways with men, not on a faith divorced from reason. Yet the voice of fideism has been heard in his lines "All is best, though we oft doubt, / What th' unsearchable dispose / Of highest wisdom brings about" (1745–47). And, when this has been taken as Milton's own voice, it has been found too weak a philosophical consolation either to counter or to elevate the dramatic effect of Samson's tragic suffering.[3]

This voice, however, belongs neither to Milton nor to Samson, but to the Hebrew Chorus. Within the last two decades the Chorus, once generally assumed to speak for Milton, has been recognized by several critics as often inferior to Samson in understanding or moral strength.[4] Most commentators who interpret Samson's experience as regeneration have tried to identify a gradual spiritual growth in the Chorus occurring parallel to Samson's,[5] but there are some awkward problems involved in the attempt to demonstrate the Chorus' regeneration in detail. Barker reminds us that the Old Testament Hebrew Chorus has a specific historical identity and point of view toward Samson's experience to which neither Milton nor the reader is confined, and that even its final comment, may not stand as our key to the play's meaning.[6] In extending this argument, I wish to show not only that the "Chorus of Danites" represents the whole Hebrew people, bound by the law of Moses in its service to Jehovah, but also that, just as Samson serves as a model for the regenerate Christian, so the Chorus embodies a mentality found in all ages and all too common, in Milton's view, among the Christians of his own day.

To recognize the Chorus' function we should review what it meant, to

Milton, for a people to be in bondage to the law. Milton's political writings show how the abstract theological distinction between bondage and liberty operated in regard to the actual controversies of seventeenth-century society. In the prelatical debates, he argued that Anglicans attempting to preserve episcopal succession were in effect trying to retain the Jewish priesthood, an institution of the Mosaic law that had been abrogated by the coming of Christ. They were holding to the literal rather than the spiritual meaning of priesthood, turning "the inward power and purity of the Gospel into the outward carnality of the Law" (*CPW* 1:766).

The distinction between the inward power, the spirit, of the Gospel and the "carnality," the letter of the law, formed, as we have seen, the basis for Milton's later defense of revolution and of regicide as well. The whole philosophical disagreement over the right of revolution was at its heart a disagreement over what a law of God is, and, indeed, what the nature of the Christian diety is. Royalists, seeking a scriptural injunction against revolution, quoted as divine law the words of St. Paul: "There is no power but of God" (Romans 13:1), interpreting "power," in England's case, to refer to its current governor, the king, and concluding that God's law enjoined absolute obedience, even if the king were a tyrant. Milton answered that this interpretation of Paul's words could not be correct, for, if it were, it would contradict that most fundamental law of God's creation, by which not only kings but all people are created free in his image (*TKM, CPW* 3:209–11). The royalists, as we have seen, were willing to accept such a contradiction as a divine paradox and to base their argument on the idea that God can break even his own laws because he can do anything, being God and therefore omnipotent. Milton, however, held that God, being not only all-powerful, but rational and good as well, does not contradict himself (*CPW* 6:146). Moreover, Christ's sacrifice means in part that the Christian's prelapsarian powers of right reason are restored sufficiently from the bondage of sin for him or her to resolve apparent inconsistencies within faith, including interpretation of God's decrees. Milton saw many in his day fail to recognize this gift and its attendant responsibility when they mistakenly considered particular literal laws to be pure manifestations of God's will and thus absolutely binding. He stressed in all the controversies, as well as in the *De Doctrina*, that "God made no absolute decrees about anything which he left in the power of men, for men have freedom of action": "Here we have a rule given by God himself! He wishes us always ... clearly to appreciate the condition upon which the decree depends. ... For if the decrees of God ... were interpreted in an absolute sense without any implied conditions, God would seem to contradict himself" (*CPW* 6:155–56). "To appreciate the condition upon which the decree depends" is to interpret the literal terms of a law in accordance with the law's ultimate purpose, with its "spirit."

In his political works Milton held that the royalists' kind of piety, which believed that God (and, by extension, the king) must be worshiped and obeyed even if his commands are contradictory, had been excusable in fallen human beings before Christ's coming. But even in the time of the Old Covenant's blind loyalty to the letter of the law, God had foreshadowed the New Covenant in special instances. Liberty, Milton pointed out in the *De Doctrina*, "was not unknown in the time of the law" (*CPW* 6:536). It was "not unknown to the descendants of Abraham, even under the law of servitude, in that they were still called sons of God" (*CPW* 6:496). That liberty consisted in their using reason to interpret the letter of the law in the spirit of love in which law was given: "possessing this liberty they refused to be bound even by the ceremonies of religion, whenever charity demanded that they should do otherwise. *Thus all the people who had been born in the desert on the journey, they had not circumcised,* Josh. v. 4: and David, when faint with hunger, ate what it would not otherwise have been lawful for him to eat, I Sam. xxi. 6, compared with Matt. xii. 4. Psal. cxix 45: *I will always walk in freedom because I seek your commands*" (*CPW* 6:496).

In spite of these exceptions among the Hebrews, the chosen people of God—represented in *Samson Agonistes* by the Chorus—lived in a divinely imposed bondage until the coming of Christ. The law bound them in a special relationship to God, with different moral expectations than are found in the New Covenant. We need to understand the terms of this Old Covenant before we can appreciate the nature of Samson's struggle to move, like Israel in the desert and David under persecution, through that law to liberty.

Adam, once fallen, learns the function of the Old Testament law in book 12 of *Paradise Lost*. "This yet I apprehend not," he confesses there to Michael,

> why to those
> Among whom God will deign to dwell on Earth
> So many and so various Laws are giv'n;
> So many Laws argue so many sins
> Among them; how can God with such reside?   (280–84)

Having sensed the mercy shown in God's continuing relation with fallen humankind, he seeks to understand the terms under which this mercy can be reconciled with God's justice. Michael explains the two functions of the

Mosaic law in preserving it. First, the law preserves the moral sense which, since the Fall, must entail a realization of sin and guilt:

> And therefore was Law given them to evince
> Thir natural pravity, by stirring up
> Sin against Law to fight;

and second, the law leads fallen humankind, through near despair at their inability to keep Moses' law, to a faith in God's ability to restore them to harmony with the law of their original being:

> that when they see
> Law can discover sin, but not remove,
> Save by those shadowy expiations weak,
> The blood of Bulls and Goats, they may conclude
> Some blood more precious must be paid for Man,
> Just for unjust, that in such righteousness
> To them by Faith imputed, they may find
> Justification towards God, and peace
> Of Conscience, which the Law by Ceremonies
> Cannot appease, nor Man the moral part
> Perform, and not performing cannot live.   (289–99)

Man is to come, through a strict belief that he *must* keep the law, to a realization that he *cannot*. This contradiction is the Mosaic law's imperfection—that inherent characteristic which calls forth its own eventual need for abrogation and identifies it as a temporary tool of God, not the eternal law of being. The contradiction is summed up in the relation between its ceremonial and moral parts. Humans were given the ceremonial observances, which they could keep even in their fallen state, both as signs of fulfilling a covenant and, at the same time, in that their function is atonement, as reminders of their inability to keep the moral commandments which were the essence of that covenant.

> So Law appears imperfet, and but giv'n
> With purpose to resign them in full time
> Up to a better Cov'nant, disciplin'd
> From shadowy Types to Truth, from Flesh to Spirit,
> From imposition of strict Laws, to free
> Acceptance of large Grace, from servile fear
> To filial, works of Law to works of Faith.

As the first function of the law is to "discover sin, but not remove," so its second function is to lead its truest followers to transcend its own limits by the grace of a God who makes fallen people's efforts to keep a perfect law acceptable "works of faith."

What is most important for a reader of Milton's drama to understand is that the second function of the law can come into being only after the first function has had its full effect. This does not happen for the Chorus in *Samson*: they are servants under bondage, not yet fully aware of the sin in themselves which the law discovers but cannot remove, pious followers of the Lord, but incapable of faith. Samson, however, reaches the limit of the old law and hence is able to transcend and fulfill it. As he becomes capable of facing in himself a tremendous sense of guilt, so he proves capable finally of a relentless belief in the existence of that justice which includes within itself the mercy of a chastising Father (see Hebrews 6.5–10). In the course of the play he moves away from the condition of the Chorus, out of bondage and into sonship, as an example of pre-Christian adoption. The resulting liberty demands from Samson, as from a Christian, a greater degree of perfection than the law demands from the Chorus. For he must weigh each deed and motive against his right reason and will not be excused for acting or willing blindly, out of piety. "It is not a less perfect life that is required from Christians but, in fact, a more perfect life than was required of those who were under the law" (*CPW* 6:535).

To perceive the process of Samson's growing superiority over the Chorus, we must recognize that from the beginning the Chorus, as well as Samson, is a bearer of guilt. Its sin of servility directs Milton's reading of the Biblical Samson story. The Chorus sings in awe of Samson's famous feats of physical strength, but it does not mention why these were done. In Milton's view, they were never merely acts of personal revenge or glorification, but were all occasions seized by the natural and appointed leader of a people for their national deliverance. The Bible does not show Samson speaking of his achievements or purposes to his people; and Milton interprets this silence as Samson's own kind of dedication, which "Us'd no ambition to commend my deeds, / The deeds themselves, though mute, spoke loud the doer; / But they persisted deaf" (247–49). The Israelites' inability to see beyond Samson's sheer physical accomplishment is revealed in the contrast between what they and Samson say happened at Ramath-lechi. In their view,

> Then with what trivial weapon came to hand,
> The Jaw of a dead Ass, his sword of bone,

> A thousand foreskins fell, the flower of *Palestine*,
> In *Ramath-lechi* famous to this day.   (142–45)

Samson echoes some of their language when he describes how he, "with a trivial weapon fell'd / Their choicest youth" (263–67), but he says that the moral point of what happened on that battlefield was not his strength or even God's glorification by his strength but rather the people's betrayal of him and of "God's proposed deliverance": "Had *Judah* that day join'd, or one whole Tribe [such as his own tribe of Dan], / They had by this possess'd the Towers of *Gath*" (265–66).

A cause pursued only to the point at which either personal ease is attained or personal safety seems threatened had always betokened for Milton, as it does for Samson, evidence of selfish motives governing the pursuants even though the cause itself might be righteous. In the earliest attempts at ecclesiastical reform, a young Milton had urged: "Let us not dally with God when he offers us a full blessing, to take as much of it as wee think will serve our ends, and turne him back the rest upon his hands" (*Of Reformation, CPW* 1:602). In the greater responsibility of regicide, where larger numbers fell away, he had charged: " 'Tis true, that most men are apt enough to civill Wars and commotions as a noveltie, and for a flash hot and active, but through sloth or inconstancie, and weakness of spirit either fainting, ere their own pretences, though never so just, be half attain'd, or through an inbred falshood and wickednes, betray oft times to destruction with themselves, men of noblest temper joyn'd with them for causes, whereof they in their rash undertakings were not capable" (*TKM, CPW* 3:912). And in the last moment of his political freedom, an aging Milton still reasoned: "Most just it is doubtless, if it com to force, that a less number compell a greater to retain, which can be no wrong to them, thir libertie, than that a greater number for the pleasure of thir baseness, compell a less most injuriously to be thir fellow slaves. They who seek nothing but thir own just libertie, have alwaies right to winn it and to keep it, when ever they have power, be the voices never so numerous that oppose it" (*Ready and Easy Way, CPW* 7:455). Earlier judges of Israel, deserted by their followers, furnish Milton's Samson, as they had Milton himself, with examples that help him place his situation in perspective and philosophically accept his own lonely struggle for freedom:

> But what more oft in Nations grown corrupt,
> And by thir vices brought to servitude,
> Than to love Bondage more than Liberty,
> Bondage with ease than strenuous liberty;

And to despise, or envy, or suspect
Whom God hath of his special favor rais'd
As thir Deliverer.   (268–74)

The Chorus understands Samson's words only in a general sense and
remembers from history the cases of Gideon and Jephtha. It fails to see the
comparison Samson is drawing between those earlier leaders and himself
for the same reason that it had seen Ramath-lechi merely as an exhibition
of physical glory. Thus, it is unable to obey him when Samson admonishes: "Of such examples add me to the roll" (290); for if the Danites add
Samson's to the case of Gideon, then they must add themselves to the
example of the men of Succoth and of Penuel: if Samson is like Jephtha,
then they are the modern "ingrateful Ephraim." To recognize their own
guilt in this manner would mean that they would also have to recognize
their duty no longer to submit to Philistine rule, and they have not the
courage or freedom of mind. Thus, they are in danger of falling into the
ranks of those peoples, "conquered . . . and enslav'd by War" whom
Michael describes to Adam in book 11 of *Paradise Lost*:

therefore cool'd in zeal
Thenceforth shall practice how to live secure,
Worldly or dissolute, on what thir Lords
Shall leave them to enjoy.   (803–806)

And with fear repressing their awareness of their own guilt, they are
unable rationally to justify God's treatment of their leader. Their vision of
Samson's experience is "carnal," to use Milton's own word for the servility
of people unable to follow the spiritual essence of a law, and they are
bound in the tangles of the letter.

The Chorus displays the effect on its faith of its carnal vision when it
starts offering advice to Samson in a speech beginning "Tax not divine
disposal" (210). Despite the efforts of some critics to fit this speech into a
reading of the Chorus' regeneration, it remains intractable, and to understand its real function we must note how Milton carefully arranges it to
compare with a statement by Samson that precedes it and to contrast with
one that follows it. When we first meet Samson, we find his mind weighed
down in the bonds of his suffering flesh. The Chorus' lament about the
inadequacy of the "inward light," which "alas / Puts forth no visual beam"
(162–63), is paralleled by Samson's faulty judgment about the nature of his
God-given strength: "God, when he gave me strength, to show withal /
How slight the gift was, hung it in my Hair" (58–59). The Chorus'

conclusion—viewing Samson as a "mirror of our fickle state" (164)—in effect denies the justice of God's governance of the world by equating his providence with "fortune" (169); for the metaphor of fortune's wheel, although intended as a reminder of God's omnipotence, when applied by the Chorus to Samson's case, denies God's justice. A just God does not reward evil or punish virtue; if a man feels an affliction to be from God— if he experiences a sense during his tribulations of heaven's desertion— then he must accept his suffering as merited and its justice as comprehensible; he must seek out its cause and its cure. The spiritual fall of a moral creature is always the result of sin (cf. Hooker, *Laws* 421; 5.76.7–8).[7]

Likewise a just God could not have created a rational creature with too little wisdom to detect temptation. This truth is not, however, what Samson accepts as his first answer to the challenge to God's justice when he interrupts his reasoning about the problem:

> But peace, I must not quarrel with the will
> Of highest dispensation, which herein
> Haply had ends above my reach to know:
> Suffices that to mee strength is my bane,
> And proves the source of all my miseries.   (60–64)

Because his reasoning is stopped here by piety and not by a rational answer, he finds himself again quarreling with God's dispensation a few lines later and falls into the same carnal confusion about the analogy between the literal light of sight and the metaphoric light of the soul (92) that the Chorus will be in when we first see it.

In trying to accept the easy answer of piety, Samson is willing to believe that God created him with a wisdom inadequate to the task he was given to do—that is, that the Creator was the source of his "default" (45) and that, therefore, the God whose will for him he had thought he understood is in fact inscrutable. This assumption of God's inaccessibility to rational understanding enables Samson for the moment to limit the perspective of his meditation to the pain of his own physical and emotional torment instead of seeking to understand its ultimate cause. This limitation is exactly what the Chorus advises him to impose upon his thoughts when he raises the question for them. The admonition "Tax not divine disposal," taken by itself, might mean, "God gave you sufficient wisdom; his disposal is just"; but the explanation that follows contradicts this interpretation, saying in effect, "God gave many men insufficient wisdom." It says that "wisest Men / Have err'd, and by bad Women been deceiv'd, / And shall again, pretend they ne'er so wise" (210–12). So "Tax not divine disposal" means, "God appears to be unjust, but is actually inscrutable, and must not be questioned."

The Chorus' resulting advice is that Samson limit his thoughts to the human, carnal level: "Deject not then so overmuch thyself, / Who hast of sorrow thy full load besides" (213–14). This had been Samson's own conclusion earlier, that he had nothing left, in the face of inscrutability, but to dwell on all his miseries, "So many, and so huge, that each apart / Would ask a life to wail" (65–66). Now that this kind of piety is urged by a voice other than his own, he sees more clearly the moral weakness that it excuses in a person and begins to suspect the truth of the morality it ascribes to God, even as he is known to human perception. Thus, here Samson renews his effort to understand the human fault behind his fall. He will not assign the blame to "bad Women," as the Chorus advises, but acknowledges, "of what now I suffer / She was not the prime cause, but I myself" (233–34). This is not yet a full realization of guilt; for in spite of the shift of attention from Dalila's fault to his own, Samson goes on to blame himself for a weakness that is closer to a psychological failing than a moral sin, being "vanquisht with a peal of words (O weakness!) / Gave up my fort of silence to a Woman" (235–36). This sort of weakness Manoa calls "frailty" (369), which so understood would be, as Manoa (368–72) and the Chorus (164–75) think, incommensurate with his punishment, the affliction of a seemingly unjust God.

Samson's answer to Manoa's suggestion that his punishment is too severe has been read as identical in meaning to the Chorus' "Tax not divine disposal." Actually it speaks directly against the opinion of the Chorus and marks another step in Samson's growth away from the blindness of its piety, which in the play's beginning he was tempted to share. Instead of accepting an unjust or inscrutable God, he continues to look for justice accessible to human understanding and is thus forced to reason back from the magnitude of the punishment to what must necessarily have been the magnitude of the offense:

> Appoint not heavenly disposition, Father,
> Nothing of all these evils hath befall'n me
> But justly, I myself have brought them on,
> Sole Author I, sole cause; if aught seem vile,
> As vile hath been my folly, who have profan'd
> The mystery of God giv'n me under pledge
> Of vow. (373–79)

Many readers who recognize that Samson's sense of his own guilt is here becoming more truthful and profound do not see how this growth is related to the concerns, seemingly superficial by comparison, of the Chorus and Manoa over the illegality of his Canaanite marriages and the ceremonial defilement of the feast of Dagon. Holding to God's literal commandments, which are its sure link with heavenly disposition, the Chorus wants to suggest that the crime for which Samson suffers, however disproportionate to the penalty it may seem, is his twice breaking the law that forbids intermarriage. In addition it implies that its own continued captivity may, in spite of Samson's efforts in battle, also be a part of its leader's punishment for these marriages. The Chorus' conception of sin serves to point out, by contrast, Samson's depth. But it also points out issues that Samson, with a growing ability to reason rightly, must carefully interpret, since even full Christian freedom from law never means law's abandonment or denial, but its fulfillment, that is, its truest interpretation.

His marriage to the woman of Timna, Samson can assure the Chorus, had God's approval; and although he undertook on his own mistaken initiative to marry Dalila, his motivation was at least partly virtuous, seeking God's will. It is revealing of the nature of the Chorus' limitation that, even though the great sin Samson confesses was with Dalila, and not in his marriage but in his betrayal of the secret, the Chorus returns to consider the ceremonial breach in the Timna marriage, which God specifically urged, as the issue that is its stumbling block to accepting God's justice. The Chorus' self-absolving legalism prevents it from searching wisely for God's consistency. Its inability to reason toward an answer is primarily a moral rather than an intellectual failing; it is the absence of *recta ratio*. Just as Samson searches his soul for the sin commensurate to his punishment, the Chorus should be examining its own moral life for the reason why "*Israel* still serves" the Philistine tyranny. As long as it cannot see its own moral guilt, it cannot recognize the moral nature of Samson's sin and, thus, the appropriateness of God's punishment. The Chorus' only recourse, therefore, is to blind interpretation and obedience of the literal law, however contradictory that may appear, in order to maintain its covenant with God. In its concern to prevent divine "glory's diminution," it finds itself, as Milton had found all too many of his own countrymen, defending God's power at the expense of his goodness:

> As if they would confine th' interminable,
> And tie him to his own prescript,
> Who made our Laws to bind us, not himself.

In contrast to the Chorus' sense here, we know that Milton believed God's eternal laws to bind first of all God himself. The Chorus, however, does not possess the concept, held by Hooker, Milton, and Goodwin, of eternal, immutable law—the concept of a Deity accessible to right reason. The Hebrews see God absolving appointed persons from obedience to those laws which set Israel apart as a nation, and reason that God

> . . . hath full right to exempt
> Whom so it pleases him by choice
> From National obstriction, without taint
> Of sin, or legal debt.   (310–13)

In their reference to both parts of their law, the moral ("sin") and the ritual ("legal debt"), they have a tool for understanding the way by which God can reasonably exempt from literal obedience to fulfill spiritual intent, but they cannot use it because they see God's right as based on his omnipotence rather than on the justice which defines his divine nature. Hence, they conclude piously: "For with his own Laws he can best dispense" (314). Because he is the creator of the laws as well as of physical nature, they reason, he has the power to do with them what he will. "Best" implies goodness as well as power, however, and their next instinct is to seek God's rational justification.

> He would not else who never wanted means,
> Nor in respect of the enemy just cause
> To set his people free,
> Have prompted this Heroic *Nazarite*,
> Against his vow of strictest purity,
> To seek in marriage that fallacious Bride,
> Unclean, unchaste.   (315–21)

God *could*, because he can do anything, have found a legal means for Samson to begin Israel's deliverance, they reason; and it seems to them that "in respect of the enemy," he *should* have. Their own reasoning has left them as confused as those impious "by their own perplexities involved," and they conclude that because they cannot understand God's reasons, those must be unfathomable to human beings: "Down Reason then." But even as they try to close the door to reason, they glimpse but cannot comprehend the way in which right reason would lead them to a fuller faith. They understand that God never told Samson to break a moral law ("unchaste") in marrying, only a ritual ("unclean").

What they do not go on to recognize about the Timna marriage is that through it (in Milton's version) Samson, as he was divinely urged, did his part to fulfill the purpose that underlay the ceremonial law against marrying a Gentile. That purpose was to preserve God's people from falling captive to the false gods and morals of the heathens. And the result of Samson's first marriage *was*, at the instigation of the oppressor, a battle to liberate Israel; but the Israelites' only willing part in it had been to bind their leader and surrender him as hostage. And since the Chorus cannot face the fact that God had "wanted . . . just cause" in respect of the Israelites themselves to set his people free, it cannot, as it studies Samson's history, grasp the spirit behind the laws either of marriage or of national identity and is thus stopped in the contradictions of the letter (322–25).

In Samson's fuller confession of his true guilt before Manoa, we can discern the insight he has attained by thinking through with right reason the same questions the Chorus has been trying to solve with uncomprehending piety. He has thought about the way his first marriage, in which he had acted in harmony with God's will, stood in relation to his second, in which he had sinned. It was true that he had broken the ceremonial law in marrying Dalila without God's specific prompting, but in that offense he fell deceived: "I thought it lawful from my former act" (231). His recognition of this fact helps him to face more clearly where his much worse "weakness" (235) had lain, in conscious sin ("warn'd by oft experience" [382]) against the spirit of the ritual law that had forbidden the marriage. In failing to shake off Dalila's snares, he had fallen, not deceived, but fully capable of understanding the servitude into which he was yielding himself (386–419).

With his mind thus free from spiritual blindness toward the issues of his marriages, Samson immediately goes on to perceive the more serious moral reason behind what, in his father's eyes, is the grave ceremonial offense of being the occasion for a great feast honoring Dagon. He faces the full extent of his guilt again by allowing his reason to grasp the essential correspondence between the letter and the spirit of the law. As Samson sees how, in telling the ritual "holy secret" (497) of his strength, his moral sin had been uxoriousness, the betrayal of his own relationship to God, so too he sees how his occasioning ritual honor to Dagon, the result of the captivity into which his sin drew him, is a betrayal not merely of ritual, but of his God-given moral relationship to his people (448–57). For although the fact of their political captivity is their own fault and not his, the same moral weakness that binds them in physical subjection renders them all the more vulnerable to a religious confusion from which he, as their leader, has an even greater responsibility to protect them.

Most readers agree that, at the end of the encounter with Manoa, Samson and the Chorus have reached the greatest degree of despair they experience in the play. But the nature of what each experiences is not at all the same. Whereas Samson suffers guilt because of his deepened awareness of God's justice, the Chorus suffers fear because it worships a God it believes to be, by human ethical standards, unjust (667–704). Its petition for Samson, at the end of its "God of our Fathers" speech, is the fearful appeal of an essentially barbarian superstition to an all-powerful Deity for a special favor:

> So deal not with this once thy glorious Champion,
> The Image of thy *strength*, and *mighty* minister.
> What do I beg? how hast thou dealt already?
> Behold him in this state calamitous, and turn
> His labors, *for thou canst*, to peaceful end.
>
> (705–09, emphasis added)

Because of its inability to make moral sense of Samson's relation to the ritual law, it is thrown back into blind obedience (bondage) to that law and absolute subjection to an inscrutable Deity.

Samson, on the other hand, has progressed in his rational faith to the limits of the Old Testament law. Freed from dependence on the ritual letter, he is still tied to his irreparable breach of the moral law, but now it is with the realization that there is no channel in the Mosaic law by which what virtues he has (as Manoa fondly hopes) can compensate for his wrongs. Thus, for a reason exactly opposite that of the Chorus, he has come to view his story from now on as taking place on two levels, the divine (461–62) and his own. "Hopeless are all my evils," he believes, "all remediless" (648). And as long as he is surrounded only by others bound by the same law, he can progress no further. Having understood the relation between the ritual and moral law, and between the letter and the spirit, he knows that "Law can discover sin, but not remove." He is thus in a position to understand the necessity for the abrogation of the moral law as well, in order that in "righteousness / To them by Faith imputed, they may find / Justification towards God, and peace" (*PL* 12.294–96). So when Manoa tells Samson that his insistence on punishment is not pious, Samson is not wrong in persisting on his penitential course; for he is ready to move beyond piety. As his own people have shown him the negative limits of that law whose servant they are, so now it will take the Philistines to reinforce his knowledge of the necessity for law and lead him to the realization that God himself operates by a more perfect law than that by which Samson now judges himself. He will move in the encounters that follow to an understanding of the law as liberty.

DALILA'S relation to the Mosaic law is ambiguous. Although she is married to a Hebrew, she comes from a nation not bound to Jehovah or his decrees. Both Samson and the Chorus recognize the legal responsibility of a Hebrew to divorce an unrepentant infidel, but Samson is not, like the Chorus, legalistic in his treatment of Dalila; and, in contrast to it, he grows spiritually from the encounter.

The Chorus' only possible solution to the puzzle of Dalila's arguments is to ignore them; for, as we have seen, it cannot make the discrimination between higher and lower laws necessary to follow an argument either from "Love's law" or "public good." As the Chorus could not reason rightly about its own guilt, and thus about Samson's guilt, so it cannot ascribe genuine moral responsibility to Dalila. Instead, as it was earlier willing to ascribe unfairness to God by believing it a flaw of created nature that wise men can be morally deceived, so now it looks for a natural inconsistency in women in general: "Is it for that such outward ornament / Was lavish't on thir Sex, that inward gifts / Were left for haste unfinish't?" (1025–27). Its words recall, in their phrasing, those of Adam, who, pondering on the effect of Eve's beauty on him, had wondered innocently whether Nature "at least on her bestow'd / Too much of Ornament, in outward show / Elaborate, of inward less exact" (*PL* 8.537–39). But the Chorus would have been unable to understand Raphael's answer, as could Adam, who knew in his wife the power of reason that can "declare unfeign'd / Union of Mind, or in us both one Soul" (603–04). Such had been Milton's definition of marriage in the divorce tracts. In the *Tetrachordon*, he had qualified Paul's injunction that wives should be subject to their husbands, saying, "Neverthelesse man is not to hold her as a servant, but receives her into a part of that empire which God proclaims him to, though not equally, yet largely, as his own image and glory: for it is no small glory to him, that a creature so like him, should be made subject to him." Milton went even further in pointing out that the same spirit in which God had ordered the woman subordinate to the man may require exceptions to the literal rule: "Not but that particular exceptions may have place, if she exceed her husband in prudence and dexterity, and he contentedly yeeld, for then a superior and more naturall law comes in, that the wiser should govern the lesse wise, whether male or female" (*CPW* 2:589).

The Chorus cannot conceive of such a governing relation. As it interprets God's placing the man above the woman in marriage, the law "Gave to the man despotic power / Over his female in due awe" (1045–55). Its view of the marriage relation is simply an extension of its view of its own relation to a God whom it is ready to consider despotic, a God who contradicts himself but is all-powerful and therefore not to be questioned.

Samson, however, governs Dalila not despotically but by granting her moral liberty. In contrast to her assertion that "love's law" is, for a lover, higher than—or at least an excuse from—other responsibilities, he insists that genuine love would have "taught," not contradicted, moral "reasonings." Genuine values, Samson has come to believe, are not contradictory, are no impediment to moral choices. Thus, although he refers to the custom by which a foreign wife adopts the country of her husband, he does not make custom the basis of his discussion. Instead, he bases his urging for her repentance and for his divorce from her on natural law, implying that Dalila, while his wife, could have retained her "Philistine" nationality and even her worship of "Dagon" if those names had represented conditions that were genuinely national and religious according to universal criteria—if, that is, her governors had not commanded betrayal of marriage "against the law of nature, law of nations" and her priests had not demanded Dagon be served by "ungodly deeds." In the course of these speeches to Dalila, Samson voices a growing vision that his God is not only tribal, but universal, and that God's moral law extends beyond national rules to all people.

Samson's confidence in the universality of God's justice is the source of the renewed spiritual vigor he shows in the encounters with both Dalila and Harapha. The Chorus is like Dalila in not recognizing its own guilt; but it more closely resembles Harapha, who, unlike Dalila, has never considered issues of guilt and moral responsibility beyond a blind, literal faith in the given rules of his country and religion. Harapha's wish to have been in the field of battle at Ramath-lechi manifests a perception of that event that is the same as the Chorus'. For both, the battle would prove which side was stronger. Harapha thinks of Samson's God only in terms of his strength and favor to Samson, as do the Hebrews, not in terms of the justice of his cause. Like the Chorus in its "what is man" speech (667–704), he conceives of Samson's defeat and suffering as the inexplicable loss of the favor of that Deity: "whate'er he be, / Thee he regards not" (1155–56). Also like the Chorus, Harapha does not understand the sin against his divine gift and responsibility that Samson explains in lines 1168–77. The closest he can come to seeing justice in the situation is to turn to the official pronouncements of his own governors, by which Samson is "A Murderer, a Revolter, and a Robber" (1180), "Due by the Law to capital punishment" (1225).

Samson reasons through these charges to demonstrate his own justice—in the same terms by which he has demonstrated God's justice in punishing his sin—not according to Philistine decrees, but according to universal truths. He refers to the right of human beings, created free, to self-government, even though this responsibility has been betrayed, in his case, by the "servile minds" of his own compatriots. As long as Samson had considered God's justice in relation only to his own offense, he could not see beyond his own punishment and sought death as an escape from pain and humiliation. When, having recognized the depths of his own guilt, he is directed to view the workings of God's providential justice not only toward, but through and beyond himself, he is rewarded with the insight that God's consistency encompasses not only his sin and its punishment, but his repentance and pardon. While the Chorus is worrying about the further afflictions to which Harapha's "malicious counsel" may lead, Samson has gained distance enough from his own suffering to suspect that all the while God's justice is working on his sin, it is also judging the Philistines' wickedness; and that since they have been enemies so closely locked in action, they may all as sinful people meet their punishment in a way that allows the just cause to triumph, and that he may die in God's service: "Yet so it may fall out, because thir end / Is hate, not help to me, it may with mine / Draw thir own ruin who attempt the deed" (1265–67).

The Chorus is inspired by Samson's courage—"Oh how comely it is and how reviving" (1268)—but it is unable to credit him accurately for what he has accomplished. For he has proven "Victor" not merely, as it realizes, "over all / That tyranny or fortune can inflict," but over these as the appearance of God's desertion (1290–91). By rejecting the notion of the arbitrariness of "fortune" and relentlessly pursuing full knowledge of his guilt and that of others, Samson has been rewarded for his faith in God's righteousness with the discovery of what he has gropingly sought, a rationally and morally governed universe. That discovery has brought with it victory over the ultimate enemy, over his own sin and despair. He is now ready to meet in his future not what will "chance" to become of him (1294–96), but what God will offer.

It seems at first incredible to Samson, after the subtleties of sin and guilt he has mastered, that he should next be challenged by the Philistine officer's command with simple idolatry in its most easily recognizable form. Hence the simplicity and civility of his first answer: "Thou knowst I am an *Ebrew*, therefore tell them, / Our Law forbids at thir Religious Rites / My presence; for that cause I cannot come" (1319–21). When this answer is not accepted, he sees the torturous intent of the enemy, and his immediate response is what we saw in him at the opening of the play, personal chagrin at humiliation: "Do they not seek occasion of new quarrels / On my refusal to distress me more" (1329–30).

Samson has one last barrier to break down before he attains liberty. This temptation has seemed an insult both to his intelligence and to his will to keep the law; to give in to it would be the "worst of all indignities," indignities, that is, to Samson himself. The purpose behind the law that forbids his presence at the ceremonies, however, is not to prevent embarrassment to Samson, but to maintain the right relation between God and his people. The significance of his presence in the pagan temple would be in what it symbolized, as his uncut hair was the sign and not the source of his strength.

The Chorus recognizes the crisis—"matters are now strain'd / Up to the height, whether to hold or break" (1348–49)—and it speaks more than it knows. "Matters" include not only the fate of Samson, but the adequacy of the old law. With the exit of the officer, Samson moves more quickly than he could have earlier from the issue of personal humiliation to its real source, sin, from self to God: "Besides, how vile, contemptible, ridiculous, / What act more execrably unclean, profane?" (1361–62). The Chorus counters: "Where the heart joins not, outward acts defile not" (1368). But Samson points out that the conditions for this maxim do not yet apply to his case: "the *Philistian* Lords command. / Commands are no constraints. If I obey them, / I do it freely" (1371–73). If in exercising his freedom, as the Chorus suggests, he were to act from its persistent motive, "fear of man," he would be breaking the spirit as well as the letter of the law. Although it is true that he would not be feeling ceremonial reverence for Dagon, what he would be feeling would be no better; his cowardice would be a moral wrong. It is significant that at this point the Chorus can see no answer except destruction for Samson: "How thou wilt here come off surmounts my reach" (1380). If they were in Samson's place, fear would be their motive, as it has been up to now; accordingly, the right thing for them to do would be to obey the ceremonial law as its loyal servants, and suffer the consequences from the Philistines.

But at this moment of seeming impasse, Samson, because he is ready, is shown the other side of the coin. If his motives *are* God-centered, it becomes more important for him to obey the spirit than the letter. The creator of the ceremonial law can set it aside if the higher moral law, the condition upon which the ritual decree depends, is to be served: "Yet that he may dispense with me or thee / Present in Temples at Idolatrous Rites / For some important cause, thou need'st not doubt" (1377–79). Here, Samson is not—as was the Chorus when it said God "made our laws to bind us, not himself"—subduing his reason either to fear or to piety. God knows that he has not been afraid of death or of anything the Philistines can do to him, except humiliate him. Samson must be recognizing that pride is a stronger motive in him for keeping the ceremonial law than "fear of man" would be for breaking it. As soon as he condemns the fear motive to the Chorus, he can see that, although such fear has been the source of their failure to pursue a thorough knowledge of their own guilt, it has never tempted him—and that he must face what has. When he sees that God can dispense with the act of going to the temple, he sees that he must dispense with his pride. He must become, as Arnold Stein puts it, a "Fool of God."[8]

Samson's experience throughout the play has been preparing him to receive "Some rousing motions in me which dispose / To something extraordinary my thoughts" (1382–83). The "motions" are divine inspiration, to be sure, but Milton's God inspires rational creatures with reason. In Samson's case, it is the right reason that can perceive not only logical relations, but the hierarchical ones that are logic's preconditions, and that can thereby reconcile seeming contradictions: "I with this Messenger will go along, / Nothing to do, be sure, that may dishonor / Our Law, or stain my vow of *Nazarite*" (1384–86). The essence of the law of Moses as well as of the Nazarite vow will not be sacrificed in their abrogation, but fulfilled. Samson presumably does not know, when he leaves the Chorus, how God will enable him to accomplish their fulfillment. But his final words to the Chorus reveal the perception of a hierarchy of values that has restored his right relation to the Israelites and has set him free: "Our God, our Law, my Nation . . . myself" (1425).

The final scene with Manoa, the Chorus, and the Hebrew messenger is weighted with ironies. Some the Hebrews learn in the end to recognize, and some remain known in full only to the (fit) audience. Among the second kind are the references to Samson's liberty. Manoa arrives to tell the Chorus what hopes he has "to work his liberty." When he hears that Samson is dead, he cries: "O all my hope's defeated / To free him hence!" There is a bitter irony intended in his comparison of death's role and his own, "but death who sets all free / Hath paid his ransom now and full discharge" (1571–73). Samson, however, views his death not merely as punishment or payment of debt, but as the restoration of his right reason ("Reason also is choice," *PL* 3:108), the birth of his liberty. It is the sign of the just God's continuing presence with him that frees him to act truly "of [his] own accord," using his punishment as service.

The Chorus enters into Samson's victory as deeply as its bondage to the law permits. Its faith in their world's predictability has been restored by the literal fulfillment of the promise of Samson's birth. But rather than a rational faith like Samson's, it remains a blinded piety, as its reference to "dire necessity" makes clear. George M. Muldrow, taking the Chorus at this point as Milton's spokesman, tries to identify its words here as referring "to some law of inevitable physical causation and not to any mysterious power of fate in the universe."[9] But while Muldrow is right to think that Milton could not have believed in a Christian fatalism or fideism, the majority of readers are right to recognize that this is the belief of the Chorus. Martin Mueller has identified the truly tragic center of the drama in this perception by the Chorus of a universe shrouded in mystery, "which willing acceptance can mitigate but the terror of which it can never entirely remove."[10] Mueller, however, attributes to Samson, and hence to the audience, a belief that Milton gave in this play only to Samson's contemporaries. By the play's ending calm of mind has been restored to the Chorus and Samson. But there remains a sense in which the God of Milton, now known to the audience through Samson, must say that the Old Testament Hebrews have "serv'd necessity, / Not mee" (*PL* 3.110–11). The difference between Samson's faith and the Chorus' fideism can be seen most clearly if we recognize the relation of each to the catastrophe. For Samson it is but the outward manifestation and reward of his faith, of his new knowledge of God that was achieved before the summons of the Officer. For the Chorus the catastrophe is the precondition of its restored belief that "All is best." Many readers have thought the Chorus' *felix culpa* resolution to the contradictions with which its faith has been confronted to be Milton's as well. With the destruction of the temple, the mystery has been revealed, it is suggested: God must have wanted Samson to sin all along so that he could engineer the catastrophe.

But understanding God's ways does not give the ability to predict future events. This view of the message of the angel of Samson's birth reduces God to the level of the pagan oracles, and faith to the level of fortune-telling. To understand God, we must deal with essence, not time. A subsequent event cannot justify a former event, an end cannot by itself justify a means. Any event, end or means, is justified by the rightness or wrongness of its own nature and of the appropriateness in the circumstances in which it is deployed; it must be judged according to the law of all nature. Samson's marriage to the woman of Timna and his going with the officer are justified as breaches of ceremonial law *not* because they lead to the play's catastrophe, but because they are done in true communion with God's will according to "the condition upon which the decree depends," the spirit, of the very laws that were literally broken. The marriage with Dalila is not justified, for it is done for self-centered, not God-centered, reasons, using a license, not a liberty, to break the law. That it too leads to the destruction of the Philistines does not excuse it. Only

Samson's penance and God's responding grace can do that. The Chorus never is able to make these distinctions, and its view of a God who keeps his promise to a favored nation only by violations of his own law, inexplicable except as means to that desired end, never accurately describes Milton's God. The Chorus cannot experience a full faith in God's justice as long as it does not understand experientially what justice means.

In the end the Chorus reveals the service Samson has performed for it. He has cured what had been his "chief affliction, shame and sorrow" (457), to have brought "diffidence of God, and doubt / In feeble hearts, propense enough before / To waver" (454–56). The simple piety it expresses in its final song, however, is its own, not Samson's and not Milton's. The Israelites "oft doubt"; and because they lack the full knowledge of guilt prerequisite to liberty, they will doubt again. That the Hebrews' liberation will therefore be short-lived, however, does not invalidate the justice of Samson's cause, or the justice of the Philistines' punishment, or the basis for the Israelites' dimly understood hope. For Samson truly "died in faith, not having received the promises, but having seen them afar off" (Hebrews 11:13). And he has achieved "a more perfect life than was required of those who were under the law" (*CPW* 6:535).

ALTHOUGH many agree that Samson experiences spiritual regeneration, the political dimensions of Milton's drama have caused difficulty for readers in our age. In the Western world today, politics is no longer understood as a religious endeavor and national values are generally held not to depend on universal truths, but to be related to the needs and desires of individual nations. In particular, readers have questioned the logic of the judgments Samson expresses in his encounters with Dalila and Harapha who are Philistines. Why, it is asked, is Dalila wrong in using her marriage to attack the enemy in the Philistine cause, but Samson not wrong in wanting to have so used his two Philistine marriages in the Hebrew cause? And why is Samson not justly viewed by Harapha as a criminal and an enemy to the Philistine state? Some believe that to look for reasonable solutions to these questions is futile because Milton is simply expressing, through Samson, his own nationalistic and religious dogmatism.[11] A second, less censorious group regards Milton's presentation as dogmatic only on the divine level of the play, as following Scripture, and holds that from his human perspective Milton presents an action which in itself does not explain the divine prejudice.[12] Most proponents of this view find Samson's and the Philistines' self-justifications equally valid relative to their own countries and invalid relative to each others', while they find God, on an entirely separate and inaccessible level of values, using whom he chooses for his own inscrutable purposes.

Like other scholars who find Milton solidly within the rationalist tradition of Western thought,[13] I do not believe that *Samson Agonistes* supports a dogmatic or fideistic picture of the poet. Nevertheless, I readily concede the pressures within the work itself that foster such readings. No art can accurately reflect and interpret experience without containing and accounting for the appearances that often hide or blur—and, unprobed, may easily be taken for—reality. While the artist risks being misunderstood when he effectively dramatizes misleading appearances, he would be derelict to the subtlety of his vision of experience if he did not. Such literature obliges the reader to probe its dramatic context carefully for evidence to corroborate the ethical judgments that frame the incidents before concluding of the artist, especially of Milton, that he has consciously or unwittingly constructed an action that affects our feelings and judgment in ways contradictory to his expressed intentions. Let us again use Milton's prose discussions of analagous situations from his own time as commentary on the issue of revolution in his play. This gloss helps to illustrate the extent to which both Milton's historical and his literary partisanship are accessible to our rational analysis. It reveals the political positions assumed by Dalila and Harapha to be parodic versions of Samson's genuine commitment to the public good.

In defending the English parliamentary cause against the bishops and later against the king, Milton had stressed the dangerously deceptive potential of the argument, as used by bishops and royalists, from "public good." In *Of Reformation* he defined the only true government, proclaiming, as Aristotle had recognized, that "to govern well is to train up a Nation in true wisdom and vertue"[14] and that the validity of anyone's claim to be acting in the public interest can be tested against this criterion of natural law, which is available to all human understanding. He then argued vigorously to unmask "men conspiring to uphold their state" by claiming to represent the public good: "This is the masterpiece of a modern politician, how to qualifie, and mould the sufferance and subjection of the people to the length of that foot that is to tread on their necks, how rapine may serve it selfe with the fair, and honourable pretences of publick good" (*CPW* 1:571). As we have observed, the Hebrew people, before the beginning of Milton's play, have already yielded their own nation to such pretences when, contrary to Samson's urging and example, they accepted the argument of the Philistine rulers that it was for their own "good" that they surrender him and thus achieve peace. What they have done in so yielding is to equate their "good" as a people not with "true wisdom and vertue" but with *ease*. Fearing the difficult means, they have lost sight of the valid end of their self-government, allowing their sufferance and subjection to be molded to the length of the Philistine foot.

This distinction between the ends and the means of government should be kept in mind when we consider the claim for relativism in the play, that is, the claim that "good" cannot be regarded as an absolute thing but must be defined vis-à-vis the will of the individual ruler and his public. It has been charged that Samson's judgment of Dalila's betrayal of him as "wedlock treachery" is simply a case of "the pot calling the kettle black"[15] and, as a corollary, that the Hebrew "Jael [to whom Dalila compares herself] was just as bad in non-Israelitish eyes"[16] as Dalila was in Hebrew eyes. How does Samson's willingness to use his marriages to combat the Philistines differ from Dalila's willingness to use her marriage to allow the Philistines to attack Samson? The answer to judging the means both used in serving their respective nations cannot be found, in Samson's as in Milton's world, without reference to the cause represented by each government. Since every citizen is both a private person and a member of a nation, he or she is morally responsible for two realms: the individual and the collective. This is why Milton could point out that while God, in judging the participants in the English civil war, might condemn either side for wrongdoing and thus fail to grant it the victory, his judgment against the revolutionaries would not be because they had revolted, but because they had failed as private persons to defend their public cause with full integrity. " 'Tis true," he said, "on our side the sins of our lives not seldom fought against us, but on their side, besides those, the grand sin of thir Cause" (*Eikonoklastes, CPW* 3:532).

Samson's private sin in yielding his secret to Dalila has fought against him in God's judgment, and therefore against his nation's cause. That cause, however, as Samson knows throughout his ordeal, has been the right goal for a genuine governor: to free his people to live righteous lives. When he fails to maintain his personal freedom and private good, he becomes unable to defend the public good. When he judges Dalila, Samson claims that her crime was the same as his, even though her nationality is different; her private sin, indirectly and perhaps even unwillingly, rendered service to a sinful public cause. When Dalila, however, instead of repenting her private sin, defends it as a public virtue, then she surrenders herself entirely to the service of tyranny, supporting it directly and willingly in both her private and public roles.

How could Dalila at first have judged the admonitions of the Philistine lords and priests? A passage from *Of Reformation*, in which Milton warns of private sin corrupting public judgment, is a helpful gloss. Just as the true role of a governor is to train a nation in wisdom and virtue, so the governed of a nation have the responsibility to demand and adhere to such training: "Well knows every wise Nation that their Liberty consists in Manly and honest labours, in sobriety and rigorous honour to the Marriage Bed . . . and when the people slacken . . . then doe they as much as if they laid downe their necks for some wily Tyrant to get up and ride" (*CPW* 1:588). Dalila's possessive desire for power over Samson, as well as any other dishonest desires that motivated her, can be understood as "slackening" (as can Samson's yielding to his wife's importunings). In this slackened condition, her mind could not control her response to the demands of the Philistine governors. Samson tells Dalila, however, that when her rulers told her that in order to serve her nation she should dishonor her own marriage, they—through that very request—could be seen to violate the right purpose for government in rational law, that is, the training of its citizens in virtue, here "rigorous honour" in marriage:

> if aught against my life
> Thy country sought of thee, it sought unjustly,
> Against the law of nature, law of nations.   (888–90)

Since their means revealed them to be in violation of the universal purpose of government, they could not be regarded as valid governors:

> No more thy country, but an impious crew
> Of men conspiring to uphold thir state
> By worse than hostile deeds. . . .   (891–93)

The idea that a nation ceases to be a nation in the true sense when its actions violate the purposes for which governments are established may help us understand a statement by Samson about which there has been some question. When Samson tells Dalila that the Philistines have violated "the ends / For which our country is a name so dear" (893–94), to what or whom does "our" refer? Is he calling Israel her country as well as his, since by custom the wife adopts the husband's country? Such a legalistic explanation misses the point that Israel, like Philistia, has violated its true governing function by conceding to its tributary alliance and, as Samson tells Dalila, is also "Not therefore to be obeyed." "Our country," it would seem, is not a nationalistic concept but an ideal one to which Samson would have himself and Dalila devote themselves, if necessary, against both of the deviant states.

But was not Samson's plan to use his marriage to Dalila in warring against the Philistines an unjustified means to serve nationalistic ends? From the reasoning by which Samson judges the crime of Dalila and her governors, we can see how his love for her and his campaign against the Philistines could never have been morally contradictory. Although he wanted to use his position as Dalila's husband to oppose Philistine tyranny, he would not have acted against *her*, would not have sought "aught against [her] life," in violation of his marriage. He is guilty of and repents a private sin against himself and God, that of uxoriousness; this sin of his life has fought against both him and his cause. But because Dalila refuses to repent her own sin against Samson in the violation of her marriage, enrolling instead as a Philistine heroine, her sin is no longer merely private. She seeks sanction for a private sin as public duty, an action which only compounds her guilt: "but on their side, besides those [private sins], the grand sin of thir Cause."

In her surrender to a tyrannous cause, Dalila forfeits her personal liberty of conscience, "which above all other things," Milton always stressed, "ought to be to all men dearest and most precious" (*Ready and Easy Way*, *CPW* 7:456). A free conscience is one trained up in wisdom and virtue; its protection is the only legitimate function of government and the only ground for a citizen's obedience. Liberty of conscience is the point of Milton's irony in having Dalila compare her deed to that of Jael, the heroine of the Hebrew Song of Deborah (Judges 4 and 5). Jael's husband, Heber the Kenite, was not taking part in the war of Deborah, Judge of Israel, and her general Barak against the Canaanites (Judges 5:17). Jael did not react with cowardice as did the Hebrew people of Meroz,[17] who, when recruited, were afraid to support Barak in battle (Judges 5:23). Jael is "blessed above women" in Deborah's song (Judges 5.24) because, without being directed by any force outside her own conscience, and holding it wrong for the Canaanites to oppress the Hebrews, she went against the official neutrality of her tribe to perform her higher public duty. In so doing she exercised both insight and courage, wisdom and virtue—that combination which comprises right reason. This is exactly what Dalila, lacking a free conscience, has failed to do, what Samson now urges her to do as he calls for her repentance, and what he has done himself in defiance of Hebrew national "policy." When Dalila seeks glory in Philistia instead, she is "conspiring" with the Philistine rulers to uphold her state with "pretences of publick good."

Samson's second Philistine visitor does not concern himself with rhetorical pretences to public good, but with sheer power. Harapha holds simply that the power of government should go to whoever has the superior means, the strength, to wield it—regardless of the end or purpose for rule. His terms have been tacitly accepted by the Hebrew people out of their own fear of such strength. "Knowest thou not that the Philistines are rulers over us?" the men of Judah had said to Samson before Ramath-lechi (Judges 15.2). "Is not thy Nation subject to our Lords?" Harapha accuses Samson. The argument he implies for obedience to Philistine tyranny is similar to that of the seventeenth-century royalists: one obeys the king absolutely, even if he is a tyrant, simply because he *is* the ruler in power.[18] Remember that Milton's contemporary antagonists had argued that God wills the order of the state to be preserved at all costs, that they quoted St. Paul, Romans 13:1: "there is no power but of God." Milton, however, had replied that Paul's words "must be understood of lawfull and just powers, els we read of great power in the affaires and Kingdoms of the World permitted to the Devil" (*TKM, CPW* 3:209–10).

In the past, when resisting Philistine power, Samson was a warrior somewhat like the proud, unthinking Harapha in that he took his cause essentially for granted and gloried mainly in his own renown (523–32). And here, in the encounter with Harapha, he does not immediately reach a full Miltonic solution to the challenge posed, but answers the Philistine warrior in his own terms, offering as his self-justification for revolution under Jehovah, the omnipotence of that God. Since Harapha assumes that the strongest should rule, Samson demands a duel to "see . . . whose God is strongest."

Harapha will not argue with the notion of a deity's power, but feels confident that the Hebrew deity, "whate'er he be," is, like the Philistine deity, analogous to earthly rulers who wield their power not according to universal standards of "wisdom and vertue" but arbitrarily. Speaking from the vision of a human world subject to gods whose only known attribute is power, he attempts to undermine the confidence of one against whom divine power has apparently turned: "Presume not on thy God, whate'er he be, / Thee he regards not, owns not" (1155–56).

Again Samson challenges Harapha to combat, but this time he speaks out of a different world-view from Harapha's when he explains to the Philistine that his suffering is merited by his own sin and is evidence of a just God's presence, not desertion. That he punishes sin shows God to be a governor to whose wisdom and virtue power is a means, not an end. Thus Samson challenges Harapha a second time, inspired by trust not merely in God's power but in God's justice, and assured that Harapha's god is not a genuine deity. As Samson had told Dalila, no true god would demand, as the Philistine priests said Dagon did, to be served by "ungodly deeds, the contradiction of their own deity" (896–99).

Though Harapha cannot understand Samson's argument because he has no concept of sin, virtue, or law beyond that of his warrior's code, he makes an effort to defeat Samson in his line of argument by resorting to the official propaganda of his political leaders, who, unlike the politically simple warrior, present themselves not only as most powerful, but as defenders of the public good:

> Fair honor that thou dost thy God, in trusting
> He will accept thee to defend his cause,
> A Murderer, a Revolter, and a Robber.   (1178–80)

These criminal terms would label Samson a violator of the private and public good, but Samson refutes the charges on the grounds that all his acts of violence against the Philistines were political, not personal, not crimes at all, but battles for liberty and service to God.

Harapha's charges, in forcing Samson to correct his foe's notion of what constitutes a private and a public act, lead the Nazarite to discover the means of readmittance to grace and the service to Abraham's race that was promised by the angel of his birth (28–29). He has already begun to consider the implications of the distinction between private and public acts in regard to his domestic history. In divorcing Dalila, he realized and accepted how fully his private sins have fought against his cause. From his examination of his private role at that time, he had been left feeling that not only Dalila but he also was hopelessly condemned. Now, in the political confrontation with Harapha, however, the other emphasis can be explored. As he defends his past public acts, Samson finds a basis for the hope that God may yet again use him in a public role simply because of the justice of his cause, which exists regardless of his or the Hebrews' unworthiness, and because of the "grand sin" of the Philistine cause. And, as we have seen, the hope that God will still use him is identical with a hope for divine grace.

The details of Samson's self-defense here have caused the play's readers some difficulty. Arnold Stein fits Samson's answer about the thirty men at Askalon somewhat awkwardly into an otherwise very illuminating discussion of Samson's "discipline of justice"; he thinks that Samson is being merely legalistic by saying that the Philistines struck first. The point of Samson's answer, though, is not just when he struck at them, but why. He attacked them, he says, not as private persons "who never did [him] . . . harm," but as political agents of the Philistine tyrants. John Broadbent thinks that Samson's claim to special status as a "person rais'd" is illogical, that it "evades by mere assertion and contradiction the complicated issues raised even by political, let alone religious, resistance movements."[19]

To understand why Samson's claim can be considered reasonable and not "mere assertion," we must return to the English revolution for a rather detailed look at an historical analogue in which the criterion for a valid political-religious resistance movement is identified, in the English case, as the genuine preservation of the public good. When King Charles prayed in *Eikon Basilike* that God would not judge him for his people's blood spilled in the civil war, Milton treated that prayer as an admission of guilt. "God *imputes* not to any man," he said, "the blood he spills in a just cause" (*Eikonoklastes, CPW* 3:533).

In defending the regicides, Milton often had to explain how the revolutionary parliament could prove the justice of its cause, how it could—when there was no official court above the king—lawfully try, condemn, and execute Charles. After arguing that Charles, by waging civil war against the English people, had forfeited his kingship and should be judged as a private person for the murder of many Englishmen and the oppression of liberty, Milton went on to develop the distinction between a public and a private person in relation to Charles's judges and executioners.

In addition to the reference to Romans 13, as evidence of God's forbidding anyone to disobey or touch a king royalists adduced the examples of Ecclesiastes, David, and Christ. "Ecclesiastes," Milton answered, "is instructing neither the Great Sanhedrin nor the Senate [equivalents of Parliament, thus public persons] but private persons. He commands observance of the king's orders, especially because of the oath of God: but who gives his oath to a king unless the king in turn swears by the laws of God and of his country?" The preacher, then, did not command obedience to a tyrant's power as a matter of principle, but merely offered a practical consideration to private citizens: "In his wisdom then Ecclesiastes here warns private citizens against contending with their king: for it is wholly ruinous to strive even with a man of wealth or power in any form" (*A Defence, CPW* 4, pt. 1:346–47). This in fact had been the policy of Christ, Milton replied to those royalists who piously invoked Christ's answer to the tax collectors as divine sanction for an absolute monarchy. Christ did not pay an unjust tax because he was acknowledging the governor's right to tax unfairly, or urging obedience to the kings of this world, but in order "to avoid causing trouble for himself as a private citizen by angering the collectors, knowing as he did that in the course of his life on earth he had a far different duty and task to perform." Christ had a public role that no mere human can imitate, because no human has the sinless private life necessary to the performance of that sacrificial duty. Christ's public task, in taking upon himself the penalty for human sin, was to reveal to human-kind the divine foundation for their liberty of conscience, which, accord-ing to Milton, requires not only private but also public expression: "Thus in I Corinthians 7, Paul makes this assertion not of religious liberty alone, but also of political: '. . . You are bought for a price; be not the slaves of men.' It is then vain for you to urge us to slavery from Christ's example, for, at the cost of his own slavery, he put our political freedom on a firm foundation" (*A Defence, CPW*, 4, pt. 1:, 374–76). Whereas Christ thought it unwise as a practical matter to risk allowing his public cause (that is, laying a religious foundation for all men's political liberty) to become vulnerable to the charge of being a private crime (a citizen not paying his taxes), David, when he spared King Saul, did so because he did not want to turn what was really a private strife into a public cause: "And if *David* refus'd to lift his hand against the Lords anointed, the matter between them was not tyranny, but privat enmity" (*TKM, CPW* 3:216).[20] When Saul did become tyrannous, the practical problems involved in David's status as "a private citizen" prevented his acting (*A Defence, CPW* 4, pt. 1:402–03). So David could be in this respect no example to the English Parliament, who took their inspiration, Milton said, rather from Ehud and "the heroic Samson," men to whom God had given both the right cause and the power to assume a public role.

When he cited these last two examples, Milton was aware of the royalist objection to them, particularly in the case of Ehud's slaying the Moabite king Eglon. Salmasius, he knew, would insist on a difference between the Israelites' defending themselves against a foreign Moabite conqueror and the English revolting against their own king. Milton's defense of the regicides' claim to be "persons rais'd" was based simply on the justice of their cause, which was determined by the universal criterion of the tyrant's tyranny, not by the relative criterion of his national origin. The Israelites' "enemy became their king," he said: "our king became our enemy." "It matters not whether Eglon was a foreigner and our man a native, since they were both enemies and tyrants. If it was right for Ehud to slay the one, it was right for us to punish the other." Then he continued with the example of Samson: "Samson therefore thought it not impious but pious to kill those masters who were tyrants over his country, even though most of her citizens did not balk at slavery" (*CPW* 4, pt. 1:401–02).

In his drama Milton gave to Harapha the royalist (and relativist) con-fusion about political resistance movements. Harapha views Samson's attack on the thirty men at Askalon as the crime of a private citizen against other private citizens, implying robbery as the motive for the attack and personal revenge as the motive for robbery. But while Samson had indeed entered into his relation with his Philistine wedding guests as a private person, and as such had proposed his bridegroom's riddle, it was not he but the Philistine "Politician Lords," whose agents the men turned out to be, who turned what had been meant as a personal contest into a public cause. They,

> Under pretense of Bridal friends and guests,
> Appointed to await me thirty spies,
> Who, threat'ning cruel death, constrain'd the bride
> To wring from me and tell to them my secret,
> That solv'd the riddle which I had propos'd.   (1196–1200)

When Samson saw that the Philistines were using the private occasion of his marriage to treat him as a political enemy, he first experienced what he was to learn to his greater sorrow with Dalila: that it had been, as a practical matter, foolish of him to expect to be able to deal as friends, in a private relationship, with some of the Philistines, while he was as a public person at war with the powers of their nation.

Although most readers interpret as a lie Samson's claim that his choosing a wife from among the Philistines had "argued [him] no foe" (1193), it is not necessary to do so. Certainly it was poor judgment for Samson to trust his Timnan wife, much less to seek private friendship with her compatriots, all the while he was planning open and, when necessary, violent opposition to their government's policy toward Israel. Undoubtedly Samson's personal pride in his role as champion aided his failure to be more careful in his private relation and caused him to regard his marriages as being for his personal enjoyment ("pleased / Me" [219–20]) as well as for his public purpose ("what I motioned was of God" [222]). The role of Samson's prideful inconsistency is magnified in his relationship to Dalila, where, "like a petty god" (529), he based his marriage on his own rationalization against divine law ("I thought it lawful from my former act, / And the same end" [231–32]) rather than on divine dispensation from the law.

Hubris, however, is not hypocrisy. Moreover, there are close parallels between Samson's relation to his enemies in this matter and Milton's in his own past political struggles. As Samson believes his marriage had "argued him no foe" and that it would have been possible to befriend individual Philistines even while seeking to end Israel's oppression, so too Milton, as a young man first entering political controversy, had in the antiprelatical tracts argued ardently—and had surely then believed, along with his Presbyterian mentors—that his advocacy of religious reform need not conflict with the genuine interest of the monarchy. This claim, through preposterous from Charles's point of view, would have been perfectly reasonable from the point of view of the ideal magistrate whom the young Milton envisioned (see *Of Reformation*, book 2). The problem for Milton was that while religious reform would have benefitted an ideal monarchy, it could not coexist with the current Erastian establishment. When the depth and complexity of the conflict became clear to him during the next eight years, he viewed the Stuart monarchy as being in irreparable conflict with its own purpose for being. Thus, even though Milton had held himself to be a royalist in 1641, he was not arguing dishonestly when he urged from 1649 on that the king himself, and not the revolution, had betrayed the English crown and nation. Charles's actions had shown that he, rather than the Puritans, was England's foe.

So too, as Samson explained to Dalila, the Philistine "Politician Lords," not Israel, had been Philistia's true foe. If the Philistines had measured up to true nationhood, permitting religious and civil liberty, Samson's revolution could have ceased; Israel would have been liberated peacefully. In truth, the Philistines had, in Samson's marriage, genuine reason to see a possibility for peace with their mighty opponent. This argument, which is outrageous from Harapha's unidealistic point of view, is as unpractical for Samson's relationship to Dalila and the Philistine rulers as was Milton's own unhappy first marriage choice for himself. Yet all the while Milton was devoting his creative energy to defending the Commonwealth cause, he was actively, if painfully, supporting his wife's royalist relatives who came to him for help.[21] And there is no reason to doubt that he means to show Samson embroiled, with similar good, if mistaken, intentions, in a similar tangle of public and private roles. Samson, besides being a husband, is the leader of Israel; in that capacity he saw that he must assert his own and his people's political freedom at Askalon. Nevertheless, the contest of the riddle became a political and violent fight for freedom only when that freedom was abused. The thirty garments were taken not as loot, but as Samson's sign to the Philistines that the treachery visited by them on his wife had been recognized as a political blow and that their tyranny would be opposed with unremitting political revolution, "force with force," "in their [political] coin."

"But I a private person," Samson anticipates Harapha's next objection, "whom my Country / As a league-breaker gave up bound, presum'd / Single Rebellion and did Hostile Acts" (1208–10). He answers that a person is not necessarily acting privately when he is the sole defender of his

cause, but only when his cause is a private one (like the young David's) or
when he has not the practical power (as Ecclesiastes warned) to defend a
public cause:

> I was no private but a person rais'd
> With strength sufficient and command from Heav'n
> To free my Country. . . .
> I was to do my part from Heav'n assign'd,
> And had perform'd it if my known offense
> Had not disabl'd me, not all your force.   (1211–19)

From this point on in the drama Samson is once again enabled, notwithstanding the sins of his life, to act in his public role.

Samson's self-justification to Harapha and his judgment of Dalila rest
upon fine distinctions between public and private action that are not mere
assertion or rationalization. That Milton intended them to be regarded as
valid is hard to deny since they correspond to arguments upon which he
had based the justification of his own Puritan movement.[22] But the poet's
intentions are not confirmed only by his political prose, and the validity of
Samson's arguments rests not only on their logic but also on their plau-
sability and efficacy in dramatic terms. Within the embracing dramatic
context rational political insights come to Samson only as a result of the
spiritual experience of deep humility, repentance, and renewed faith.
Though pride bars Dalila and Harapha from access to his inspired understanding, hope is held out for the reader who, participating in the liberating effect of Samson's acceptance of merited death, may share his higher
vision of a universe governed by wisdom and virtue.

IN *INTERPRETING* Samson Agonistes, Joseph Wittreich refers to the emer-
gence in recent literary criticism of a new, or alternative, *Samson Agonistes*
in which Milton's Samson is seen not as the regenerate Pauline man of
faith but as the tragically flawed embodiment of an Old Testament world
view—"that primitive Hebraic element which persists in Renaissance
Christianity"—which is here rejected. It is contrasted with a New Testament world view—"a new ethical system and an improved moral
consciousness"—embodied in the Christ of his *Paradise Regained*.[23] Unlike interpretations that assume an inscrutable deity and tragic human
experience, a central assumption of this reading of the drama is that
Milton's own Christian humanism led him, after the defeat of the English
revolutionary cause, to reject war or any physical violence as a viable

course of action in any cause. Samson's violent acts, therefore, are seen as wrong, and the drama contains Milton's pacifist criticism of "royalists and revolutionaries alike."[24]

From this assumption about Milton's humanism, it follows that Milton's God could not have moved Samson to pull down the pillars of the Philistine Temple; that Samson's "rousing motions" come not from God but from his own desires; and that when Milton has Samson announce his final deed by saying that he undertakes it "of [his] own accord" (1643), the poet means for us to recognize not the free and faithful exertion of a man's will in God's cause, but the proud and blind assertion of a man's will operating without divine sanction. Helen Damico suggests that had Samson at the play's end been genuinely filled with God's spirit, Milton would have had him say, "Of my God's accord."[25] Wittreich believes that in *Samson Agonistes* Milton is criticizing the antinomian claims of seventeenth-century Puritans, whom he believed, by the time he wrote the drama, to have been false prophets.[26]

That Samson's final faith is both humanist and antinomian has been the import of the foregoing sections of this chapter. In Chapter 4, we considered how, in the absence of intrinsically authoritative external laws, one can know when a decision to act is based on the direction of God's spirit dwelling in one's heart and when it is based on personal desire? In the case of Milton's Samson, revisionists generalize from the Chorus' "Oh dearly bought revenge, yet glorious!" (1660) to say that the rousing motions must be based on personal desire in Samson to exercise a pent-up brute violence in search of personal vengeance.

The seventeenth-century antinomians' answer to the trial of spirits had been that the presence of God's genuine spirit will be known by its fruits in the believer and that "if any man sin more freely because of forgiveness of sins, that man may suspect himself to be forgiven."[27] Yet antinomian liberty is not always bound to those fragments of the whole law that are expressed in the Mosaic code; its task is to seek the course of action that will embody the spirit of the whole law, which is charity. Wittreich's and Damico's insistence that Samson's "transgress[ing] moral and religious law" is a sign that his prompting does not come from God reveals that the antinomian nature of Milton's belief in Christian liberty is not understood by these readers. Damico expresses their logical problem: "it is difficult to believe that a God who has restrained his omnipotence and abides by the laws he himself has created would perversely instigate his creatures to unlawfulness (*Paradise Lost*, III, 95–128)" in marrying a non-Jew and later in going to the idolatrous temple.

However, these same readers believe that the "strong motion" which

Milton's Christ feels leading him into the wilderness in *Paradise Regained* comes from God. Why do they believe this? Not just because the protagonist's name is "Jesus" (the name "Satan" has not stopped readers from believing that character to be the hero of *Paradise Lost*), but because "in obeying his prompting, the Son of God breaks no law in entering the Wilderness."[28] Since Milton considered it very important that Christ *did*, at other times, break laws—such as healing the sick on the Sabbath—these readers could respond reasonably: but Christ broke a law only if in doing so he fulfilled the higher purposes of the whole law in charity, divine love for human beings. Christ was acting creatively to fulfill the honor of the law, the spirit of God.[29]

Samson is shown by Milton to have been a very great sinner, his personal sins being all the more grievous because of his public role, his divine calling and great gifts. On this matter both regenerationist and revisionist readings must agree. The revisionist's concern is, at its heart, with the play's catastrophe. Irene Samuel puts the issue most straightforwardly: the regenerationist readings "focus exclusively on Samson as though no one else were involved and dismiss the victims of his wholesale murderousness as 'God's enemies.' "[30] Now, if in response to his "rousing motions," Milton's protagonist, instead of pulling down the pillars of the Temple, had stood between them and preached reformation and reconciliation to the Philistines (suffering martyrlike their scorn and violence), then presumably the divine origin of Samson's rousing motions would be in less doubt. It would not be so bad that he was breaking a ceremonial law by his presence there if his behavior were in accordance with a "higher ethic" than that of the Old Testament (as ascribed by Wittreich to Jesus in *Paradise Regained*). On the other hand, if the poet had chosen to convey unambiguously that the motion was from God and that God wanted Samson to pull down the roof on the Philistines—and at the same time that Samson's sinful heart had been utterly cleansed of any desire for revenge and was filled only with self-sacrificial courage—what would the revisionist response be? That both Samson and the Philistines were shown by Milton to be victims of a cruel God? A belief that Milton must have meant to show an evolutionary ethical consciousness in his pairing of *Samson Agonistes* and *Paradise Regained* is not unlike Empson's belief that Milton must have meant to show an evolutionary deity.[31] It is based on the feeling that a God who could will the wholesale, violent destruction of the Philistines, or of any people, cannot be the God that Milton, the humanist, or Milton, the creator of *Paradise Regained*, believes in; by enlightened standards such a God is, as Empson said, wicked.

Many critics, in particular some from Christian backgrounds, know intuitively, in response to such objections, that the God who moved Samson to pull down the pillars is the Christian God—whether orthodox or not. However, it is not helpful to readers who do not share this perception to assert simply, as C. S. Lewis is reputed facetiously to have done, that Christian readers are "supposed" to share the Chorus' jubilation in the drama's final moments,[32] or, as Wendy Furman has done, that there exists a "twentieth-century antagonism between Biblical and 'humanist' values."[33]

Early in this chapter, in agreement with Arthur Barker, I explained why I do not think that Milton has given us in *Samson Agonistes* a play whose central spiritual action is bound to the dispensation of the period of the Law. For Milton, the Old Testament God is the New Testament God. All of his great poems, whether set B.C. or A.D., are about Christian liberty; there is no irony at the heart of Samson's experience. The God of *Samson Agonistes*, who wills the political destruction of Philistia and the sudden death of Philistia's leaders, is the Christian God of *Paradise Lost* and *Paradise Regained*. This is not to say, however, that the concern about the issue of the Philistines' destruction may be dismissed as unimportant.

Seventeenth-century Puritans worried deeply about the people God destroyed. The classic disputed case was the Pharaoh of the Exodus, whose heart, the Bible says, God hardened. John Goodwin filled many pages of his *Agreement and Distance of the Brethren* (1652) and his *Exposition of Nineth Romans* (1653) explaining that "hardened" cannot mean "predestined to damnation" and that, in fact, we cannot know whether even Pharaoh is damned. Rather than returning to those voluminous controversies, I shall consider three twentieth-century Christian humanist treatments of the issue. The first, by Madeline L'Engle, is a meditation on the same story:

> You sent evil angels to the Egyptians
> and killed countless babies in order that Pharaoh—
> whose heart was hardened by you (that worries me, Lord)
> might be slow to let the Hebrew children go.
> You turned back the waters of the Red Sea
> and your Chosen People went through on dry land
> and the Egyptians were drowned, men with wives and children,
> young men with mothers and fathers (your ways are not our
>   ways),
> and there was much rejoicing, and the angels laughed and sang
> and you stopped them, saying, "How can you laugh
> when my children are drowning?"[34]

Milton means for us to rejoice in Samson's repentance and redemption. At the same time he may well be asking of his readers, "How can you laugh with the Chorus while God's Philistine children are dying?"

L'Engle's solution lies in the same conception of the deity that Goodwin offered to Parliament: in God's amazing creativity in the face of sin, his astounding solution to the dilemma that all human sin poses to justice, that is, the Incarnation (see Chapter 3):

> One small enormous thing: you came to us as one of us
> and lived with us and died for us and descended into hell for us
> and burst into life for us—
> and now do you hold Pharaoh in your arms?

Pain, including the pain of dying, is not—as Nisroch is shown to believe in book 6 of *Paradise Lost*—"the worst / Of evils" (462–63). "I am forced to admit," L'Engle considers, "that my best work has been born from pain. . . . It is pain and . . . failures which keep me from pride and help me to grow."[35] Hooker quoted St. Augustine: "wee pray accordinge to the generall desire of the will of man that God would tourne [tribulations] away from us, owinge in the meane while this devotion to the Lord our God, that if he remove them not, yeat we doe not therefore imagin our selves in his sight dispised, but rather with godly sufferance of evils expect greater good at his mercifull hands. For thus is vertue in weaknes perfected" (*Laws* 201: 5.48.13). Weakness must accept suffering whose goal is virtue's perfection and sanctification. Weakness is a tool of God and must never be used either, as Samson remonstrates to Dalila, as an excuse for sin or, as Samson himself must learn, as an excuse for despair.

The archetypal Scriptural embodiment of this insight is found in the story of Abraham and Isaac, the purest instance of antinomian love. That Milton decided to make Samson the subject of his tragedy, rather than Abraham, must have been because of the very purity and steadfastness of Abraham's faith in this story. Milton's notes show that the original focus of his tragedy "Abram from Morea" was to have been not Abram's own experience, which is spiritually very powerful but contains no ambiguity, but the agonizing doubts experienced by his family and friends concerning his faith and God's justice when Abram departs with Isaac for the sacrifice. The friends, in Milton's version, were to be shown "discoursing as the world would of such an action divers ways, bewailing the fate of so noble a man faln from his reputation, either through divin justice, or *superstition*, or coveting to doe some notable act through zeal" (*CPW* 8:558). The mature Milton retained these confused questionings for his Chorus in

Samson Agonistes, but complicated the story enormously by choosing, instead of the faithful Abraham and his friends, the guilt-ridden Samson and his servile compatriots. This is the same utter artistic integrity that gave to Satan all the immensely attractive appearance of beauty that humans can experience in meeting evil. Milton does not shrink from dramatizing to the fullest the divine beauty retained and perverted by an evil being, or the evil remaining in and challenging the man of faith.

Along with "Abram from Morea," Milton considered at length a possible "Sodom Burning." The two stories go together thematically in their insistence that the reader not make those assumptions that "the world would" about, in the case of Abraham, God's mercy or, in the case of Sodom, God's justice. The notes for "Sodom Burning" (or "Cupid's funeral pile" [*CPW* 8:558]) show a faithful Lot, warned by angel visitors of the impending destruction of Sodom, trying to convey his faith in these heavenly messengers to his kinsmen; "heer" once again "is disputed of incredulity of divine judgments & such like matter" before "the Angels doe the deed with all dreadfull execution" (559). It is interesting in light of the concern shown by *Samson Agonistes'* readers for the Philistine nobility, that in this sketch for a tragedy, Milton considered having "the K[ing] and nobles of the citty . . . come forth and serve to set out the terror," not for sudden, last-minute dramatic effect, but only after the Angels, still disguised as beautiful men, and "pittying [the] beauty" of the Sodomites, "dispute [with their priests, who serve "Venus Urania or Peor"] of Love & how it differs from lust [,] seeking to win them." Then in "the last scene to ye king & nobles when the firie thunders begin aloft the Angel appears all girt with flames which he saith are the flames of *true love* & tells the K[ing], who falls down with terror, his *just suffering*" (559; emphasis added).

Milton chose finally to focus on Samson's agon, substituting the Philistines for the Sodomites, but a twentieth-century Christian humanist playwright, Christopher Fry, undertakes the stories of Abraham and Sodom in his screenplay for the film "The Bible." To tell the story of Abraham at Moriah, he invents an extra-Biblical account of the journey of Abraham and Isaac to the mountain so that he can take them through the desolation of destroyed Sodom. In this scene Abraham tells Isaac, as they make their way through charred rubble and bones, that God "overthrew these cities, and all the plain, and all the inhabitants of the cities." When Isaac asks, "All the inhabitants of the cities . . . the children also?" Abraham stumbles away, "raving." Isaac's question reflects his father's own agony. His original answer to God's command that he sacrifice Isaac had been, "Wouldst thou I do even as the Canaanites, who lay their first-born on fires before idols? Art thou truly the Lord my God?"—the God who has promised that my seed, through Isaac, child of old age, will be the innumerable keepers of the Covenant?

Abraham's agony finds its answer in Sodom, before he reaches Moriah and is given a ram for the sacrifice. Fry's Sodom scene is a version of John Preston's optimistic assurance to the Puritans at Cambridge in the face of the righteous' suffering: "There are many things that God, the great Governour of the world, must bring together" (see Chapter 3). " 'Shall not the judge of all the earth do right?' Abraham raves,'Has it not been told from the beginning, God is he that sitteth upon the circle of the earth; that stretcheth out the heavens as a curtain, and spreadeth them out as a tent wherein to dwell; that bringeth the princes to nothing. He shall blow upon them, and they shall wither.' " It is at this point that Abraham shares with Isaac "the promises" (Hebrews 11:17): "My Son. The Lord God appeared unto me, and said unto me, 'I am the Almighty God; walk before me and be thou perfect; behold, my covenant is with thee, and I will make thee exceeding fruitful.' " In these words Fry shows Abraham's completed renewal of faith. The dialogue on the mountain in Moriah can then be very brief. Abraham binds Isaac, who submits:

ISAAC: (Quietly) Is there nothing he may not ask of thee?
ABRAHAM: Nothing.

This is the illumination of antinomian Christian liberty: There is nothing he may not ask. God, who "sitteth upon the circle of the earth," made the Law to bind first of all himself. But we, unlike him, cannot see round all the corners of his providence. A lesson Abraham learns and Isaac inherits is that suffering is inevitable for God's servants and sons, as well as for the fallen princes of this world. As a screen direction for the scene in Sodom indicates, the suffering comes from sin: Isaac asks, "Were the children also wicked?" and *From a skull emerges a snake, which swiftly writhes away.*[36]

At stake is not whether one suffers or dies, but whether one suffers in faith, trusting, as Abraham does, that the seeming contradiction of a law is accounted for by the highest purpose of the whole law, God's love. Abraham, Fry shows, is prepared to kill his son, not in spite of the fact that he loves Isaac, but *because* he loves him. This is the purest antinomianism. Abraham's greatest gift to his son is not protection from fear or pain. It is not even his life. It is his faith, his relation with God, the source of all moral being. Fry's Abraham at his nadir in Sodom calls on his memory of God's covenant with him—as Milton's Samson recalls the promises of his birth. It is this covenant that he must give to Isaac, even if it turns out to require his son's death. The flames that destroyed Sodom as well as the flames that consumed the sacrificial ram on Moriah were, as Milton would have had his angel say, the "flames of true love."

One of the most striking twentieth-century discussions of this perception is in *The Cost of Discipleship* (1937), written by Dietrich Bonhoeffer while he was deepening his involvement in the German underground resistance to Naziism. Bonhoeffer treats Luke 14.26, "If any man cometh unto me, and hateth not his own father, and mother, and wife, and children, and brethren, and sisters, yes, and his own life also, he cannot be my disciple." He insists, "We must face up to the truth that the call of Christ *does* set up a barrier between man and his natural life." Bonhoeffer does not believe that Christ calls men to "a new ethical system." When we renounce the world, "it should not be as though . . . we were exchanging a lower ideal for a higher one." Rather, "it is the call of Jesus, regarded not as an ideal, but as the word of a Mediator, which effects in us this complete breach with the world"—as Abraham was given Isaac to love, Bonhoeffer tells us, "through the Mediator and for the Mediator's sake."

God calls us to love, in this way, not only our own people but also—and even more so—our enemies; and not just those who hate us as individuals or nationals but those who embody that enmity "which exists between the People of God and the world," such as the Philistines or the Nazis. "The will of God . . . is that men should defeat their enemies by loving them."[37] However, for Bonhoeffer as for Milton and Goodwin, such love did not mean enduring passively until the apocalypse.[38] Wittreich refers repeatedly to Milton's treatise *Of Civil Power in Ecclesiastical Causes*, which argues against the civil magistrates' penal authority in matters of religious belief and expression, as if it were a pacifist tract arguing against the use of violence under any circumstances.

But Milton was arguing against the use of force in matters of conscience. The destruction of the Philistine temple was not done to force the Philistines' conscience but to punish their evil (Samson's evil is being punished too) and to free the Israelites from their religious and political oppression. The Philistines in this drama are "forcers of conscience," tyrants against whom free people have an obligation to fight.

Wittreich also reads Samson's reference to "Philistian gold" as Milton's directing us to the scriptural account of Jesus in Gethsemane, where, Wittreich says, Jesus' refusal to be defended by his disciples' swords against the Roman soldiers is evidence of Milton's pacifism.[39] In *Of Civil Power*, however, Milton himself refers directly to the scene in Gethsemane in order to discuss Jesus' words *"if my kingdom were of this world, then would my servants fight, that I should not be deliverd to the Jewes*. This proves the kingdom of Christ not governd by outward force," Milton says, repeating the main point of his treatise. "And yet," he is careful to add, lest anyone think he is arguing for a political pacifism here, "disproves not that a Christian commonwealth may defend itself against outward force in the cause of religion as well as in any other; though Christ himself, coming purposely to dye for us, would not be so defended" (*CPW* 7:258). Milton's position on this matter had not changed since the 1640s, when he believed with William Walwyn that the very depth of the love we should feel for the Christ who sacrificed himself for our sin should fill us with love for others, and consequently with courage to battle the oppressors of his children.[40]

Bonhoeffer never lost his belief that "men should defeat their enemies by loving them." He found no contradiction between this faith and his activism. "We must take our full share of responsibility for history . . . because we know that it is a responsibility laid upon us by God,"[41] he wrote just before his imprisonment at the end of 1942, ten years after he had made his first public statement of opposition to Hitler's National Socialism and five years after, as a well-known international figure, he had refused asylum in the United States and England and returned to Germany at the outbreak of war to offer leadership to the German church.

Bonhoeffer's leadership took the form simultaneously of intensive moral and theological teaching and of intensive underground attempts at the overthrow of the Nazi government. After 1939 he did not believe, as Milton shows the young Christ of *Paradise Regained* imagining, that he could "make persuasion . . . teach the erring Soul" (*PR*, 1.221–24).[42] "The seat of faith [of "a true knowledge of God"] is not really the intellect but the will" (*De Doc.*, *CPW* 6:476). Thus teaching cannot cure moral blindness. "Folly," Bonhoeffer wrote in 1944, referring the German people's support of Hitler, "is never amenable to reason": "We shall never again try to reason with the fool, for it is both useless and dangerous. To deal adequately with folly it is essential to recognize it for what it is. This much is certain, it is a moral rather than an intellectual defect. . . . Once [the fool] has surrendered his will . . . there are no lengths of evil to which the fool will not go, yet all the time he is unable to see that it is evil. . . . But it is just at this point that we realize that the fool cannot be saved by education." "What he needs," Bonhoeffer concludes, as does Milton's mature Jesus, "is redemption."[43]

Redemption is the unique task of God, of the divine love that may come as flames over Sodom or as a voice on Moriah. A justified concern of revisionist readers of *Samson Agonistes*, however, is that the child of God who attempts in God's service active and even violent opposition to evil will become morally polluted by the very attempt. (Certainly the Samson

who confesses that he has walked "like a petty God" has come to understand this danger.) Confining one's actions to observance of duty under
the law and to the patient sufferance of evil, they believe, is the morally
safer—and more Christlike—course.

On July 20, 1944, members of the German resistance failed in their
attempt to assassinate Hitler. "The failure of the plot," his friend Eberhard
Bethge tells us, "was a dreadful blow for Bonhoeffer." "Today," Bonhoeffer wrote on July 21, "I can see the dangers of *The Cost of Discipleship*,
though I am prepared to stand by what I wrote."[44]

One danger of misinterpretation and misapplication lies in the area of
"Civil Courage": "The subordination of all individual desires and opinions
to the call of duty has given [to Germans] meaning and nobility to life. . . .
This readiness to follow a command from above [a governor] rather than
our own private opinion . . . was a sign of legitimate [moral] self-distrust.
But the German . . . [has sought] deliverance from his own will through
service to the community. . . . He forgot that submissiveness and self-sacrifice could be exploited for evil ends. Once that happened . . . he could
not see that in certain circumstances free and responsible action might
have to take precedence over duty and calling." Bonhoeffer's answer for
the Germans addresses our attempt to evaluate the combined spiritual
experience of Milton's Chorus and Samson: "Only now are we Germans
beginning to discover the meaning of free responsibility. It depends upon
a God who demands bold action as the free response of faith, and who
promises forgiveness and consolation to the man who becomes a sinner in
the process."[45]

"At the cost of his own slavery," Milton wrote, Christ "put our political
freedom on a firm foundation" (*A Defence, CPW* 4, pt. 1:376). Especially
during the last years of his own struggle for political freedom, Bonhoeffer
wrote on July 21, 1944, he "had come to appreciate the 'worldliness' of
Christianity as never before." He had "discovered . . . that it is only by
living completely in this world"—not by trying to be an untainted "saint"
awaiting the apocalypse—"that one learns to believe. It is in such a life that
we throw ourselves utterly into the arms of God and participate in his
sufferings in the world and watch with Christ in Gesthemane." These
words can be taken as a guide to understanding the relation between
Samson Agonistes and *Paradise Regained*. "How can success make us arro-
gant or failure lead us astray, when we participate in the sufferings of God
by living in this world?"[46] Milton's deeply repentant Samson, after "arrogance" in success and "straying" in failure, in the end realizes in himself the
pure love of God by taking action. How can he know that his rousing
motion comes from God? He can know from the depth of his own

repentance and his sense of God's return: "no man can know at all times [the spirit] to be in himself," Milton said (*Of Civil Power*, *CPW* 7:246). But there are some times when one can know.

"To do and dare—not what you would, but what is right. Never to hesitate over what is within your power, but boldly to grasp what lies before you . . . only in the deed there is freedom. . . . Out into the storm of event . . . and freedom will receive your spirit with exultation."

Samson dies of course, and the success of his cause is short-lived: Where then is his freedom? "Helpless," Bonhoeffer wrote as he foresaw accurately that his own death was imminent upon the failure of July 20, "you see the end of your deed. Yet with a sigh of relief you resign your cause to a stronger hand, and are content to do so." His meditation shows how naturally the action undertaken "of one's own accord," that is, in freedom, is simultaneously "of God's accord." "For one brief moment you enjoyed the bliss of freedom, only to give it back to God, that he might perfect it in glory."

To perfect human freedom in glory is the task of the Christ of *Paradise Regained*. In Milton's brief epic we see the process by which God's Son invests all deaths—including those of Samson and the Philistines—with the meaning that death held for Bonhoeffer, and for Milton's Samson, as the last of the "Stations" "on the road to eternal freedom."[47]

SIX

The Birth of Christian Liberty:
Paradise Regained

IN THE final prophetic books of *Paradise Lost*, the Archangel Michael, though he hides all terror (11.111), imparts to Adam and Eve an awe-inspiring knowledge "of themselves, of God" (*PR*, 4.309), knowledge that Milton held to be prerequisite for spiritual growth into liberty. To their knowledge of original liberty, of its steadfast sustenance by loyal angels and its loss by angelic and human sin, Milton has Michael add, by introducing history, the insight that only with full recognition and acceptance of guilt (*PL*, 12.285–306) is found the beginning point for spiritual growth into original liberty and beyond. If Milton's readers have been filled with faith, knowing that their own goal, like that of their first parents, involves attainment of internal paradise, these same readers are left at the epic's end, like Adam and Eve, with the world all before them to choose their way (12.646). Although they are newly enlightened, their steps are yet wandering and slow. To these readers Milton gives his companion poems *Paradise Regained* and *Samson Agonistes*. The last poems are intensely focused on the dynamics of their protagonists' interior experience. Utterly bound to this interior focus is a need for action in the world—for Milton's Christ as much as for his Samson and for those of Milton's contemporary readers who drew upon the inner light.

Though meaningful public action must have seemed next to impossible to the compatriots for whom Milton published his poems in 1671, the poet offered no ground for them or succeeding generations to believe that the loss of an external Paradise in the east of Eden can have resulted for us solely in an interior or allegorical private garden to tend. It is true that while the prelapsarian possibility that humankind could have made a genuinely sacramental kingdom out of the things of this world was once very real, it is now lost, as Michael explains to Adam (*PL*, 11.317–48), with sin. In its place Milton's angel holds out the prospect of a "Paradise within," which is the result, the reward and natural accompaniment, not of withdrawal from the world but of "Deeds" undertaken in it (*PL*, 12.582). "What dost thou in this World?" Satan demands of Christ (*PR*, 4.372) in one of his ironically intended rhetorical questions, whose answer, as the tool of Providence, crystallizes a profound revelation. While Christ is not *of* this (Satan's) world, as the Savior will tell his disciples in the days shortly to follow, he came in order to act *in* it (John 15–17), and they too must work on earth for the Kingdom—"only in the deed there is freedom."[1]

Milton shows us the protagonists of *Paradise Regained* and *Samson Agonistes* at their moments of greatest ambiguity. For Christ, as for Samson, the question is: Now, in fallen and mutable time, in the flux of events, in the midst of history, what am I to do? What now, in this particular configuration of circumstances, is my mission? A paramount issue for the reader of both poems is: How can anyone find out, in any moment of time, what particular form one's mission should take? Given faith, how does one learn to undertake works?

In Milton's experience and observation, cultivation of the inner light had been closely tied to a commitment to social and political activism. At the same time, as we saw in the separation scene, people who choose the full liberty of the Spirit have no casuistry of precedents and formulae to apply to decisions for action. Although laws and precedents are part of their equipment, their guide is the very much more dynamic "Providence" (*PL*, 12.647). This Providence, who gives to humans both texts and the course of events to read and the spirit necessary to understand them, is often unpredictable. His unpredictability never means, however, as we have seen, that his ways are not rationally accessible. In Milton's radical Christian humanist view, providences exist, for rational beings, not to be experienced blindly, but to be read.

Reading is a philosophical preoccupation of the late twentieth century; its recent sophistication has refocused some scholars' most pressing questions about *Paradise Regained*. Whereas earlier readers were distressed over the denial by Milton's Christ of the classical learning that had nurtured the poet himself,[2] post-modern readers want to identify in the poem a Miltonic "deconstruction" of texts, or of the very idea of a text. To his assertion that a reader must bring to any book a "spirit and judgment equal or superior" to that offered by its author, Christ adds a parenthetical question "(And what he brings, what needs he elsewhere seek)" (*PR*, 4.325). This question has become a crux for critical arguments that the internalism of Milton's Christ removes any moral or spiritual necessity for reading at all. The reader's "inner authority," William Cain suggests, "is not required to exercise itself [even] on texts like *Paradise Regained*." "The fit [that is, redeemed] audience," argues William Kerrigan from another angle, because they are illuminated by the inner light, "will require no education within the work itself."[3]

Reading is the context of Raphael's admonition to Adam, "be lowly wise" (*PL*, 8.173), an admonition reinforced by Michael as "the sum / Of wisdom" (12.575–76). "Lowly" means "in this world"; it means that we have a ready check by which we can ascertain whether the hermeneutic self is on a valuable track or not. We are to ask at all times, "Toward what actions in the world, toward what deeds, are my questionings directed? In what way do I intend them to build a holy society?" Since Milton's humanistic antinomianism does not hold out a possibility of either non-engagement or irrational engagement, it follows that, while no particular text or experience is a priori necessary to moral growth, everyone's "inner authority" does need texts and events on which to exercise itself. Such exercise maintains the paradise within, through individually chosen deeds answerable to divinely given faith and understanding.

"I mean / To exercise him in the Wilderness," God tells the angels (*PR*, 1.155–56). One does not come to texts or events to *seek* the spirit, but to *exercise* the spirit, to focus it on the tasks of this world. The paradise within—a perfect spiritual commitment—which Adam and Eve leave the mount in Eden to regain and toward which Samson stumbles faithfully, Christ knows himself to possess. When Milton's readers understand with his Christ that they are not at all of this world, then once again, as in Eden and as with the regenerate Samson, everything in the world is at the same time fully dispensable and fully available for their use. The deeds answerable to a complete spiritual steadfastness manifest responses of antinomian creativity to the providences of an always dynamic world.[4]

Milton made his commitment in the world of his day to the English revolutionary cause. In this he resembled his Samson. Whereas Samson, like Jephtha, pursues his cause by arguments and feats of strength, Christ's challenge is almost wholly (right) rational and verbal, like Milton's own. The Restoration brought him the deepest political disappointment. Nevertheless, at the same time the poet must have seen in this providence a benefit for his own mission, for it enabled him to refocus the truths he had been defending—in the debates about the Commonwealth, toleration, tithing—into their true proportions, and to hand over their defense (with his "right hand") to Christ himself.

The format of the debate, with which Milton had become so familiar, survives into *Paradise Regained*. Though debate had been the form of a great deal of Milton's prose writings from the ecclesiastical apologies through *Eikonoklastes* and the *Defences*, their composition had been a trial for him, as the tracts written in debate form are for today's readers, who prefer the more tightly organized *Areopagitica* and *Tenure of Kings and Magistrates*. Milton considered his *Defence* against Salmasius his greatest contribution, but he was not hesitant to acknowledge the tedium and waste involved in following someone else's argument, as when he allowed himself this aside to Salmasius: "This is all I could find worth answering in nine pages which were surely long enough in all conscience; the rest was either the same old oft-refuted stuff dragged out again, or had no bearing on the issues of this case. If then I answer with unusual brevity, the cause is no lack of diligence on my part, for despite my disgust, I do not let myself grow slack, but rather your continual foolish prating so completely devoid of sense or substance!" (*A Defence, CPW* 4, pt. 1:519).

The *Defence* (1651) exhibits a patience learned by Milton since his first entries into public controversy. In *Of Reformation* (1641) he had given vent to his impatience at worldly objections to reform, wanting to answer them not with political practicality but with spiritual truth. To the charge that the proposed reform could not stand with common law, which had episcopal government woven into it, he had exclaimed: "In Gods name let it weave out againe. . . . Tis not the common Law, nor the civil, but piety, and justice, that are our foundresses; they . . . farre above the taking notice of these inferior niceties with perfect sympathy, where ever they meet, kisse each other" (*CPW* 1:605–06).

Yet Milton always believed, despite their frustrating inconvenience, in the value of these controversies. With Walwyn and other radical humanists, he shared the view that truth is best approached not by sermons or speeches, "which are apt to deceive" a passive or anxious hearer, "but by conferences, and mutual debates, one with another, (the best way for attaining a right understanding)."[5] He waged his last pamphlet battle in 1673, the year before his death, to argue as he had in *Areopagitica* (1644) for the right of debates to exist: "There is no Learned man but will confess he hath much profited by reading Controversies, his Senses awakt, his Judgement sharpn'd, and the truth which he holds more firmly establish't. If then it be profitable for him to read; why should it not at least be tolerable and free for his Adversary to write? In *Logic* they teach, that contraries laid together more evidently appear: it follows then that all controversies being permitted, falshood will appear more false, and truth the more true: which must needs conduce much, not only to the confounding of Popery, but to the general confirmation of unimplicit truth" (*Of True Religion* [1673], *CPW* 8:437–38).

When, on the eve of the Restoration, the advocates of censorship had pointed out that in Revelation 2.20 the church of Thyatira is blamed for allowing the "false *prophetes to teach and to seduce,*" Milton had answered: "that seducement is to be hindered . . . by instant and powerful demonstration to the contrarie; by opposing truth to error, no unequal match; truth the strong to error the weak though slie and shifting. Force is no honest confutation; but uneffectual" (*Of Civil Power* [1659], *CPW* 7:263). To the end of his life, he held that faith, which he had shared with Saltmarsh while the first Charles was still king, that error cannot be combatted with the magistrate's sword: "And what if the *Prince of Persia* withstand for a while? *Truth* is otherwise armed from heaven: Though *Satan* be in the wilderness with *Christ,* yet Christ shall conquer. . . . The Gospel dares walk abroad with boldness and simplicity."[6]

Milton had learned discouraging practical truths since 1642, when he had believed the perception and championing of truth possible for all people. By 1671 tyranny was reinstalled, and the claims he had earlier made with confidence about all Christians—such as that schisms are sent to test the faithful, "For if there were no opposition where were the triall of an unfained goodnesse and magnanimity?" and "vertue that wavers is not vertue" (*Reason of Church Government, CPW* 1:795)—he held to be absolutely true only of Christ. But his belief in Christian liberty, and in the Christian's need to build a holy society, had not changed even though "the *Prince of Persia* withstand for a while."

In defeat one needs more than ever to hold to and confirm "unimplicit truth." Surely the impetus for the form of *Paradise Regained* grows out of this experience. If every learned man[7] has "much profited by reading Controversies" and if, "controversies being permitted, falshood will appear more false and truth the more true," then the most valuable debate that we could witness—even as we seek another avenue for our action— would take place between Christ, the incarnation of truth, and the devil, truth's most talented opponent.

The value to the witness of a "controversy"—in contrast with the value to the reader of a doctrinal statement such as the Westminster Confession—lies in the fact that the reasoning involved does not take place in the abstract but in a concrete situation and is thus an exemplum, where the reasoner's "sense of rational structure" is "acquired by example rather than by rule."[8] This most fundamental exercise of human *recta ratio* Milton gives to the human Christ and his readers. "This man," the Father explains to Gabriel at the beginning of book 1,

> ... henceforth I expose
> To Satan; let him tempt and now assay
> His utmost subtlety. . . .   (1.142–44)

Throughout the poem we see Satan's "seducements" met by "instant and powerfull demonstration to the contrarie":

> ... Israel's true King ... to the Fiend
> Made answer meet, that made void all his wiles.
> So fares it when with truth falsehood contends   (3.441–43)

—"truth the strong [with] error the weak though slie and shifting."

UNDERLYING the overt issues of that ultimate controversy—Christ's physical need, his kingship, or his supernatural powers—Milton develops a question of basic concern to both Satan and Christ: the meaning of Christ's sonship. The terms of the question were set by the Father at Christ's baptism when he "pronounc'd him his beloved Son" (1.32). To "all the Angels and Ethereal Powers, / They now, and men hereafter" God explains what he is providing to the witnesses of this encounter, who

> ... may discern
> From what consummate virtue I have chose
> This perfect Man, by merit call'd my Son,
> To earn Salvation for the Sons of men.   (1.163–67)

The concept of the sonship of every Christian is fundamental in all Milton's discussions of Christian liberty. Following Biblical precedent, the loyal angels are termed "Sons" by Milton in *Paradise Lost* (11.80, 84). Hooker explains the Biblical sense: It is their imitation of God's goodness, their free and rational morality, that "is intimated wheresoever we finde them termed the sonnes of God" (*Laws* 71; 1.4.1.j). Since the fall of Adam, it is through their deliverance by the Son of God—through "Christ our Liberator"—that believers find their own original sonship renewed in adoption and are once again free to be what they were created to be: "that being made sons instead of servants ... we may serve God in love through the guidance of the Spirit of truth" (*De Doc., CPW* 6:537; cf. Hooker, *Laws* 244; 5.56.12, on Christians as "Sonnes of God"). Milton's source was St. Paul: "you have not received the spirit of slavery again in fear; but you have received the spirit of adoption, through which we cry Abba, Father" (Rom. 5:15); "you are not a slave anymore, but a son" (Gal. 4:7).

As the familial term implies, such adoption alters not only the believer's status vis-à-vis God but also the believer's relationship with God. Saltmarsh explained it thus: "In our first man [fallen] *Adam* we had to do with . . . [God] onely in a way of *subjection* and *righteousnesse*; But now in our second *Adam*, in a way of *sonship* or adoption, and *free-grace*." In terms that Satan can never understand, Saltmarsh explains the relation between grace and glory: "And thus the soul is to look on him, and consider him in *grace*, not in *glory*."[9] Sonship is what transmits God's glory to fallen men and women as his grace. Sonship also yields an enlarged capacity for moral commitment: "It is not a less perfect life that is required from Christians, but, in fact, a more perfect life than was required of those who were under the law" (*De Doc., CPW* 6:535).

Within the vast compass of *Paradise Lost* Milton treats Christian liberty as it appears in all the phases of human society that he treated in his prose: worship, marriage, government, and the kingdom within. As in his prose writings he was forced finally to surrender the outlying areas in which the liberty of Sons of grace ought to be exercised and to retreat to a defense, in the pamphlets on conscience, of the Christian identity itself, so, after the wide-ranging freedom of *Paradise Lost*, Milton turned in his last poems to the source of the Christian's liberty. Like St. Paul, he viewed Samson (along with Noah and the sons of Seth [*PL*, 11.808, 622]) as a prototype for the liberty given Christians by their adoption as sons of God; in *Samson Agonistes* he portrays the mind of this hero in the process of its growth out of bondage. In *Paradise Regained* Milton takes as his subject the very Son of God to show his Christian readers the birth of their liberty in the mind of its creator.[10] The theme functions for Milton both dramatically, by providing the basis for a struggle in the mind of the protagonist, and emblematically, in the implications of that struggle for the drama of everyman who comes after him. We see God, physically bound to natural law and to human history, in the person of his Son encountering Satan, bent on the ultimate evil and sent by God's providence to serve as the Son's stimulus to reason toward his enactment of humanity's salvation.

Christ's antagonist in the brief epic understands no more of the nature of liberty now than he did when, in *Paradise Lost*, we saw him rebel against the source of his own powers. Satan has, during the ages of his rule over Hell, hardened in a slavery to his own destructive purposes that has reduced his originally willed refusal to recognize spiritual truth to a habitual, involuntary literalism. Thus, as his account of the baptism reveals, he can understand nothing of God's symbolism, of Christ's sonship:

> And out of Heav'n the Sovran voice I heard,
> This is my Son belov'd, in him am pleas'd.
> His Mother then is mortal, but his Sire,
> Hee who obtains the Monarchy of Heav'n,
> And what will he not do to advance his Son?   (1.84–88)

Still the believer in "divine right" rule as monarchy obtained by sheer strength, he thinks he understands the threat posed by Christ's "elevation." Satan translates the Baptist's spiritual claim to fit the people "Purified to receive him pure" into practical political terms that refer to outward signs of glory, "rather, / To do him honor as their King" (1.74–75). And he cannot account for the symbol of the grace he denies, the dove, "whate'er it meant" (1.83).

In the course of the temptation Christ gives Satan a full demonstration of what his sonship means: in his free obedience to the law of right reason, he is what humans and angels were created to be, the image of the Father. Satan can, however, no more here than in Heaven, know the spiritual truth which only acknowledgment of his own guilt and repentance would make possible. In book 4, just before he begins the temptation to "wisdom," he reveals his hopeless inability to learn, saying, "Sons of God both Angels are and Men" (4.197).

Satan, like Adam, had been a Son of God; but both fell long ago from sonship into bondage. Fallen human and angel were still servants of God's law, either willingly as Adam and later the Jewish people under the covenant, or unwillingly as Satan is at this moment and has been throughout human history (1.410). Some individual persons in history, like Samson, have attained the spirit of adoption. But the only beings who at the moment are Sons of God, and not merely bondservants, are the unfallen angels and Christ.

That Milton thought of the historical Jesus as conscious of still living under the Law is clear from his analyses of Jesus' conduct in affairs of church and state. In *The Likeliest Means* he answered the proponents of the state-supported church who argued that Jesus told the Pharisees they ought to have paid tithes (Matt. 23.23): "our Saviour spake then to those who observ'd the law of *Moses*, which was not yet fully abrogated, till the destruction of the temple" (*CPW* 7:290). The young Christ of *Paradise Regained*, like the singer of the first Psalm, delights in the law of the Lord:

> . . . myself I thought
> Born . . . to promote all truth,
> All righteous things: therefore above my years,

> The Law of God I read, and found it sweet,
> Made it my whole delight, and in it grew. (1.204–08)

Satan's awareness that Christ's relation to the Law bears upon the meaning of his coming is emphasized by his parody of that delight:

> Hard are the ways of truth, and rough to walk,
> Smooth on the tongue discourst, pleasing to th' ear,
> And tunable as Silvan Pipe or Song;
> What wonder then if I delight to hear
> Her dictates from thy mouth? (1.478–82)

Christ's struggle, not only with Satan's attempts at confusion, but with the inadequacy and yet necessity of the law, must be the reader's dilemma as well. For through Christ, Christians, when they become adopted sons, co-heirs, become also "kings and priests with him" (*Likeliest Means, CPW* 7:288); as they share Christ's offices, they must see how he came to understand them himself. This understanding has been Milton's goal in making his epic "to tell of deeds, / Above Heroic . . . unrecorded left through many an Age" (1.14–16). The simple facts of Christ's temptation in the wilderness have not been "unrecorded"—that Christ obeyed, was perfect man, and was therefore demonstrated to be the redeemer—Milton summarizes the scriptural record in lines 1–7 and 17–32 of book 1. What has "remain'd so long unsung" is *how* Christ performed these deeds of obedience. Because the duty of Christians is not only to hold the faith that at the final judgment Christ will redeem them but also to serve him now in active obedience, Milton wants his readers' rational imaginations to apprehend that Christ's own human obedience was creative, not passive only—and that his obedience is both the source and model for the reader's own spiritual liberation and public action.

MILTON shows Christ's state of mind and spirit at the beginning of his encounter with Satan. It is highly active and intensely receptive as he sorts through the "multitude of thoughts" that "swarm" in him from his reading of Scripture as well as of God's specific providences in his own miraculous birth and now, most recently, in the Baptism and God's own voice, by which he knows that he is to begin his ministry. Christ fully accepts that he is the prophesied Messiah and that his way will require suffering to transfer sin's weight to himself. But he has yet to learn how to make himself into the bearer of this burden. He must not simply wait to die on the Cross; he must sort out his thoughts and experiences to begin the ministry that will invest the Cross with its meaning.

Satan's first temptation is to distrust God's providence. Barbara Lewalski points out that the temptation to turn stones to bread "alludes to the issue of ministerial tithes and clergy support which will continue to plague the Church throughout its history."[11] That issue, as Milton described it in *The Likeliest Means*, was essentially a challenge to a Christian minister's trust in God's providence. Milton had urged that ministers should live off the voluntary offerings of the people they teach. When challenged "This would be well anough . . . but how many will so give?" he answered: "as many, doubtles, as shall be well taught; as many as God shall so move. *Why are ye so distrustful*, both of your own doctrin and of Gods promises" (*CPW* 7:314; emphasis added). In *Paradise Regained* Milton's purpose is not primarily to refer the reader back to the issue of the tithe, but to subsume the greed and spiritual insecurity of state-supported clergy into its place with all forms of distrust in the ultimate order of things as we watch the Son trust God in the face of the devil.

In this first encounter Christ's belief that "what concerns my knowledge God reveals" (1.293) enables him to perceive the relevance of Scripture to his present situation. He perceives, as soon as Satan begins to speak falsely, the hypocrisy of the "aged man in Rural Weeds," who tries by appealing to a lesser law of nature to debase a prophet's sojourn in the wilderness. "No Man or Angel can know how God would be worship and serv'd unless God reveal it," Milton argued in defense of each Christian's right to understand the Scriptural revelation of God's will. And one must trust in the adequacy of that revelation to answer all questions experience will raise: "According to that of St. *Paul, Though wee or an Angel from Heaven preach any other Gospel unto you . . . let him be Anathema*" (*Of True Religion, CPW* 8:419). Christ begins by applying against Satan's carnal suggestion the highest related spiritual truth from Scripture: "is it not written / . . . / Man lives not by Bread only, but each Word / Proceeding from the mouth of God, who fed / Our Fathers here with Manna?" (1.347–51).

In the discussion of Satan's own relation to truth which forms the aftermath of the stones-to-bread temptation, Christ accepts the challenge of analyzing the events raised by Satan for discussion. He will sort and label guilt so as to keep straight the true and universal meaning of those moral qualities claimed here by Satan to have underlain his own deeds. Christ understands that the basis of Satan's historical success in tempting fallen human beings is the same that enabled the angel himself to fall and remain committed to his own damnation:

> For lying is thy sustenance, thy food.
> Yet thou pretend'st to truth . . .
> . . . . That hath been thy craft,
> By mixing somewhat true to vent more lies.   (1.428–32)

Throughout the temptations to follow, Satan will continue trying thus to corrupt the meaning of the literal laws of Scripture and of nature. Christ will answer by penetrating to their spiritual truth.

At this point the first act of the ministry Christ is in the process of discovering occurs. It is his ministry to the Gentiles: "henceforth Oracles are ceased" (1.456). Now he intends to put right reasoning ability, "an inward Oracle," based on faith in God's truth, into all "pious Hearts" (1.463). He knows that he is the sinless Messiah, destined to "work Redemption for mankind, whose sins' / Full weight must be transferr'd upon my head" (1.266–67)—that he will be the means by which God's justice can encompass mercy and still maintain his truth. In this knowledge is the understood precondition that makes possible his swift, impeccable untangling of Satan's arguments. When this truth becomes known to human beings as the gospel, it will free them from the chains of fallen reason in which their sins hold them, giving them Christian liberty. "Truth liberates," Milton said in the *De Doctrina*, and he quoted John, "you will know the truth, and the truth will make you free" (*CPW* 6:536).

Satan's first attempt, on his return, is to induce Christ to break some part of the Jewish ceremonial law. Christ's reference to other prophets that have gone without food in the wilderness suggests to Satan that he should try to make Christ confuse the manna from heaven and food the ravens brought with any food miraculously produced and so eat at the devil's table, in effect eating food "offer'd first to Idols." Lewalski quotes Calvin on this point: "Now to be present at a feast which was celebrated in honour of false gods, was a kind of indirect renunciation of the true God." This is what Samson had feared doing: "Our Law forbids at thir Religious Rites / My presence" (*SA*, 1320–21).

Christ is neither deceived by the gift from the Idol nor tempted to give in to the hunger to which we have just heard him reconcile himself. His refusal, however, must be not only an act of will, but of reason. Since Satan comes back to tempt him with "Permission from above" (1.495), Christ sees that it must be the plan of Providence through the temptations to reveal knowledge to him. Thus Christ's rational challenge is to refuse Satan's offer in such a way as to answer all possible ways in which the offer is wrong and to learn from it what his mission really is. Christ avoids refusing the gift on the lesser basis of the unclean meats and avoids idolatry of spirit by simply rejecting the giver himself.[12] But Satan has managed to weave more than the ceremonial law into the terms of his offer. He has appealed to the law of nature and Christ's peculiar relation to physical nature as a Son of the Creator and a prophesied king:

> Hast thou not right to all Created things,
> Owe not all Creatures by just right to thee
> Duty and Service, nor to stay till bid,
> But tender all thir power?   (2.324–27)

Of course Satan, not Nature, has tendered this banquet; but Christ must see what he can learn from the argument abstracted from Satan's personal error. He is, as an unfallen human being, in the position of Adam and Eve in Eden, a governor of the rest of nature. His answer encompasses the moral question of rulership as well as questions of ritual law: he will govern "temperately" according to just reason. He will not abuse his power as king of creation to make creatures perform to no purpose. "Said'st thou not that to all things I had right?" he begins his answer, suggesting Satan's meaning of the term "right" as "the ability to compel." His next question returns the term "right" to its moral sense by distinguishing power from will: "And who withholds my pow'r that right to use?" (2.379–80). We may understand his answer to this question about the ruler's will to be: "I myself withhold my power from commanding nature needlessly to disrupt its normal laws." The issue thus settled has not been between Christ and nature, but how Christ's relation to nature compares to Satan's.

As this answer reveals to Satan the intensity of Christ's interest not in pleasure or comfort but in his own ruling power, the tempter moves on to what concerns Christ more intimately than the physical conditions which had seemed most immediate. Satan begins the "manlier" temptations "such as have more show / Of worth, of honor, glory, and popular praise; / Rocks whereon greatest men have oftest wreck'd" (2.225–28), those that came first into his mind in the Council and are much nearer his own spirit. When he begins in the long political temptation of the kingdoms to offer what he himself truly values, his temptations become more skillful—and more self-revealing. He gets off to a weak start by offering riches; it is an action parallel to his building his palace in the North of Heaven to gain the external properties of glory.

Christ's patient reply (2.432) shows him testing for himself the several hypotheses Satan's suggestion implies. Here we first meet a rhetorical formulation we shall hear again (2.457; 3.188; 4.128): "What if . . ." Al-though Christ's answer contains philosophical reflection—"Riches are needless"; "he who reigns within himself . . . is more a king"—the thrust of his thinking is, in a personal hypothesis, constructed in interaction with the stimulus that Satan, as the tool of Providence, has offered: *What if* I reject both wealth and a realm? *If* I do, my reason must not be the fact that a kingdom is burdensome to the king. The most important spiritual truth about a crown's weight is that a true king is the bearer of his people's burdens. But if bearing the burdens of others is more important than exercising control over others, then what is the spiritual truth about ruling, about wielding power? Surely, at base, it involves kingship over the very "Passions, Desires, and Fears" out of which human actions spring—a task that begins with the individual self, and which "every wise and virtuous man attains." But not all men are kings over themselves, nor can the nations be full of self-ruled people until the ultimate divine source of such self-rule is known—"But to guide Nations in the way of truth . . . is yet more Kingly" (2.473–76).

Christ has gained some insight into his kingly mission through these reflections. Satan does not perceive the growth in Christ's awareness; but he is readily "convinc't / Of his [own] weak arguing and fallacious drift" (3.3–4). He remembers well the sense in which a Crown, "Golden in show, is but a wreath of thorns." He too has believed that a leader must not seek ease for himself. He has claimed as his own "Honor, Virtue, Merit, and chief Praise / That for the Public all this weight he bears" (2.463–64). As, ages ago, he had chosen the rule of Hell rather than the treasures of Heaven, so now again he recognizes that what really attracted him is the feeling of glory that power brings, and this is what he offers next:

> . . . glory the reward
> That sole excites to high attempts the flame
> Of most erected Spirits, most temper'd pure
> Ethereal, who all pleasures else despise,
> All treasures and all gain esteem as dross,
> And dignities and powers, all but the highest?   (3.25–30)

For the archrebel, glory, not grace, is the highest treasure, gain, dignity, and power. Satan is exposing to Christ the motives and beliefs that un-derlay his own rebellion and dictatorship. When his simple naming of them is rejected, he is compelled to reveal their theological roots.

Milton believed himself to have witnessed this confessional process in Charles's *Eikon Basilike*, where he saw exposed "more of Mysterie and combination between Tyranny and fals Religion, then from any other hand would have bin credible. Heer we may see the very dark roots of them both turn'd up, and how they twine and interweave one another in the Earth, though above ground shooting up in two sever'd Branches" (*Eikonoklastes, CPW* 3.509). In *Paradise Regained* Satan, by exposing his understanding of the Father's glory, reveals the roots of "th' abominable terms" he will set at the end of his offer of the kingdoms. The passage from *Eikonoklastes* continues to observe that "the Kings of this World have both ever hated, and instinctively fear'd the Church of God," true religion, because it teaches liberty and its members are the "Children of that King-dom, which as ancient Prophesies have foretold, shall in the end break to peeces and dissolve all thir great power and Dominion." Satan is *the* King of this World and fears what he supposes will be the earthly kingship of God's Son. "Ere in the head of Nations he appear / Their King, their Leader, and Supreme on Earth" (1.98–99), Satan wants Christ, in claiming his empire, to do so in the very pattern by which his tempter fell, by assuming the divine right of kings, which Milton called "fals Religion."

"Why move thy feet so slow to what is best," Satan will urge, "That thou who worthiest art shouldst be thir King?" (3.224–26). In Heaven, Lucifer had felt himself "worthiest" to rule. Now he wants Christ to assert his worth by a similar belief in his extraordinary powers:

> . . . wert thou sought to deeds
> That might require th' array of war, thy skill
> Of conduct would be such, that all the world
> Could not sustain thy Prowess, or subsist
> In battle, though against thy few in arms.   (3.16–20)

If you think you are worthiest, take power and glory. This was and is Satan's view of how God rules. He refuses to understand why such an assertion of power by one angel over others was wrong, but he knows that a similar challenge to God's rule over humans would, as his was, be considered rebellion and be crushed.

Christ interprets Satan's suggestion as taking its model from earthly rulers who have claimed divine right in the crudest sense, who, seeking glory, destroy their fellow human beings and "then swell with pride, and must be titl'd Gods" (3.81). Like Satan, earthly tyrants claim to be "Great Benefactors . . . Deliverers" and are worshiped until they are in turn met by "Conqueror Death" who reveals them scarce men, "Rolling" like Sin's allegorical lower half "in brutish vices, and deform'd" (3.82–86).

With this answer Satan, "murmuring," must offer his own justification;

he and all his earthly imitators seek glory by a supposed analogy with the rule of God himself:

> Think not so slight of glory: therein least
> Resembling thy great Father; he seeks glory,
> And for his glory all things made, all things
> Orders and governs . . . (3.109–12)

To this Christ answers that no such analogy is possible between human and divine rule. The very reason that God deserves and receives glory is the same reason that humans ought to seek glory not for themselves, but *for* God. To draw political correspondences between links in the chain of Being and their source is to vitiate the true chain. God is glorious because He is perfect goodness; humans, if they are good, seek God's glory. This service to God is what comprises human goodness. Thus, when Charles I had tried to claim for himself the title of martyr, Milton had denied him that right: "Martyrs bear witness to the truth, not to themselves. If I beare witness of my self, saith *Christ*, my witness is not true" (*Eikonoklastes*, *CPW* 3:575). "I seek not mine," says the Christ of *Paradise Regained*, "but his / Who sent me, and thereby witness whence I am" (3.106–07).

Once the issue of divine right is raised, Christ is given the terms he needs to work out the basis for his own kingship, which will be not a false analogy but a true imitation of the Father's. Glory is not right, or to be sought by human beings, because God receives it; rather, God receives glory because it is right for him as Creator and sustainer of the universe to do so. The act of Creation is the source of God's authority and hence of his glory, "And reason since his word all things produc'd" (3.122). As a human ruler over fellow creatures, Christ reasons, he could never merit the authority that is in the Creator by virtue of his power to create, or the attendant glory that is His because in his creation he works "to show forth his goodness." "But why should man seek glory? who of his own / Hath nothing" (3.134–35). Such a false imitation of the Father's rule cannot be the motive for Christ's own prophesied kingship. Once again Satan recognizes truth in Christ's words about higher standards of glory and the inviability of divine right. This part of the definition of a governor, however, he must hear not with pride, but shame, "struck / With guilt of his own sin, for he himself / Insatiable of glory had lost all" (146–48).

There is at this point in the discussion of kingship an irony known only to the reader: that Christ is the only king who does rule by divine right. He is the only man for whom an analogy between heavenly and earthly rule holds true. "As to your saying it [monarchy] was 'patterned on the example of the one God,' " Milton had demanded of Salmasius, "who, in fact, is worthy of holding on earth power like that of God but some person who far surpasses all others and even resembles God in goodness and wisdom? The only such person, as I believe, is the son of God whose coming we look for" (*A Defense, CPW*, 4, pt. 1:427–28). Yet there is no paradox involved here. Christ is like God in his essence and for that very reason will not imitate external traits which are not fitting to the context in which he is to govern on earth. Even though Christ in his divine nature, unlike other human governors, is the actual Creator of his subjects, his goodness, like the Father's, limits and directs the exercise of his power. It is the role of an earthly governor to rule a people according to laws, according to "reason abstracted as much as might be from [the] personal errors" which result from humans' first loss of the natural liberty that was theirs with unfallen reason. Christ is soon to imitate the Father's rule in its essence by restoring human nature to that harmony with the law of its being that enables liberty.

The full discovery of this mission, however, is yet to come to Christ in the wilderness. In his reply to the temptation of glory, he has laid down the fundamental motive, though not yet the means, for his kingship: humans "Who for so many benefits receiv'd / Turn'd recreant to God" (3.136–37) may still—"so much bounty is in God"—be advanced by grace to true glory if they will "advance his glory, not thir own" (3.142–44). To enable fallen human beings to "advance his glory" will be the motivation for Christ's rule.

In light of this motive, we must return to the beginning of the temptation of glory, to those words of Christ about political man, "the people," that have caused a problem of interpretation for many readers. Christ is refusing Satan's offer of Empire for glory's sake:

> For what is glory but the blaze of fame,
> The people's praise, if always praise unmixt?
> And what the people but a herd confus'd,
> A miscellaneous rabble, who extol
> Things vulgar, and well-weigh'd, scarce worth the praise?
> They praise and they admire they know not what;
> And know not whom, but as one leads the other;
> And what delight to be by such extoll'd,
> To live upon thir tongues and be thir talk,
> Of whom to be disprais'd were no small praise?
> His lot who dares be singularly good.   (3.47–57)

Christ's several references to "the people" in *Paradise Regained* are too often referred to as if they all said the same thing, when in fact they do not and must be read in context. This statement is the most frequently quoted. S. B. Liljegren, who suspects that Christ is an incarnation of Milton's own ambitious drives, suggests that the hero of *Paradise Regained* "does not want to save mankind out of love. He simply wants to achieve a splendid career and the means to do so is the feat of saving a few valuable souls, but mankind at large, the 'miscellaneous rabble,' he despises." Liljegren expresses the problem felt by a number of readers of these lines, "It is difficult to imagine the Christ who is speaking thus as willing to die for publicans, shoemakers, and tailors."[13] Christ's reference to "the people" here is not based on social class. If it were, it would jar surprisingly not only with the gospels, but with Milton's stress in *Paradise Regained* on the fact that the apostles were "Plain Fishermen, (no greater men them call)" (2.27). It is even more important for us to understand the context of Christ's reference. Satan has not asked Christ to die for the people or to do anything in their behalf, but rather to manipulate and then use their opinion as a standard by which to fashion and measure his kingdom. In the tone of Christ's answer to this suggestion we do hear the voice of Milton's more vitriolic prose. Satan is urging Christ to be the same kind of publicity agent for himself that Charles I was in *Eikon Basilike* when he used prayers as an oratorical device to win the people's sympathy and favor. Such a ruse, Milton asserts, in *Eikonoklastes* would not be able "to stirr the constancie and solid firmness of any wise Man, or to unsettle the conscience of any knowing Christian ... but to catch the worthless approbation of an inconstant, irrational, and Image-doting rabble; that like a credulous and hapless herd, begott'n to servility, and inchanted with these popular institutes of Tyranny, subscrib'd with a new device of the Kings Picture at his praiers, hold out both thir eares with such delight and ravishment to be stigmatiz'd and board through in witness of thir own voluntary and beloved baseness." It is demogoguery that Satan is urging and Christ is rejecting. In the same passage, which closes *Eikonoklastes*, Milton continues his reference to the people to hold out hope for those who, while mistaken in their admiration, may yet be saved from slavery: "The rest, whom perhaps ignorance without malice, or some error, less then fatal, hath for the time misledd ... may find the grace and good guidance to bethink themselves, and recover" (*CPW* 3:601). To be the vehicle for "grace and good guidance," not to be an Idol of the people, will be the purpose of Christ's rule. In Milton's own experience the "Image-doting rabble" had turned out to be the majority; but that Charles II was able to regain their

favor did not prove the merit of that king. Milton's human Christ in
Paradise Regained is still the Christ of *Paradise Lost*, whose motive for
accepting God's vicegerency over angels and humans is true glory:

> . . . this I my Glory account,
> My exaltation, and my whole delight,
> That thou in me well pleas'd, declar'st thy will
> Fulfill'd, which to fulfil is all my bliss.   (*PL*, 6.726–29)

Though he cannot persuade Christ "to seek wealth / For Empire's sake
nor Empire to affect / For glory's sake," Satan keeps in mind the prophesied kingdom and formulates his next offers on a pattern he perceives in
Christ's own thoughts on kingship, revealed in answer to the temptation
of wealth (*PR*, 2.439–79). Christ had seen models of good leadership in
the Hebrew Judges Gideon and Jephtha, and in King David; in the
Roman worthies; and in the idea of governing the inner man by saving
Doctrine. So Satan offers next the Parthian army as a means to the Throne
of David, then Rome, and then the learning of the ancient Gentile World.
By doing his best to induce Christ wrongly to apply these models to his
own mission, Satan providentially provides him the opportunity to analyze the real worth of each in relation to himself.

As he draws Christ's attention to a consideration of these versions of a
kingly mission, Satan presses the issue of timeliness, of urgency in the
pursuit of "Zeal and Duty" (3.172). As always with Satan, the approach of
this mightiest adversary is very close to the truth he aims to pervert, and very
close to issues at the core of Milton's understanding of the English people's
experience. Satan's complex rhetoric on the subject of watchfulness here
reflects the ambiguity and heartache experienced by adherents of the Good
Old Cause on the matter of reading the providences. The case of the
republican Lieutenant General Ludlow gives us a feel for the dilemma.

Viewing the Protectorate as the product not of God's providence but of
Cromwell's pride and ambition, Edmund Ludlow refused to take the
Engagement of loyalty, telling Cromwell frankly: "If Providence open a
way and give an opportunity of appearing in behalf of the people [against
the Protectorate], I cannot consent to tie my own hands beforehand."[14]
Ludlow believed that Cromwell and the major generals had wrongly made
themselves the occasion for which they should have waited, arrogating
power to themselves that should have remained with the people in a
commonwealth. Major General Lambert demanded to know how Ludlow
intended to decide when he had found an authority that would oppose the
Protectorate and would better "employ its power for the good of

mankind"; for, he pointed out, "all are ready to say they do so, and we our selves think we use the best of our endeavours to that end." Ludlow's answer was "that if they did so, their crime was the less, because every man stands obliged to govern himself by the light of his own reason, which rule, with the assistance of God, I was determined to observe." Ludlow was uncompromisingly a man "who reigns within himself," advocating that kingship "which every wise and virtuous man attains."

Late in 1656 Cromwell again sought Ludlow's support, with no success. In Cromwell's view a compromise was necessary for logistical reasons. In Ludlow's view, the means used by Cromwell's compromise would under-mine the end. Cromwell insisted, "I am as much for a government by consent as any man, but where shall we find that consent? Amongst the Prelatical, Presbyterian, Independent, Anabaptist or Leveling Parties?" The question was meant to be rhetorical, to make the point that consent was not politically viable. But Ludlow answered him literally: "Amongst those of all sorts who had acted with fidelity and affection to the publick." The forcing of political, as of religious, consciences was not an option for him. The opposing parties—or, rather, their virtuous members—must consent freely to an instrument of government, and Ludlow himself must remain free and ready to move in response to God's providence. At the same time, retreat to the private life is not an option; the political effort must somehow go ahead.

At the beginning of his kingdoms temptation, Satan speaks to the dilemma of an uncompromising political integrity like Ludlow's:

> If Kingdom move thee not, let move thee Zeal
> And Duty; Zeal and Duty are not slow,
> But on Occasion's forelock watchful wait.
> They themselves rather are occasion best.   (3.171–74)

This claim is very close to a Miltonic definition of public commitment—very close and therefore deadly in its error. "Occasion's forelock," as we should recognize from Milton's other angry allusions to the illusory terms "Fate" and "Chance," is a satanic substitute for "God's providence." The zealous servants of God are perilously placed, this language reveals; from waiting on the providences, they may come to believe that "they them-selves rather are" the providence.

The solution to this danger is to keep the spirit always first, before the letter. "So shalt thou best fulfil, best verify / The prophets," Satan tells Christ, as if "fulfil" meant "prove the accuracy of," as if faith were the same thing as fortune telling. Yet the confusion had belonged to good people in

Milton's day. Ludlow's *Memoirs* recount a visit in 1656 with the Fifth Monarchist Major General Harrison, who offered as his reason for having supported Cromwell his belief that he was fulfilling Daniel's prophecy, "that the saints shall take the kingdom and possess it." Ludlow recalls that his own reaction to this reasoning was to cite Daniel further, where he says "that the Kingdom shall be given to the Saints of the most High" and to point out that "if they should presume to take it before it was given, they would at the best be guilty of doing evil that good might come from it" which was ultimately impractical "because we cannot perceive that the Saints are clothed with such a spirit, as those are required to be to whom the kingdom is promised."[15]

When Satan concludes with the pragmatic exhortation "Reign then; what canst thou better do the while?" (*PR,* 3.180), we may hear his words, rhetorically intended, as providentially literal, prompting for Christ a hermeneutical activity like Ludlow's: Before the coming of his kingdom, what must Christ do first, "the while"? He must invest that Kingdom with its spiritual meaning.

What happens next in the drama of Christ and Satan is subtle and extremely interesting. Christ reflects, in response to the question of his taking action, that his kingdom will await the time given by providence, and he prepares himself for suffering, the passion. Then he focuses directly on Satan:

> But what concerns it thee when I begin
> My everlasting Kingdom? Why are thou
> Solicitous? What moves thy inquisition?
> Know'st thou not that my rising is thy fall,
> And my promotion will be thy destruction?   (3.198–202)

Though "inly racked," the tempter does not miss a rhetorical beat. His response is to try the very opposite tack of that which he has been pursuing. *My* crime, he says, invoking a sense of predestination, will be punished no matter what *you* do, "whether thou / Reign or reign not" (3.214–25). The implication is: God is almighty; he does *not need* you. And then, even though he does not need you, you *could* win his (arbitrary) favor, being the favorite. Since you are in such a secure position, why not be a little generous—rather than hostile—toward me, Satan, who can do you no harm and who suffer so deeply.

In this prelude to the kingdoms temptation, we see Satan give Christ (although they are turned exactly backward in Satan's version) the seeds of the insights he now needs: first, that God *does need* Christ for the accomplishment of Satan's destruction; and, second, that the means of Satan's destruction will be in Christ's role as intercessor with the Father. These insights will mature as the meaning of the Kingdom is refined.

Christ's kingdom will ultimately contain both power and glory. Its power and glory are parodied in the violence of war that is offered with the Parthian alliance and in the corruption of luxury with the Roman Empire. Milton had warned the English people in his *Second Defence* against ever again submitting themselves to men unworthy to rule. "How could they suddenly become legislators for the whole nation who themselves have never known what law is, what reason," he asked them to consider, "who think that all power resides in violence, all grandeur in pride and arrogance" (*CPW* 4, pt. 1:682). On the eve of the Restoration, Milton was still tenaciously defending religious freedom from the same influences that were now indeed removing civil liberty. "Two things there be," he repeated, "which have bin ever found working much mischief to the church of God, and the advancement of truth; force on the one side restraining, and hire on the other side corrupting the teachers thereof" (*Of Civil Power, CPW* 7:245). These two basic means—"force" and "hire"—are what Satan here offers Christ, embodied in the great powers of his time.

Christ's understanding of his relation to "the people" he is to govern is developed next in terms of the ten lost tribes of Israel, whom, Satan says, it will take a military victory to regain. His suggestion that it is Christ's "Duty to free / Thy country from her Heathen servitude" (3.175–76) recalls the prayer of the Apostles who expect a political and military as well as spiritual Messiah—an heir of David under whom "the Kingdom shall to *Israel* be restor'd":

> God of *Israel*,
> Send thy Messiah forth, the time is come;
> Behold the Kings of th' Earth how they oppress
> Thy chosen, to what height thir pow'r unjust
> They have exalted, and behind them cast
> All fear of thee; arise and vindicate
> Thy Glory, free thy people from thir yoke!   (2.42–48)

That prayer sounds, not surprisingly, like the Old Testament psalms that Milton translated, for instance, Psalm 82:

> Rise God, judge thou the earth *in might*,
>   This *wicked* earth redress,
> For thou art he who shalt by right
>   The Nations all possess.   (8–9)

And the messianic prayer of the psalmist was, when he translated it, not separated in Milton's mind from his hopes for the state of England, in expectation of which he had prayed in the early tracts: "when thou the Eternall and shortly-expected King shalt open the Clouds to judge the severall Kingdomes of the World, and distributing *Nationall Honours* and *Rewards* to Religious and just *Commonwealths*, shalt put an end to all Earthly *Tyrannies*, proclaiming thy universal and milde *Monarchy* through Heaven and Earth" (*Of Reformation, CPW* 1:616). Milton himself in those early days of the Reformation thought in the Apostles' terms that God should vindicate his glory by restoring to power the righteous in his Church: "O perfect, and accomplish thy glorious acts; for men may leave their works unfinisht, but thou art a God, thy nature is perfection, shouldst thou bring us thus far onward from *Egypt* to destroy us in this Wildernesse though wee deserve; yet thy great name would suffer in the rejoycing of thine enemies, and the deluded hope of all thy servants" (*Animadversions, CPW* 1:706).

When the Apostles of *Paradise Regained* pray for a king in the line of David, they are expecting a ruler of a kind unique to their race. "These kings," Milton explained, differentiating the English monarchy from that of Saul, David, Solomon, and Joash, "as well as the rest of the descendants of David, were, I confess, appointed both by God and by the people; but all others everywhere I assert to have been appointed by the people alone. . . . It is then in a very special manner that the throne of David is called the throne of God" (*A Defence, CPW* 4, pt. 1:357–58). The Jewish kings prefigured Christ in that they ruled by a partial "divine right." From this distinction Milton argued eight years later against an English magistrate's right to use force in matters of religion, as the kings of Judah sometimes had done, that the Jewish kings had had to rule a people under bondage to the ceremonial and national, as well as moral and civil, law and its punishments, but state religion no longer befit the government of the religious life of a society under the gospel. The Israelites' original request for a king had been for idolatrous reasons, as God explained to his prophet Samuel: "They have not rejected thee, but they have rejected me, that I should not reign over them, according to all the works which they have done wherewith they have forsaken me, and served other gods." And Milton found the English people still wanting a king for an idol, asking for an earthly master over them. Of God's words to Samuel, he wrote in 1651: "The meaning clearly is that it is a form of idolatry to ask for a king who demands that he be worshipped and granted honors like those of a god. Indeed he who sets an earthly master over him and above all the laws is near to establishing a strange god for himself, one seldom reasonable, usually a brute beast who has scattered reason to the winds. Thus in I Samuel 10:19 we read: 'And ye have this day rejected your God, who himself saved you out of all your adversities and your tribulation, and ye have said unto him, Nay, but set a king over us'; and in 12:12: You sought a king 'when Jehovah was your king.' . . . That hero Gideon also, himself greater than a king, said: 'I will not rule over you, neither shall my son rule over you; the Lord shall rule over you' (Judges 8); just as if he had been teaching them that it was not for any man, but for God alone, to rule over men" (*A Defence, CPW* 4, pt. 1:369–70).

By the time wrote he *Ready and Easy Way* Milton had come to understand that it would not be, as he had hoped in *Animadversions*, a vindication of God's glory in a Christian era for God to save his professed followers, "though wee deserve" defeat. Rather, at this juncture, God's glory will be served by his faithful adherence to the law of justice. On the eve of the Restoration, Milton knew that the people's "wilfull sins" had provoked God's judgment on them to give them over to the captivity they desired. In respect of the enemy, God had just cause to prevent the Restoration, but in respect of the English people, he did not. At this point in his political career Milton's thought sounds not like Satan's temptation, but like Christ's judgment of the captive tribes. England in 1660 would draw down on herself God's denouncement against the Israelites who clamored for a king: "They had thir longing; but with this testimonie of God's wrath; *ye shall cry out in that day because of your king whom ye shall have chosen, and the Lord will not hear you in that day. Us if he shall hear now, how much less will he hear when we cry heerafter, who once deliverd by him from a king, and not without wondrous acts of his providence, insensible and unworthie of those high mercies are returning precipitantly, if he withhold us not, back to the captivitie from whence he freed us" (*Ready and Easy Way, CPW* 7:450). Thus, Lewalski is right to see in the exercise of civil power over the church under the Restoration "a contemporary analogue" to the situation of the ten tribes.[16] If we use our knowledge of this analogue to look at the Parthian temptation, we may see what part Christ's judgment of his mission to the ten tribes plays in his growing awareness of the nature of his true kingdom.

When he refused Satan's offer of wealth as a means to kingship, Christ made clear his determination to eschew not only riches but many aspects of kingship itself because of the corrupting, enslaving influence they may have over the person into whose hands they place power. He wanted all the glory of kingship attributed to the Father, who alone is worthy of it. Thus, Christ will not be persuaded that he himself should be more eager to seize a throne than Israel's first king, "he who seeking Asses found a

Kingdom." If he takes power with any doubt or confusion about his own motives, he leaves himself vulnerable to those influences that corrupted Saul, of whom God had truly declared: "Ye shall cry out in that day because of your king." Now, in refusing Satan's offer of Parthian military might, Christ is still concerned first of all with consciously preserving his own freedom, without which he can have no reason to govern others.

Resort to war, unlike possession of wealth, is a sign not only that one may become corrupted, but that one already has. War is "argument / Of human weakness, rather than of strength," Christ maintains; and the reader of *Paradise Lost* may recall how no battle but the sheer presence of Christ in the war in Heaven finally put to flight millions of warring angels. At this moment Christ is without that memory and must work out the meaning of true strength in human terms. As he meditates here on the subject of war, he is working out a refinement of his view, twice earlier expressed, that persuasion is a better governor than force. As a youth, Christ had desired to bring truth and justice to power in all the world, but had thought it "more humane, more heavenly, first / By winning words to conquer willing hearts . . . the stubborn only to subdue" (1.221–26). When offered wealth for Empire's sake, he has held it more kingly "to guide Nations in the way of truth by saving Doctrine" and explained:

> . . . this attracts the Soul,
> Governs the inner man, the nobler part;
> That other o'er the body only reigns,
> And oft by force, which to a generous mind
> So reigning can be no sincere delight.   (2.473–80)

Now he recognizes that not only foreign powers, but even the ten tribes would have to be forced into the temple (*CPW* 7:269), not truly governed in the spirit. While he has been considering force, his response to the Parthian temptation, as was his response to the earlier temptations, has been to answer in terms of the motives and power of the governor. This concentration is brought into sharp focus when he challenges Satan's own motives for wishing him to govern: "But whence to thee this zeal?" As it had been to the great harm of the Israelite people that Satan had persuaded King David to number them, so from ill will to the people and to him, Satan is urging that Christ assume rule on his terms: "such was thy zeal / To *Israel* then, the same that now to me" (3.406–13).

At this point, however, Christ must move from preserving the high freedom of the potential governor to consider the condition of those Satan wants him to govern. He must apply his notion of governing the inner

man to his own national case not just of "the erring Soul" he had imagined
as a boy, "Not wilfully misdoing, but unaware / Misled" (1.224–26), but of
a people "Who wrought their own captivity, fell off / From God to
worship Calves . . . Nor in the land of their captivity / Humbled themselves, or penitent besought / The God of thir forefathers" (3.415–21).
Christ here recognizes a fundamental characteristic of right reason: that
the problem with the inner man is not one of intellectual error, but of the
will (cf. *CPW* 6:475–76). All of the "saving Doctrine" that he could offer
as their ruler would fall useless on the unwilling ears of those who might
rationalistically keep the letter of the law in "Circumcision vain," but
would join "God with Idols in their worship" (3.425–26). Such a people
would inevitably be captive to whoever ruled them, "which to a generous
mind / So reigning can be no sincere delight." And yet, he must remember,
God has allowed Satan to discuss them for a reason; these may be included
in the people he is to govern, even though he knows his rule is not to be
in Satan's terms. If he is to rule them and at the same time preserve his own
liberty to be perfectly good, Christ reasons, the people themselves will
have to repent. This change in their hearts could happen only through the
Father's grace; and Christ senses from Scriptural prophesies and promises
that this grace will come to be, though he does not yet perceive a relation
between such a restoration and his own kingship.

> Yet he at length, time to himself best known,
> Rememb'ring *Abraham*, by some wond'rous call
> May bring them back repentant and sincere
> And at their passing cleave the *Assyrian* flood,
> While to their native land with joy they haste,
> As the Red Sea and *Jordan* once he cleft,
> When to the promis'd land thir Fathers pass'd;
> To his due time and providence I leave them.   (3.433–40)

How that "wond'rous call" will come through him to be the call of the
gospel, Christ has yet to learn.

At this point, Milton's Christ experiences the dilemma of the English
radical humanists and their kin throughout history. Utterly committed to
building a holy society, to responding to God's call for his kingdom's
coming on earth, they were simultaneously aware that they must not either
act precipitously or fail to act. They must learn how to find the right time
and way to act. "Each act is rightliest done, / Not when it must, but when
it may be best," says Satan, mixing humanist truth into his overarching lie

(*PR*, 4.475–83). What is the true, providential meaning of "best" if it is not Satan's strategic ducks in a row?

The English revolutionaries' answers varied, demonstrating the enormous difficulty of the problem. Saltmarsh, the antinomian Army preacher, when he perceived that good and holy men might be sacrificed for party unity, wrote to the generals at Putney, where the future of the revolutionary cause was being debated: "let not the wisdom of the flesh intice you under the disguise of Christian prudence."[17] He was not here saying "Do not act"; rather, he was strenuously insisting that the generals find a way to settle the Commonwealth's government that did not betray these men and what they stood for in the cause.

Saltmarsh did not live to struggle further with this mission. But we have seen the republican Edmund Ludlow's struggle with the same issue as he refused to accept the Protectorate, obstructed its initial promulgation, and several times over personally refused to take the Engagement, which he viewed as a "reestablishment of that which we all engaged against."[18] Dealing with Ludlow, Cromwell was faced politically and practically with the dilemma we saw Hooker struggle with ecclesiastically and theoretically: the reforming Christian humanist cannot resort to force; opposing sides must consent. Ludlow, like Milton, insisted that at the same time we must refuse to act in an unacceptable way we also nevertheless must remain committed to action. There can be no public life without individual virtue and no private virtue without a public commitment.

John Goodwin, like Milton, decided to support Cromwell's leadership as a vehicle for action; yet he kept sharp watch to preserve individual freedom. Goodwin was candid about the terms of his combative loyalty. In opposition to Cromwell's appointment of his Triers and Ejectors (1653), he asserted: "Men in authority can hardly be sufficiently jealous over themselves, lest they conceit their power to be more extensive than it is; or that in the exercise of it they intrench upon some of the appropriate royalties of God. . . . My great design in giving unto Caesar that which I know to be Caesar's, is, that thereby I may purchase the more equitable liberty to deny unto Caesar that which I know is not his, whensoever he assumes it."[19] Goodwin's model in this regard was the scriptural Christ, whom Milton gives us again in *Paradise Regained*, where we watch him separating his role from that of even the most righteous Christian magistrates of this world.

Christ's relation to sinful humans is further clarified by Satan's offer of Rome, whose citizens are not captives, or at war, but rulers themselves of an empire, externally free. It is true that their present governor is a "brutish monster," but Christ knows that even if he were to eschew Satan's imperial banquets and "Embassies" and try to assume Roman rule as a "wise and valient man," his task would be as impossible with these Roman people as with the ten tribes. "The happiness of a Nation consists in true Religion, Piety, Justice, Prudence, Temperance, Fortitude"—that is, in the virtues of "all sorts who [act] with fidelity and affection to the public," as Ludlow reminded Cromwell—not in "one Man," Milton had argued to the English against the need for a king at all (*Eikonoklastes, CPW* 3:542). Of Tiberius, Christ knows, "For him I was not sent" (4.131). Furthermore, as "this grandeur and majestic show / Of luxury" has debased Rome's governor, so it has also been the corrupter of her citizens. Milton viewed social and political Imperial Rome as an historical precedent for that "masterpiece of a modern politician, how to qualifie, and mould the sufferance and subjection of the people to the length of that foot that is to tread on their necks . . . by count'nancing upon riot, luxury, and ignorance" until the people are as disfigured as Io was by Juno, turned to beasts (*Of Reformation, CPW* 1:571–72).[20] Rome was perhaps history's grandest example of that process whose beginnings the Archangel Michael showed to Adam: "now I see / Peace to corrupt no less than War to waste" (*PL*, 11.783–84). Christ knows this much of his mission not just to Israel, but to all sinful people: that a kingship exercised by him, in war or peace, in any sense that the world has yet conceived would be inappropriate to his powers. The universality of this problem of government was confirmed once again, in Milton's view, when in the seventeenth century the English fell victim to the urging of their avarice and desire for the false security of one man's rule.

Warning against this possibility, Milton had demanded in his *Second Defense*: "Who would now be willing to fight, or even encounter the smallest danger, for the liberty of such men? It is not fitting, it is not meet, for such men to be free. However loudly they shout and boast about liberty, slaves they are at home and abroad, although they know it not. When at last they do perceive it and like wild horses fretting at the bit try to shake off the yoke, driven not by the love of true liberty (to which the good man alone can rightly aspire), but by pride and base desires, even though they take arms in repeated attempts, they will accomplish naught. They can perhaps change their servitude; they cannot cast it off. This often happened even to the ancient Romans, once they had been corrupted and dissipated by luxury" (*CPW* 4, pt. 1:683). And such is the judgment he attributes to Christ when he has Satan offer him the empire of Rome:

I was not sent . . . to free
That people victor once, now vile and base,
Deservedly made vassal, who once just,
Frugal, and mild, and temperate, conquer'd well,
But govern ill the Nations under yoke,
Peeling thir Provinces, exhausted all
By lust and rapine; first ambitious grown
Of triumph, that insulting vanity;
Then cruel, by thir sports to blood inur'd
Of fighting beasts, and men to beasts expos'd,
Luxurious by thir wealth, and greedier still,
And from the daily Scene effeminate.
What wise and valiant man would seek to free
These thus degenerate, by themselves enslav'd,
Or could of inward slaves make outward free?   (4:131–45)

"Or could of inward slaves make outward free?" Here we have a new recognition of what it is about "the people's"—or humankind's—wickedness that makes a worldly interpretation of Christ's prophesied kingship impossible. The Roman people are, like their emperor, made brutish monsters by their sins, and the analogy to a brute illustrates the relation between goodness and freedom. What appeared in the ten Hebrew tribes to be a weakness of will under captivity, appears in the Romans to have come back around to the flaw in reason that as a boy Christ had hoped to rectify. Only now the relation between the two weaknesses is clarified. It is the insight of *recta ratio*: degeneration of the reason inevitably follows corruption of the will; the absence of right reason, as Bonhoeffer pointed out, is a moral rather than an intellectual defect. This loss of *recta ratio* is the meaning of inward slavery. "For rest assured," Milton had warned the English, "that just as to be free is precisely the same as to be pious, wise, just, temperate, careful of one's property, aloof from another's, and thus finally to be magnanimous and brave, so to be the opposite of these qualities is the same as to be a slave." To the Christian English, Milton could give this advice: "If to be a slave is hard, and you do not wish it, learn to obey right reason, to master yourselves" (*Second Defence, CPW* 4, pt. 1:684).

Before Christ has completed his mission on earth, this option of choosing right reason is not fully available. All sinners are more or less in the position of Tiberius, whose remnant of right reason, his Conscience, remains strong enough only to torment him, but not to reform his depraved will. At this moment in history all Christ can say about the fate of

Tiberius—"Let his tormentor Conscience find him out; / For him I was not sent" (4.130–31)—is all too that he can say of the virtue, and hence freedom, of the Romans or the Hebrews or, indeed, the rulers and subjects of "All Monarchies besides throughout the world." As the Hebrews are unable to keep more than the letter of the law symbolized by "Circumcision vain," so the heathen are in essentially the same situation; their tormentor Conscience fulfills the role of the Mosaic law in discovering, but not correcting, sin. "For laws are made only to curb wickedness," Milton said to Cromwell by way of urging him to refrain from making more of them, "but nothing can so effectively mould and create virtue as liberty" (*Second Defence, CPW* 4, pt. 1:679).

Though he will not learn the means by which he can balance the composition of his own royal portrait until the end of the drama, Christ sees, in the process of his answer to the Roman temptation, that it must be the purpose of his kingdom to do what no other human government can do: to bring liberty to the inner human being, to free the soul from the chains of fallen reason and will. He first senses this active dimension of his mission in the form of a personal reaction against the Prince of this world and his Roman ectype:

> . . . then proceed'st to talk
> Of the Emperor, how easily subdu'd,
> How gloriously; I shall, thou say'st, expel
> A brutish monster; *what if I withal*
> *Expel a Devil who first made him such?*   (4.125–29; emphasis added)

Christ has previously questioned the devil's motives toward him and the people whom Satan urges he take for subjects (3.198–202, 406–12). Now he learns from his temptations that he must not only resist all falsehood in himself, but must destroy its source for all other people. The messianic prophecy of Daniel becomes suddenly relevant to his mission as Christ understands that he confronts the single source of all the evils of this world. When Christ speaks of the relation between his filling "*David's* Throne" and the "stone that shall dash / All Monarchies besides throughout the world" (4.148–50), Satan, sensing the threat, leaping to his temptations' end point before he loses his audience, dares out of desperation "to utter / Th' abominable terms" of his offer of the kingdoms of the world: his demand for worship. In doing so, he crystallizes in the mind of his antagonist the essence of his mission: to lead Nations in the way of truth he will have to eradicate from the mind and will of human beings the power of the "Evil one, Satan for ever damn'd" (4.194).

"BLESSED be the name of God for ever and ever; for wisdom and might are his," Daniel sang when God revealed to him Nebuchadnezzar's dream and its meaning. Daniel blessed God for reasons that correspond first to the kingdoms temptation and then to the one that follows it: "he removeth kings, and setteth up kings," he said, "he giveth wisdom unto the wise, and knowledge to them that know understanding" (2.20–21). Satan has been unequivocally threatened with the first of these facts. The only unclarified area remaining in which he can ply his efforts at corruption is the rule of the mind. He sees that Christ has determined to govern the "inward" man and now pursues that determination to try to deflect its direction from himself. He attempts throughout the learning temptation to insinuate the goal of external empire back into Christ's plans so that "persuasion" may become, like war, a means of subjugation. Thus, he teaches that Aristotle's greatness lay in preparing Alexander *"to subdue the world"* (4.252), that poetic harmony holds a "secret *power*" (4.254), and that the ancient orators' *"resistless* eloquence / *Wielded at will* that fierce Democraty" (4.268–69; emphasis added). Therefore, "let pass, as they are transitory, / The Kingdoms of this World" (4.209–10), Satan begins, seeking to limit the sense in which God "removeth Kings." But he concludes by suggesting that his rules of learning will render Christ a king complete, "much more with Empire join'd" (4.284).

Christ is not tempted to seek the kind of power that Satan offers in his gift of learning. But once more he must interpret the providence, he must use the opportunity provided by the temptation to judge all the problems involved with even the best side of what is offered; he must work out the reasons why all classical learning not only ought not be abused as a tool for tyrannic power, but cannot be used to free the "inward slave." "He giveth wisdom to the wise," Daniel had said, "and knowledge to them that know understanding." Christ states this idea in terms that are true for himself: "he who receives / Light from above, from the fountain of light, / No other doctrine needs" (4.288–90); but he must still work out his unique role in making this truth accessible for all people.

In his eagerness to make his antagonist fall, Satan makes Christ's task easier by pinpointing what all of his wrong suggestions have in common: the belief that "Error by his own arms is best evinc't" (4.235). In this section of *Paradise Regained* Milton was writing about two aspects of a subject he knew very well; one was the content of a vast area of study, and the other was the political and religious uses to which such learning had been put in his own age and throughout history. By the eve of the

Restoration, rulers of the English church were suggesting that Error, "Idolisms, Traditions, Paradoxes" should be adapted to in concessions that would enable the establishment of a state church; this claim staked out Milton's last prose battleground. In *The Likeliest Means* he compares the traditional arguments for tithing to mistaken attempts by the church fathers to accommodate "many rites and ceremonies, both Jewish and Heathenish" into the church, "whereby thinking to gain all, they lost all: and instead of winning Jewes and Pagans to be Christians, by too much condescending they turned Christians into Jewes and Pagans [that is, into the superstitious Roman Catholic church]. To heap such unconvincing citations as these [debates of the church councils] in religion, wherof the scripture only is our rule, argues not much learning nor judgment, but the lost labor of much unprofitable reading" (*CPW* 7:294). Milton had spent some time reading the fathers during the ecclesiastical disputes of the 1640s and had found them then not intrinsically worth studying for their form or content. Certainly, he asserted in the later battle over ministerial support, a preacher of the gospel does not need to be paid to study them: "If any man for his own curiositie or delight be in books further expensive, that is not to be recknd as necessarie to his ministerial either breeding or function. But Papists and other adversaries cannot be confuted without fathers and councels, immense volumes and of vast charges. I will shew them therefor a shorter and a better way of confutation: *Tit.* 1.9. *Holding fast the faithful word, as he hath bin taught, that he may be able by sound doctrin, both to exhort and to convince gain-sayers*" (*Likeliest Means, CPW* 7:317–18). Then, thinking back on his own youthful scholarly zeal, he added: "And yet we may be confident, if these things be thought needful, let the state but erect in publick good store of libraries, and there will not want men in the church, who of thir own inclinations will become able in this kinde against Papist or any other adversarie."

Howard Schultz points out the relevance of this "learned ministry" controversy to Christ's evaluation, for his kingdom, of humanist learning in *Paradise Regained*. Lewalski substantiates his position by applying to Christ's words the traditional Christian humanist distinction between knowledge in its own sphere, the natural order, and *sapientia*, religious wisdom.[21] Milton makes this distinction explicit when arguing that the university does not make a minister of the gospel: "what it may conduce to other arts and sciences, I dispute not now, but that which makes fit a minister, the scripture can best informe us to be only from above" (*CPW* 7:316). We have no reason from these late prose passages to think that Milton regretted the humanistic study he did for his own "other art" of poetry. An understanding of what kind of learning is appropriate to what end defines the whole value of that learning. By this standard, Milton had found Salmasius a poor scholar: "Salmasius, while a man of wide reading, possessed only immature and untried judgment" (*Second Defence, CPW* 4, pt. 1:577). When the need for learning is to evince Error, then the tool needed for both matter and method is not more error, but Truth, and Truth in her purest, "plainest" forms. In concluding his treatise *Of Civil Power in Ecclesiastical Causes*, Milton defended his procedure of arguing only from Scripture. To his textual explications, he said, "might be added testimonies, examples, experiences of all succeeding ages to these times asserting this doctrine: but having herin the scripture so copious and so plane, we have all that can be properly calld true strength and nerve; the rest would be but pomp and incumbrance. Pomp and ostentation of reading is admir'd among the vulgar: but doubtless in matters of religion he is learnedest who is planest" (*CPW* 7:272).

In *Paradise Regained* Christ finds the wisdom of this ancient observation applicable to his developing concept of inward government:

> . . . many books
> Wise men have said are wearisome; who brings
> A spirit and judgment equal or superior
> (And what he brings, what needs he elsewhere seek)
> Uncertain and unsettl'd still remains,
> Deep verst in books and shallow in himself,
> Crude or intoxicate, collecting toys,
> And trifles for choice matters, worth a sponge;
> As Children gathering pebbles on the shore.   (4:321–30)

The human "spirit and judgment," the "inward man," will be Christ's realm. It will not, after all, be his own function to rule by persuasion (4.230). All the instruction necessary for self-government, and societal government, can be found in the precepts of the moral law and the preachings of the Prophets. What people lack is the spirit and judgment necessary to implement the teachings of religion and the light of nature in their lives.[22] They lack the freedom of the "inward man."

The "many books" of "humane authors" are "wearisome," but they will not be forbidden, any more than will any other objects of this world, to regenerate Christians, who have gained "inward" freedom, just as these books are here available for use or rejection by Christ himself. The moral danger in reading without the Spirit is that readers will be distracted, by knowledge of or speculation about particular phenomena, from what must be their own primary purpose: the effort to build their own experience into a balanced picture centered in God's purpose for them in the world. When they venture away from that center of "lowly" wisdom, there is a great likelihood that they will not be able to see how all providences (the wild ass in *Job*; the stars in *PL*, 8.167–70) fit into a total balance, and that, in the face of their inability to see round all the corners of God's providence, they will be tempted to conclude with *Samson's* Chorus that God's ways are not accessible to human reason.

Once they conclude this, they are in the position of Bonhoeffer's "fool": "the fool cannot be served by education. What he needs is redemption." William Walwyn describes how he came in his own studies to awareness of this truth: "for many yeers my books, and teachers were masters in a great measure of me; I durst scarce undertake to judge of the things I either Read, or heard [in sermons]: but having digested that *unum necessarium*, that pearle in the field, free justification by Christ alone; I became master of what I heard, or read, in divinity: and this doctrine working by love; I became also, much more master of my affections, and of what ever I read in humane authors, which I speak not as glorying in myself, but in the author of that blessed principle."[23] Walwyn, whom Haller calls "a striking example of Protestant humanism on the vernacular level,"[24] was here in fact writing a radical Christian humanist's defense of his own classical and modern secular learning. Having been accused of reading Lucian, Thucydides, Plutarch, and Montaigne, Walwyn's answer was: Whether I value these authors is not the question; the question is whether I value or reject them in the Lord's service (in Bonhoeffer's words, "through the Mediator and for the Mediator's sake").[25] With Milton's Jesus, he replies: "Think not but that I know these things; or think / I know them not; not therefore am I short / Of knowing what I ought" (*PR*, 4.286–88). We cannot relate to learning, any more than to any of the other things of this world, except through the Mediator who governs the "inward man."

Milton explained in *Of Civil Power* that the "inward man" whom Christ governs is "nothing els but the inward part of man, his understanding and his will" (*CPW* 7:257), those parts which Christ had seen the Hebrew tribes, the Roman citizens, and even the greatest students of natural wisdom unable to use freely or fully. "What euangelic [true] religion is, is told in two words, faith and charitie; or beleef and practise," Milton said in order to explain why those actions related to Christ's kingdom cannot be forced by human government: "both these flow either the one from the understanding, the other from the will, or both jointly from both, once indeed naturally free, but now only as they are regenerat and wrought on by divine grace. . . . our whole practical dutie in religion is contain in charitie, or the love of God and our neighbour, no way to be forc'd, yet the fulfilling of the whole law; that is to say, our whole practise in religion" (*Of Civil Power, CPW* 7:257).

The sense in which the practice of charity means being subject to government is explained in a passage Milton quotes from St. Paul, 2 Cor. 10. 3–6: *"for though we talk in the flesh, we do not warre after the flesh: for the weapons of our warfare are not carnal; but mightie through God to the pulling down of strong hold; casting down imaginations and everie high thing that exalts it self against the knowledge of God; and bringing into captivitie everie thought to the obedience of Christ: and having in a readiness to aveng all disobedience"* (*Of Civil Power CPW* 7:258). "It is here thus magnificently describ'd," Milton stressed to the Parliament, "how uneffectual and weak is outward force with all her boistrous tooles" (*CPW* 7:259). It is also here described how the Christ of *Paradise Regained* will transform the maxim of natural wisdom that says "to give a Kingdom hath been thought / Greater and nobler" (2.481–82) than to take one. Christ will give the gift of sonship to each Christian, the ability to rule ourselves "as we are coheirs, kings and priests with him" (*Likeliest Means, CPW* 7:288) and together to govern society.

For his kingly purpose the Hebrew law and Prophets are the only accurate external tools for readying the understanding and the will. From them people can learn the truth that "the first and wisest" of the pagan philosophers knew he did not know: the truth "of themselves, of God much more." The key to a free understanding is the knowledge that God, the Creator, rules his creation with perfect consistency, with absolute truth to the law by which he created it, and is the very opposite of "Fortune and Fate . . . regardless quite / Of mortal things." The key to a free will is knowledge of the true nature of the fallen human soul, "on grace depend-ing," empty now of the springs of "virtue" which ignorant philosophers seek "in themselves." Though the philosophers are only the inheritors of original sin, their philosophy is involuntarily deluded by the same igno-rance of sin that afflicted the theories of the angels of *Paradise Lost*, newly fallen into hell:

> Alas! What can they teach, and not mislead;
> Ignorant of themselves, of God much more,
> And how the world began, and how man fell
> Degraded by himself, on grace depending?
> Much of the Soul they talk, but all awry,
> And in themselves seek virtue, and to themselves
> All glory arrogate, to God give none,

> Rather accuse him under usual names,
> Fortune and Fate, as one regardless quite
> Of mortal things. Who therefore seeks in these
> True wisdom, finds her not, or by delusion
> Far worse, her false resemblance only meets,
> An empty cloud.   (4.309–21)

Their poetry, since it cannot profit, should not wholly delight one who seeks rule over oneself. The "artful terms" that make poetic form are prostituted when made to bear a false and vicious content, "As varnish on a Harlot's cheek." A poet may find occasion to "remove their swelling epithets" and other formal devices and use them to embody Truth; but the poet, to be able to do so, must be first of all, a king with Christ. His "inward man" must be free to know the truth. What best forms a poet is not identical with what best forms a king; but it is Christ's kind of kingship alone that first frees a man to carry out any endeavor, including poetry, according to the truth of things.

> Since neither wealth, nor honor, arms nor arts,
> Kingdom nor Empire pleases thee, nor aught
> By me propos'd in life contemplative,
> Or Active, tended on by glory, or fame,
> What dost thou in this World?   (4.368–72)

The intellectual debate is over for both Satan and Christ. Satan has exhausted "all temptation" in trying Christ "to th' utmost of mere man" and has come to the end of his own ability to interpret the phenomenon he is addressing; his own vast learning has left him ignorant. He cannot conceive the sense in which Christ will assume the throne of David since, by refusing the slightest corruption in the means to his prophesied end, he will not be able to act at all in the fallen world. For Satan the fallen world is the only "Real" world, and he refuses to comprehend the reality of an "Allegoric" one (4.390).

In contrast, Christ must at this point fully realize what the Gospel of John records him as teaching later in the years of his ministry, and what Milton quoted so often: "My kingdom is not of this world." Satan's resort to the outward terror of the storm only underscores the inward strength that Christ possesses. In its reference to the outward suffering and corresponding inner strength of Christ's Passion, which it portends, it inspires the poet not to speak, for the moment, as the omniscient author of an epic but to worship, in his own voice, the subject of his poem:

> . . . ill wast thou shrouded then,
> O patient Son of God, yet only stood'st
> Unshaken. . . .
> Infernal Ghosts, and Hellish Furies, round
> Environ'd thee, some howl'd, some yell'd, some shriek'd,
> Some bent at thee thir fiery darts, while thou
> Satt'st unappall'd in calm and sinless peace. (4.419–25)

Once we have seen the Son of God's inward strength displayed thus in a drama of passive endurance, we are finally given, in the tower scene, a vision of the active power of the spirit, as Satan at last understands the identity, even if he cannot understand the nature, of the Son of God. "The Son of God I also am, or was, / And if I was, I am; relation stands; / All men are Sons of God" (4.518–20), Satan believes. But the truth is that the relation changed when both angel and humankind fell from their positions in the hierarchy of being; they stand now in relation to God not as sons, but as servants. Christ is as powerful as Satan fears; but he is "worth naming Son of God by voice from Heav'n" not because he is "more . . . than man" (4.538), but because he is fully human as humans were created to be, unfallen, free.

Thus, on the pinnacle, God's true Son does not call upon the Angels of God to catch him up; he does not fall. He is upheld spiritually from within.

> Tempt not the Lord thy God: he said and stood.
> But Satan smitten with amazement fell. (4.561–62)

As Christ stands on the pinnacle, Satan hears in the voice that utters these words to him the authority of the Father and is forced to reenact the conclusion of his first great battle with the Son. He now knows what Christ soon learns about himself from Angelic Choirs: "him long of old, / Thou didst rebel, and down from Heav'n cast / with all his Army" (4.604–06). This victory has been, like the first was and the last will be, accomplished by the "True Image of the Father" "with Godlike force" (602) of the spirit, not of the flesh. "Hee all unarm'd / shall chase thee with the terror of his voice" (626–27), with his sheer presence, just as long ago his countenance of wrath, "wither'd all thir strength, / And of thir wonted vigor left them drain'd, / Exhausted, spiritless, afflicted, fall'n" (*PL*, 6.850–52).

William Dell, the Army preacher, urged his countrymen to build a "right reformation" of the relation between church and state on a recognition that Christ "never used the power of the world; even his very punishments and destructions he executes by the word: *He shall smite the earth with the rod of his mouth, and with the breath of his lips he shall slay the wicked*: And Antichrist himself, his greatest enemy, he destroys *by the Spirit of his mouth, and the brightness of his coming*."[26]

The drama of Satan's fall in midair is tied to the intellectual form of the rest of the poem by Milton's image of the sphinx, poser of riddles. In *Eikonoklastes* Milton had criticized Charles I's false defense of his tyranny by comparing the philosophical pretences of evil kings to the unsuccessful attempts of Oedipus' predecessors to solve the riddle of the Theban Monster: "what they presume to borrow from her [Philosophy's] sage and vertuous rules, like the riddle of the *Sphinx* not understood, breaks the neck of thir own causes" (*CPW* 3:413).[27] But at the heart of active tyranny lies a vicious counsel; and when Milton took up the battle against Salamasius, he portrayed his opponent as corresponding not to the foolish riddle-guesser, but to the monstrous poser of riddles herself. Salmasius had posed rhetorical questions full of paradox designed to show the wrong of the revolutionaries' position; Milton countered by telling him to consult the English people he was insulting for the true answer to his "foolish riddles": "Then when they have acted as your Oedipus you should repay them by going to the devil as the Sphinx did" (*A Defence, CPW* 4, pt. 1:390).

But Satan himself is the source of both the false king's tyrannical will and the evil counselor's false understanding. In *Paradise Regained* Milton describes, in a vein too serious for satire, the victory of "truth the strong" over the source of all "error the weak though slie and shifting." Christ has patiently "found out" the grounds for all the shifting arguments of Satan,

> Who, knowing I shall reign past thy preventing,
> Obtrud'st thy offer'd aid, that I accepting
> At least might seem to hold all power of thee,
> Ambitious spirit, and wouldst be thought my God.   (4.492–95)

Imitating God, whose power is not exerted in things that imply a contradiction, the Son has refused to separate the power from the right of government. Thus, he has been able to understand the true nature of the human condition under the bondage of sin, and to identify the enslaver of human understanding and will as the author of sin.

"Desist," he finally orders Satan, "thou art discerned" (*PR*, 4.497). Christ has fully read the providences of his temptation in the wilderness.

> And as that *Theban* Monster that propos'd
> Her riddle, and him who solv'd it not, devour'd,
> That once found out and solv'd, for grief and spite
> Cast herself headlong from th' *Ismenian* steep,
> So struck with dread and anguish fell the Fiend.   (4.572–76)

The human Christ has found out the Truth; his victory over Satan *is* the new truth about human nature. And Truth, as Milton spent a lifetime teaching, "liberates."

"WHAT dost thou in this world?" *Paradise Regained* develops the answer of Christ and also the answer of the Christian reader to this question. But the relation between the two has caused a serious puzzle centering on the relation of Christ's kingdom to the Christian's political life. By reading the providences which God sends him through Satan's temptations, Christ maintains his own moral and spiritual integrity during the search for his mission. Traditional readings of the poem see Christ as an exemplar in this regard: "The Christian, assisted by grace, guided by providence . . . acts in the struggle for his own regeneration, and having achieved that, may act in the world to persuade others . . . The free society is a movement of individuals in process of regeneration . . . The poet cannot remake society, but he can show individuals how they can remake themselves."[28] One intent of such a reading is to point out how Milton differs from earlier aristocratic humanists, who had hoped to educate a prince who in turn would, from his central position of power, remake society. Such a statement of the lessons of *Paradise Regained* for the Christian life is incomplete, however. While it decentralizes morally responsible leadership of society away from a single commanding figure, it does not look beyond the roles of discrete individuals to consider the collective purposes of those for whom Christ paid the price of sin; it does not address the holy society. This failure encourages a belief that *Paradise Regained* models "the rejection of political and public aims in favour of the individual, private, moral aims."[29]

Andrew Milner, looking on toward the eighteenth century rather than back to the sixteenth, reads Milton's Christ as "the ideal of the isolated, discrete rational individual . . . pushed towards . . . a purely private and personal stoicism in the face of an irrational world." Milton's message, he thinks, is political quietism, although he believes, from the poet's phrasing of Christ's rejections, that "the possibility that political involvement may indeed be appropriate to other circumstances is always kept open."[30]

Herman Rapaport, on the other hand, offers an extreme reading of *Paradise Regained* as anti-political. Assuming as "a point stressed repeatedly in *Paradise Regained*" that "the governance of the gospel . . . puts an end to . . . politics," he identifies Christ's kingdom as an attempted "deconstructive solution" to politics, a denial of "the dialectical relations between . . . oppositions," yielding "a very intense violence which results from the undecidability and radical destabilization of the difference between . . . erection of power and annihilation of it." The assumption here is that since Christ's kingdom is not of this world, his followers are to deny political process, requiring that the holy society corporately sublimate the oppositions with which politics would have struggled, leaving a power vacuum into which authoritarian domination can flow. According to this view, *Paradise Regained* contributes to a definition of Milton as "one of the first political thinkers to experience . . . a proto-fascism."[31]

At this point we must ask in just what senses Milton's Christ is to be taken as exemplary and in what sense he is unique and not to serve as a model. All can agree that the Christian should follow Christ's example to "act in the struggle for his own regeneration" until "time shall be / Of tempter and temptation without fear" (*PR* 4.616–17). The problem comes with the next step. The fact that Milton's Jesus "Home to his mother's house private returned" (*PR* 4.639) tends to become separated from the angels' direction six lines earlier: "on thy glorious work / Now enter," almost as if he did not intend to fulfill this assignment. To "Home to his mother's house private" we should probably juxtapose this gospel message: "Who is my mother? . . . whosoever shall do the will of God, the same is my brother, and my sister, and mother" (Mark 3.33–35). In this answer to Mary's messenger, and throughout, the gospels show Jesus' ministry as a very public affair. Instead of retreating to a moral private life (among family, friends, fellow carpenters, local synagogue), he surrendered all private and personal relations to his cause, gathered a core of co-workers, and, with a very large number of participants at various levels, began what some theologians today call a "Jesus movement."

He did refuse affiliation with established state or church, national and international. And Christopher Hill explains incisively that Milton's Christ can be seen rejecting "one by one, temptations which had led the English revolutionaries astray—avarice and ambition, the false politics of compromise with evil, clerical pride, an ivory-tower escapism, the urge for instant solutions." In the face of an irrational world, Milton's revolutionary efforts "were in the last resort for *Christian* liberty." But, as Hill clearly recognizes, "This is not a quietist doctrine."[32]

A good deal of Jesus' mission, as the gospels show it, was given to preaching, along with healing infirmities and casting out demons. We should not confuse this preaching with the "persuasion" that Milton's young Christ had considered and that his mature Christ rejects. Many have interpreted the fact that Jesus considers it impossible "of inward slaves" to "make outward free" to mean that humanity "requires a teacher rather than a liberator." But the Miltonic interpretation is Bonhoeffer's "the fool cannot be saved by education. What he needs is redemption."[33]

Jesus' gospel preaching is not of theology or of morality, but of praxis. It is in light of such praxis that the liberation and redemption must be understood; Jesus' dying in innocence—our redemption—is the enabling of that liberationist praxis even in the midst of sin. Thus, it is not exactly that "the ethical preconditions for political liberation must first be established before political activism can be considered a legitimate enterprise." It is rather, as Edmund Ludlow observed, that "every man stands obliged to govern himself by the light of his own reason" and always, while so governing, to seek an avenue for action to be undertaken "with fidelity and affection to the publick."[34] As a practical matter, one cannot wait in privacy until "the ethical preconditions" have been established in enough of the right people to guarantee that political action will be effective. The only choice is to act judiciously, in the manner of John Goodwin, who took Christ as his model: "My great design in giving unto Caesar that which I know to be Caesar's, is, that thereby I may purchase the more equitable liberty to deny unto Caesar that which I know is not his, whensoever he assumes it."[35] This confidence in his own praxis comes as a result of the Son's crucifixion-and-resurrection, the atonement, that one public act which is uniquely possible to the Christ and which liberates sinners to act with a political freedom that Christ himself will perfect in glory.

Certainly a focus on this praxis is typical of radical Christian thought in our own day. In fact the Christology of current Latin American liberation theology, as in the work of Jon Sobrino and others, may offer a useful perspective on a traditional concern about the subject matter of *Paradise Regained*. Why did Milton not choose to treat the crucifixion in his epic about Jesus?

The crucifix is meant to be simultaneously an image of the death of an innocent man—an image, therefore, of human sinfulness—and a symbol of God's great love. Yet Sobrino finds that Jesus, when he inveighed against the idolatry of wealth and power (Luke 16.13), was defending a "God of life," warning against idolatrous divinities of death used by oppressors of the lowly effectively to deny the true God. Quoting a scriptural text central to Milton's antinomianism—"The sabbath was made for human beings and not human beings for the sabbath"—Sobrino says that Jesus' preaching unmasked the misuse of Jewish symbols of God to put others to death, and that Jesus' attack on this denial of the living God is why Jesus himself was killed. Sobrino's implication is that the same use is still being made of Jesus, to deny that Christ is the "God of life" and therefore of continuing history.[36]

Phillip Berryman assumes that Sobrino's perception of a struggle between the God of life and divinities of death was stimulated by the struggle of Oscar Romero and others on behalf of Salvadoran peasants. We know that seventeenth-century antinomians' revolutionary struggle reinforced their theological radicalism, which taught that because salvation "was purchased at an excessive price, . . . you will find it nothing [in responding to God's great love] to hazzard your lives for God . . . when tyrants and oppressors . . . pervert the truth of God into a lie, interpreting his sacred word as patron of their unjust power, as if any unjust power were of God, and were not to be resisted."[37]

"History," according to Sobrino, "is generated when one attempts to live according to God's love." God is always greater than humans can conceive; but far from leading us to quietism, God's very greatness (transcendence) should be a pull toward making love effective within human history. Rather than concentrating on Good Friday, liberation theology seeks to show connections between the way Jesus lived, his death, and the resurrection. As it was his preaching and actions that created those enemies who eventually determined to have him killed, so his message contains, in the words of Berryman's summary, "the seeds of a critique of any use of power that would bring death to human beings. Jesus' death was . . . the product of his own human decision, and the decisions of others. He was not simply acting out a prewritten script. . . . The cross . . . reveals the deepest meaning of human suffering, particularly the unjust suffering. . . . The resurrection is God's vindication of Jesus and his message. . . . Moreover, in the resurrection the real human history of Jesus' life and death sets in motion further history" (156).

Although sociological and theological differences exist between Milton's and Walwyn's radical Christian humanism and twentieth-century liberation theology, the free human decisionmaking, right reasoning, of "Christ our Liberator" plays a central role in each. The crucifixion was seen by each as having been turned by earthly powers into an idol of the forces of death, who claim that sinners must remain, in their penitence, subservient to the keeper of the idol.

Less overtly, political and social reform has been opposed by these forces with the very argument for quietism that has mistakenly been attributed to Milton. The main theological criticism of the liberation thinkers is that by Cardinal Joseph Ratzinger, whose "dualism" is, in turn, rejected by Latin American reformers. This dualism states that "liberation is *first and foremost* liberation from the radical slavery of sin . . . As a *logical consequence,* it calls for freedom from many different kinds of slavery in the cultural, economic, social and political spheres, all of which derive ultimately from sin." But the Cardinal believes that "God alone . . . has the power to change the situations of the suffering," and the growth of the kingdom of God is mistakenly identified with human liberation.[38]

Milton's view, in contrast, was that of the reformers. Jesus' life, death and resurrection—paradise regained—set in motion further history. Milton's Christ refuses Satan's proposed political solutions (as well as Satanic versions of social welfare, armies, and scholarly inquiry) not because he is instructing his followers not to engage with the issues of poverty, defense, research and teaching, or politics, but because the process of working out his rejections of Satan's temptation clarifies for him his unique course as the Mediator, the regainer of lost paradise.

"Christ himself, coming purposely to dye for us, would not be . . . defended" by Peter's sword in Gethsemane (*CPW* 7:258). But in that Christ has brought us into his kingdom—liberated from bondage to our sins—he has "made all the more possible" the political "struggle for freedom" (*CPW* 4, pt. 1:374–75). Milton's prayer was always that, under all circumstances that the world inflicts and Providence offers, some "children of reviving liberty" may continue to the end of time the work of building the holy society.

Notes
Index

Notes

Introduction

1. Christopher Hill, *The Experience of Defeat: Milton and Some Contemporaries* (New York: Viking, 1984), p. 328.
2. Robert Bellah et al., *Habits of the Heart: Individualism and Commitment in American Life* (New York: Harper and Row, 1985), p. 271.
3. For a useful explication of this point, see Mary Ann Radzinowicz, "The Politics of *Paradise Lost*," in *Politics of Discourse*, ed. Kevin Sharpe and Steven N. Zwicker (Berkeley: University of California Press, 1987), pp. 204–29.
4. *Complete Prose Works of John Milton*, ed. Don M. Wolfe et al., 8 vols. (New Haven: Yale University Press, 1953–82); hereafter cited as *CPW*.
5. Richard Bernstein presents a rich discussion of the important contributors in *Beyond Objectivism and Relativism: Science, Hermeneutics, and Praxis* (Philadelphia: University of Pennsylvania Press, 1983).
6. Christopher Kendrick, *Milton: A Study in Ideology and Form* (London: Methuen, 1986), p. 218, n. 1.
7. Bernstein, *Beyond Objectivism and Relativism*, p. 228.
8. Fredric Jameson, "Religion and Ideology: A Political Reading of *Paradise Lost*," in *Literature, Politics and Theory: Papers from the Essex Conference, 1976–84*, ed. Francis Barker et al. (London: Methuen, 1986), pp. 36–37. See also Andrew Milner, *John Milton and the English Revolution: A Study in the Sociology of Literature* (London: Macmillan, 1981); Kendrick, *Milton*; Michael Wilding, *Dragons Teeth: Literature in the English Revolution* (Oxford: Oxford University Press, 1987). Christopher Hill sees a retreat to a "first resort" in internal Christian liberty but recognizes that "this is not a quietist doctrine" (*Milton and the English Revolution* [New York: Viking, 1977], p. 421). Milner sees quietism in *Paradise Lost* and *Paradise Regained*, but renewed political engagement in *Samson Agonistes* (p. 147).
9. Jameson, "Religion and Ideology," pp. 54, 53, 37.

10. Herman Rapaport, *Milton and the Postmodern* (Lincoln : University of Nebraska Press, 1983), p. 2.
11. Kingsley Widmer, "The Iconography of Renunciation: the Miltonic Simile," *ELH*, 25 (1958), in *Critical Essays on Milton from* ELH (Baltimore: Johns Hopkins University Press, 1969), pp. 75, 86.
12. Milner, *John Milton and the English Revolution*, p. 120. Rapaport, *Milton and the Postmodern*, p. 170.
13. Milner, *John Milton and the English Revolution*, p. 123.
14. Bernstein, *Beyond Objectivism and Relativism*, p. 2.
15. Stanley Fish, "Transmuting the Lump: 'Paradise Lost,' 1942–1982," in *Literature and History: Theoretical Problems and Russian Case Studies*, ed. Gary Saul Morson (Stanford: Stanford University Press, 1986), p. 55.

ONE. Hooker, Milton, and the Radicalization of Christian Humanism

1. Richard Hooker, *Of the Laws of Ecclesiastical Polity: Preface, Books I to IV*, ed. Georges Edelen (Cambridge, Mass.: Harvard University Press, 1977), p. 1; Preface 1.1. Vol. 1 of *The Folger Library Edition of the Works of Richard Hooker*, ed. W. Speed Hill, 3 vols. (Cambridge, Mass.: Harvard University Press, 1977–81). All quotations of Hooker's *Laws* are from this edition. Citations list first the page number in the Folger Edition, then the book, chapter, and section number. Vol. 1 contains books 1–4; vol. 2 contains book 5; vol. 3 contains books 6–8.
2. See Douglas Bush, Paradise Lost *in Our Time: Some Comments* (Ithaca, N.Y.: Cornell University Press, 1945), pp. 38, 40. Cf. Herschel Baker, *The Wars of Truth: Studies in the Decay of Christian Humanism in the Earlier Seventeenth Century* (Cambridge, Mass.: Harvard University Press, 1952), pp. 201, 240–41.
3. Michael Walzer, *The Revolution of the Saints: A Study in the Origins of Radical Politics* (London: Weidenfeld and Nicolson, 1966), ch. 5.
4. My argument is corroborated by Margo Todd's recent study of the humanistic university education of the Reformers. Todd believes that "the activism and the reformist ethic of [Erasmian] Christian humanism" proved more formative than "the Calvinist doctrine of human depravity" for Protestant social theory (*Christian Humanism and the Puritan Social Order* [Cambridge: Cambridge University Press, 1987], p. 18).
5. Walzer, *Revolution of the Saints*, p. 154, n. 14. Even though he acknowledges that Hooker did not link his definition of episcopacy to the natural hierarchy (did not, like Joseph Hall forty-seven years later, claim *Episcopacie by Divine Right Asserted* [1640]), Walzer thinks he must have believed in a divinely ordained order of church and state, bishops and kings: "Surely it was natural, and not merely a matter of Elizabeth's politic piety, that the order of the church [and state] should parallel the order of the universe" (p. 153).
6. The eventual success of Jesuit proselytizers in converting such earnest Anglican rationalists as William Chillingworth and Elizabeth Falkland is offered by James Elson as evidence of the doubt and discomfort brought about by the

latitude and admitted fallibility of Anglicanism (*John Hales of Eton* [Morningside Heights, N.Y.: King's Crown, 1948], pp. 86–87).

7. See J. W. Allen, *A History of Political Thought in the Sixteenth Century* (New York: Dial, 1928), pp. 107–14, and Walzer, *Revolution of the Saints*.

8. Arthur E. Barker describes the beginning of this process in *Milton and the Puritan Dilemma, 1641–1660* (1942; Toronto and Buffalo, N.Y.: University of Toronto Press, 1976), p. 22.

9. Some political theorists in our own century have claimed that Hooker, in spite of his philosophical tendencies to the contrary, finally turned the whole of his *Laws* into an apologetic for Tudor political absolutism. At issue is whether the defense of the episcopal hierarchy in book 7 and of the royal supremacy in book 8 is consistent with earlier books, especially with the discussion of natural law in book 1. The issue can be approached by an analysis of the internal coherence of the argument of the extant parts of the eight books taken as a whole and by an analysis of the *Laws*'s publication history. Arthur S. McGrade and W. D. J. Cargill Thompson have, with different emphases, admirably resolved the matter of internal coherence by explicating Hooker's conception of the "politic society," which enabled him to give significant religious status to the English government without claiming its legal basis to be divine or its powers absolute. See A. S. McGrade, "The Coherence of Hooker's *Polity*: The Books on Power," *JHI*, 24 (1963): 163–82, and Introduction I, "Hooker's *Polity* and the Establishment of the English Church" in Richard Hooker, *Of the Laws of Ecclesiastical Polity*, ed. A. S. McGrade and Brian Vickers (London: Sidgwick & Jackson, 1975), p. 32; W. D. J. Cargill Thompson, "The Philosopher of the 'Politic Society': Richard Hooker as a Political Thinker," in *Studies in Richard Hooker, Essays Preliminary to an Edition of His Works*, ed. W. Speed Hill (Cleveland and London: Case Western Reserve University Press, 1972), pp. 3–76.

10. McGrade, "Coherence," p. 172.

11. Cf. John S. Marshall, *Hooker and the Anglican Tradition: An Historical and Theological Study of Hooker's Ecclesiastical Polity* (London: Adam & Charles Black, 1963), pp. vii, 168.

12. Raymond Houk, *The Place of Hooker in the History of Thought* (London: Routledge & Paul, 1952), p. 107.

13. See Barker, *Milton and the Puritan Dilemma*, pp. 22 and 342, n. 9. Samuel Taylor Coleridge thought that royalists and churchmen, not Puritans, might have corrupted Hooker's manuscripts and that probably "the doubt cast on the authenticity of the latter books by the high church party originated in their dislike of portions of the contents" (*Notes on English Divines* [London, 1853], p. 2; quoted in Raymond A. Houk, ed., *Hooker's Ecclesiastical Polity, Book VIII* [New York: Columbia University Press, 1931], p. 10, n. 16).

14. Robert Filmer, *Patriarcha: A Defense of the Natural Power of Kings against the Unnatural Liberty of the People* (London, 1680), p. 55. All quotations of Filmer are taken from the Folger Library copy. A modern edition was edited by Peter Laslett: Robert Filmer, *Patriarcha and Other Political Works* (Oxford: Oxford University Press, 1949).

15. W. Speed Hill, "Hooker's *Polity*: The Problem of the 'Three Last Books,'" *HLQ*, 34 (1971): 328–29.

16. W. Speed Hill, "The Evolution of Hooker's *Laws of Ecclesiastical Polity*," *Studies in Richard Hooker*, pp. 117–58.

17. "Mr. Hooker's Answer to the Supplication that Mr. Travers made to the Council," in John Keble, ed., *The Works of That Learned and Judicious Divine, Mr. Richard Hooker*, 2 vols. (New York and Philadelphia: Appleton, 1845), II, 351. Cf. *Laws* 25; 5.2.3 on the church's true enemy: "For a politique use of religion they see there is, and by it they would also gather, that religion it selfe is a meere politique devise, forged purposelie to serve for that use."

18. J. W. Allen's perceptive question about Hooker's view of toleration receives a partial answer in Hill's study of the ecclesiastical/political collaboration that produced the first editions of the *Laws*. Allen observes: "Hooker had admitted that men should not be required to 'yield unto anything other assent than such as doth answer the evidence' [II, 7]. The Puritans maintained that they were required to yield assent to propositions which could be proved false. It is difficult to see how Hooker could have hoped to convince them. His demonstration broke down at the last moment. For if the whole commonwealth doth not believe, how can it, as a Church, have authority to bind the consciences of its believing members? How can it, even, be regarded as a Church?" (*A History of Political Thought in the Sixteenth Century*, p. 198). Allen notes that Hooker "made no direct pronouncement" in the *Laws* "as to how such as stray from the truth should be dealt with" (p. 239). Hooker's identification of the positive law of church and commonwealth made it impossible to claim that sectarians should not be brought somehow to conform; but his disbelief in forced assent logically required him to say that the Christian magistrate must bring about the religious understanding of all citizens by seeing to it that they are rightly instructed until they agree to disagree on anything but the barest essentials in a broadly tolerant national Christianity. For this task Hooker offered his *Laws* to Archbishop Whitgift, Queen, and Parliament. These books, in their original intent, were conceived as a unified conciliatory vision, speaking to the psychological and rational needs of their intended audience; it was at the insistence of the Parliamentarians Cranmer and Sandys, who feared the political effects of religious dissent, that the tone and method of polemical dispute entered the *Laws* at all and caused the three last books to remain "unfinished."

19. John E. Booty, tracing Hooker's influence on Anglicanism, differs from the received view of church historians that the high churchmen of the seventeenth century were his heirs. Though these men "could and did cite Hooker as an authority with whom they could agree," Booty says, "the line of development lay not with them, but with the Christian rationalists of the Falkland group" and later the Cambridge Platonists ("Hooker and Anglicanism," in W. Speed Hill, ed., *Studies in Richard Hooker*, p. 229).

20. Elson, *John Hales of Eton*, p. 132.

21. Robert Gilmour, *Samuel Rutherford: A Study Biographical and somewhat Critical, in the History of the Scottish Covenant* (Edinburgh and London: Oliphant Anderson & Ferrier, 1904), p. 94.

22. Elson, *John Hales of Eton*, pp. 116–17.
23. F. L. Huntley, *Jeremy Taylor and the Great Rebellion: A Study of His Mind and Temper in Controversy* (Ann Arbor: University of Michigan Press, 1970), pp. 29, 82, 86–90, 101.
24. Robert Hoopes, "Voluntarism in Jeremy Taylor and the Platonic Tradition," *HLQ*, 13 (1949–50): 346.
25. *Ductor Dubitantium, The Whole Works of the Right Rev. Jeremy Taylor*, ed. Reginald Heber, 15 vols. (London: C. and J. Rivington, 1828), XII, 224.
26. Baker, *Wars of Truth*, p. 235.
27. For a helpful brief discussion of seventeenth-century British "Arminianism" and its political ramifications, see David Norbrook, *Poetry and Politics in the English Renaissance* (London: Routledge and Kegan Paul, 1984), pp. 230–34. The fullest account of the "Arminian" controversy is by Nicholas Tyacke, *Anti-Calvinists: the Rise of English Arminianism c. 1590–1640* (Oxford: Clarendon Press, 1987).
28. Barker, *Milton and the Puritan Dilemma*, p. 54.
29. See Merritt Y. Hughes, introduction, *CPW* 3:121, and A. C. Labriola, "Samuel Rutherford" in *A Milton Encyclopedia*, 9 vols. (Lewisburg, Penn.: Bucknell University Press, 1978–83), 7 (1979): 133.
30. *Lex Rex: The Law and the Prince* (London, 1644), preface.
31. Walzer, *Revolution of the Saints*, p. 5.
32. Question LXIV, quoted in Hughes, *CPW* 3:121.
33. *Ductor Dubitantium* 2.1.35; quoted in Baker, *Wars of Truth*, p. 236.
34. Quoted in *Richard Baxter and Puritan Politics*, ed. Richard Schlatter (New Brunswick, N.J.: Rutgers University Press, 1957), p. 29, n. 21.
35. Richard Baxter, *The Catechizing of Families*, ch. 5; quoted in Baker, *Wars of Truth*, p. 241.
36. Baker, *Wars of Truth*, p. 241. Baker suspects that Milton, too, being a child of the seventeenth century, probably would have denied Hooker's vision.
37. Lucius Cary, Lord Falkland, *A Speech Made to the House of Commons Concerning Episcopacy* (Oxford, 1641), p. 15; quoted in Elson, *John Hales of Eton*, p. 135.
38. See Barker, *Milton and the Puritan Dilemma*, ch. 11. The most serious recent confusion over this matter of Milton's relation to the separatists occurs in Herman Rapaport, who assumes that, "with the violent separation of church and state," God was, for Milton, banished from human politics. "Private [religious] man" was separated from "public [nonreligious] man," Rapaport says, with the result that "the social subject undergoes a disidentification with the whole to which he is related." By placing Milton with the separatists, Rapaport is able to locate him—with Descartes and Pascal—as an "underwriter" of the "cultural breakup" or " 'tragic' rupture" that eventuated, according to Lucien Goldman, in the rationalization of fascist totalitarianism (*Milton and the Postmodern*, pp. 170–71).
39. William Empson, *Milton's God* (London: Chatto & Windus, 1961); Paul Phelps Morand, *De Comus à Satan: L'oeuvre Poétique de John Milton expliquée par sa vie* (Paris: Didier, 1939) and *The Effects of His Political Life upon John Milton* (Paris: Didier, 1939); Rapaport, *Milton and the Postmodern*, p. 178.

40. *Laws* 94; 1.9.1. Hooker had explained earlier: "If fire consume the stubble, it chooseth not so to doe, because the nature thereof is such that it can doe no other. To choose is to will one thing before another. And to will is to bend our soules to the having or doing of that which they see to be good. Goodnesse is seene with the eye of the understanding. And the light of that eye, is reason. So that two principall fountaines there are of humaine action, *Knowledge* and *Will*" (77–78; 1.7.2).

41. Cf. Hooker, *Laws* 98; 1.10.3.

42. Milton displayed a similar lack of logical thoroughness, however, in his argument for divorce, where his belief in natural law led him to observe that in a marriage the wife may lead the husband if she has superior gifts. Milton allows this reversal of the positive prelapsarian pattern only if "he contentedly yield," which is rather like saying that the body politic may help itself only if "dominion doth escheate" (*Tetrachordon, CPW* 2:589). For a suggestion, on the other hand, that Hooker, under censorship, was claiming less power for a tyrant than has been believed by modern readers of book 8, see Robert K. Faulkner, *Richard Hooker and the Politics of a Christian England* (Berkeley: University of California Press, 1981), pp. 181–84.

43. Recorded in Bishop Overall's *Convocation Book* (dated 1606, printed 1690).

44. Claude Saumaise (Salmasius), *Defensio Regia, Pro Carolo II* . . . (1649), p. 19. Unless otherwise indicated, quotations of Salmasius are in my own translation from the Folger Library copy.

45. Filmer, *Patriarcha*, p. 75.

46. E. M. W. Tillyard, *The Elizabethan World Picture* (London: Chatto & Windus, 1943), chs. 6 and 7.

47. Weldon, *Originals of Dominion*, p. 6.

48. William J. Grace, in his "Preface to *A Defence of the People of England*" (*CPW* 4, pt. 1:287), fails to understand how Milton's argument at this point is based upon a logical interpretation of the chain of being and thus finds his view of Old Testament politics "narrow, private, or quaint." Grace is assuming the royalist principle of correspondences when he finds irony in Milton's interpretation of the Book of Samuel: "Amusingly enough God in support of Israel's republican principles appears rather royalistic and absolute." Republican principles, however, are not held by Milton in the abstract for their own sake, but for the sake of the higher religious principles discussed in this chapter; and there is no inconsistency involved.

49. Though by the end of his political career, Milton had learned to be less hopeful of the virtue of the English people, he never abandoned the idea of God's role that he had held in the nearly triumphant days of 1649. And, indeed, all the forms of government that he proposed were designed to maintain the supremacy of God alone, as source and protector of his laws, over at least those among the earth's "perverse inhabitants" who retained the Christian liberty required to keep them. For a detailed analysis of Milton's aims in his last pamphlets including the *Ready and Easy Way*, see Barbara K. Lewalski, "Milton: Political Beliefs and Polemical Methods, 1659–60," *PMLA*, 74 (1959): 191–202.

50. *Lex Rex*, Question XXVII; quoted in A. S. P. Woodhouse, ed., *Puritanism and Liberty: Being the Army Debates (1647–9) from the Clarke Manuscripts with Supplementary Documents*, 2nd ed. (Chicago: University of Chicago Press, 1951), p. 210; hereafter cited as Woodhouse.

51. Kendrick, *Milton*, pp. 115, 119.

52. Dennis R. Danielson, *Milton's Good God: A Study in Literary Theodicy* (Cambridge: Cambridge University Press, 1982), p. 10.

53. Jameson, "Religion and Ideology," p. 46.

54. The reason that Spenser is "a better teacher then *Scotus* or *Aquinas*" (*Aeropagitica, CPW* 2:516) is not only that he appeals to a broader audience but also, and more importantly, that his *poetry* is able to render more effectively than either a nominalistic (Scotus') or an onto-encyclopedic (Aquinas') *theoretical* work the human experience of interaction with the divine, of "providence."

TWO. Satan and King Charles: Milton's Royal Portraits

1. For full statements of such an attempt, see S. B. Liljegren, *Studies in Milton* (1918; rpt. New York: Haskell House, 1969) and Morand, *De Comus à Satan and Effects.*

2. Kendrick, *Milton*, pp. 151, 93.

3. Merritt Y. Hughes, "Satan and the 'Myth' of the Tyrant," in *Essays in English Literature from the Renaissance to the Victorian Age Presented to A. S. P. Woodhouse*, ed. Millar MacLure and F. W. Watt (Toronto: University of Toronto Press, 1964), pp. 125–48. Stevie Davies, *Images of Kingship in* Paradise Lost: *Milton's Politics and Christian Liberty* (Columbia: University of Missouri Press, 1983), pp. 3–88. See also Wilding, *Dragons Teeth*, pp. 226–31.

4. Hughes considered *Eikonoklastes* as a source for Milton's Satan, but concluded: "The experience of writing *Eikonoklastes* could contribute but little to the creation of Milton's Satanic *eikon basilike*" ("Milton's *Eikon Basilike*," in *Calm of Mind: Tercentenary Essays on* Paradise Regained *and* Samson Agonistes *in Honor of John S. Diekhoff*, ed. Joseph A. Wittreich, Jr. [Cleveland: Case Western Reserve University Press, 1971], p. 1). Although it is not necessary to argue that Milton turned back to *Eikonoklastes* or the *Defences* as a literal source for his Satan, it is important to realize that the political experience and vision informing the prose and the poetry are the same.

5. The anonymous author of *Eikon Alethine* (London, 1649) sought to discredit *Eikon Basilike* by calling it a forgery. He claimed that his purpose, besides vindicating the parliamentary cause, was to protect the memory of the king from the charge of damnable hypocrisy that he would deserve if the book were really his: "it is not infamy to say a man hath erred, obstinacy therein onely brands him: It is not I then that reproach the late king by enumerating some of his late errors; but he [the forger of *Eikon Basilike*] that makes the late king justifie himselfe in them, adding impenitency and obstiny to make them Heresies and Crimes" (Folger Library copy, pp. 1–2).

6. George W. Whiting, *Milton's Literary Milieu* (Chapel Hill: University of North Carolina Press, 1939), pp. 336–37. Also revealing of Milton's purpose is a

comparison of *Eikon Alethine*'s view of this issue with *Eikonoklastes'*. The *Eikon Basilike* portrays Charles as repenting that he had, under pressure from Parliament, agreed to Strafford's execution. The *Eikon Alethine* solves (albeit unconvincingly) the contradiction between the king's attitude at Strafford's trial and that in the book by claiming that although Charles had been sincere in condemning the guilty Strafford, thus performing a righteous act, the "forger" of the *Eikon* was villainously laying "innocent blood" on the king's head by saying that the king had thought Strafford innocent (p. 11). Milton, on the contrary, accepts both attitudes as the king's and views the contradiction as revealing of his character and dilemma as a tyrant: "No marvel then, if being as deeply criminous as the Earle himself, it stung his conscience to adjudge to death those misdeeds whereof himself had bin the chiefe Author. . . . That mind must needs be irrecoverably deprav'd, which either by chance or importunity tasting but once of one just deed, spatters at it, and abhorrs the relish ever after" (*CPW* 3:372–74).

7. Herman Rapaport thinks that this passage in the *Defence* reveals a "death squad" mentality in Milton, in which "mercy plays no role." In this passage, he says, "someone is about to be killed and this someone cries out for mercy" (*Milton and the Postmodern*, p. 177). Rapaport thus aligns himself with Salmasius' view of the king's trial and execution (a view that, according to Milton, carried "the cunning drift of a factious and defeated Party" intending "not so much the defense of [the king's] former actions, as the promoting of their own future designs" [*CPW* 3:338]). Actually, Charles did not either "plead for his life" (Salmasius [quoted in *CPW* 4, pt. 1:508]) or "cry out for mercy" (Rapaport). What Milton seeks to counter for readers of the *Defence* is a possible false interpretation of the fact that the king *failed* to ask for mercy, to repent, or to engage in any way with his accusers. Such immovability, Milton says, does not require courage when its real source is despair; "the commonest criminals," having rationalized their crimes, will reiterate that rationalization to the end. Do not be surprised by the "presence of mind" displayed in the final recitation of this rationalization, but analyze what is being said for it displays the absence of mind and moral will, the presence of "a hardened heart." Milton advises Salmasius to reconsider his interpretation of Charles's self-defense: "If you care to read his whole defence accurately rendered into French, you may change your mind" (p. 508). It would be helpful if Rapaport's attempt to link Milton to "a *thanatopraxie* of the state" were more responsive to the accounts we have of Charles's trial and execution, as in David Masson, *The Life of John Milton* (1896; Gloucester, Mass.: Peter Smith, 1965), III, 692–729.

8. For a discussion of the "Pamela prayer" controversy, see Merritt Hughes's chapter on the "Date, Occasion, and Method of *Eikonoklastes*" in *CPW* 3:150–61.

9. Cf. *Eikon Alethine*'s urging the people to distrust the rhetoric of the king's book: "Bee not cheated out of your innocency by this subtill Serpent with an Apple of *Sodom*, which at the touch of truth will fall to ashes" ("The Epistle to the Reader: To the Seduced people of England").

10. Modeling his statement about the king after the Prayer Book invocation of a God "whose service is perfect freedom," Robert Filmer had claimed, by means of what Milton considered a false analogy: "The greatest liberty in the world (if it be duly considered) is for a people to live under a monarch" (*Patriarcha*, ed. T. P. R. Laslett, [Oxford: Oxford University Press, 1949], p. 55). King Charles's version of this claim is reprinted in Masson 3:725.

11. "Space [instead of God] may produce new Worlds" (1.650); "this infernal Pit [instead of God] shall never hold / Celestial Spirits" (1.657–58).

12. Satan speculates on the creation of human beings: "Whether such virtue spent of old now fail'd / More Angels to Create, if they at least / Are his Created" (9.145–47).

13. Salmasius, *Defensio Regia*, quoted in *CPW* 4, pt. 1:310, n. 23. Cf. Milton's peroration to *Of Reformation* in which those damned in hell, "in the anguish of their torture . . . have no other ease then to exercise a Raving and Bestial Tyranny over" those most recently cast into hell "as their slaves" (*CPW* 1:617).

THREE. Milton's God: Creativity and the Law

1. John Peter, *A Critique of* Paradise Lost (New York: Columbia University Press, 1960).

2. Weldon, *Originals of Dominion*, p. 6.

3. *A Proclamation* . . . , 13 August 1660. William Haller characterizes Goodwin's philosophical orientation thus: "Here was Christian humanism, formulated in the doctrine of calling and covenant and brought to the defense of the conventicle" (*Liberty and Reformation in the Puritan Revolution* [New York: Columbia University Press, 1955], p. 253). Gary D. Hamilton brings Goodwin's views to bear on a reading of Milton in "Milton's Defensive God: A Reappraisal," *Studies in Philology*, 69 (1972): 87–100.

4. John Goodwin, *An Exposition of the Nineth Chapter of the Epistle to the Romans* (London, 1653), p. 229.

5. Empson, *Milton's God*, p. 142.

6. Psalms 19 and 119 were not translated by Milton; C. S. Lewis' discussion of them in ch. 9 of *Reflections on the Psalms* (London: Bles, 1958) suggested to me their appropriateness to this discussion. For further discussion of Milton's use of the Psalms, see Mary Ann Radzinowicz, *Toward* Samson Agonistes: *The Growth of Milton's Mind* (Princeton: Princeton University Press, 1978), ch. 10.

7. In a reading which complements this one, Mary Ann Radzinowicz discusses the kingship of Milton's Heaven as a "meritocracy" in which we witness "the politics of delegated power and the sharing of power." "Indeed," she says, "Milton's interpretation of God as king comes down to relieving God of the burden of exercising personal power" ("The Politics of *Paradise Lost*," in *Politics of Discourse: The Literature and History of Seventeenth-Century England*, ed. K. Sharpe and S. Zwicker [Berkeley: University of California Press, 1987], p. 211).

8. Empson, *Milton's God*, p. 19.

9. John Goodwin, *Redemption Redeemed* (London, 1651), p. 66; quoted in Thomas

Jackson, *The Life of John Goodwin* (London, 1822), p. 250; hereafter cited as Jackson.

10. John Goodwin, *The Obstructours of Justice* . . . (London, 1649), "Epistle Dedicatorie to . . . Parliament," pp. A2, A2v.

11. John Goodwin, *The Divine Authority of the Scriptures Asserted* (London, 1648), p. 205.

12. Goodwin, *Obstructours*, p. A2v.

13. Goodwin, *Divine Authority*, p. 205.

14. For a complementary discussion, see Diane Kelsey McColley, *Milton's Eve* (Urbana: University of Illinois Press, 1983), p. 204.

15. Peter, *A Critique*, pp. 24, 29; Empson, *Milton's God*, p. 108.

16. Stanley E. Fish, *Surprised by Sin: The Reader in* Paradise Lost (Berkeley: University of California Press, 1971), p. 188.

17. Boyd Berry, *Process of Speech: Puritan Religious Writing* and *Paradise Lost* (Baltimore: Johns Hopkins University Press, 1976), pp. 184, 179, 60, 232, 9, 10.

18. William Haller and Godfrey Davis, eds., *The Leveller Tracts, 1647–1653* (New York: Columbia University Press, 1955), pp. 283, 319, 279; hereafter cited as Haller and Davies.

19. *Walwyn's Just Defence*, Haller and Davies, p. 362.

20. Berry, *Process of Speech*, p. 10.

21. Keble, p. 294.

22. Goodwin, *Exposition of the Nineth* . . . *Romans*, pp. 231, 320, 230.

23. Fish, *Surprised by Sin*, p. 188.

24. John Preston, *The Breastplate of Faith and Love* (1630); quoted in Christopher Hill, *Puritanism and Revolution: Studies in the Interpretation of the English Revolution of the 17th Century* (New York: Schocken, 1958), p. 265.

25. Preston, *Breastplate*; quoted in Hill, *Puritanism and Revolution*, p. 265.

26. Preston, *The Saints' Daily Exercise* (1629); quoted in Hill, *Puritanism and Revolution*, p. 265.

27. John Lilburne, *As You Were* (London, 1652); quoted in Haller and Davies, p. 32.

28. Two recent attempts to situate Milton with regard to Marxist literary theory are handicapped by a failure to deal with the kind of human experiences encoded in seventeenth-century uses of the term "Providence" and "providences." Christopher Kendrick views "providence" at such a remote level of abstraction that he is able to regard it as being identical to "predestination" and to assume that the "free will" of Milton's (and other radical Christian humanists') bourgeois Arminianism, with its "dynamic sense of subject," must have been "forced [by his political experience] upon him" in conflict with what Kendrick takes to be Milton's actual faith in "the harsh predestinary God of early Protestantism." While Kendrick finds that "God's will is figured within the narrative of *Paradise Lost* as the power behind the narrative," the conception of God's will that he offers is theoretically reductive; if it were to account for the lived experience of "reading the providences," then his task of explaining the "dynamic sense of subject" in relation to God's omnipotence would have to be redone (*Milton*, pp. 95, 123, 116).

Andrew Milner, on the other hand, thinks that Milton's belief in free will abstracts God "to the level of first cause, . . . spectator, rather than . . . participant, in human history" and that Milton's faith in the Spirit within is no different from Descartes' "*cogito*, the proud and lonely self-assertiveness of the new bourgeois man." The identification of Milton's conception of natural law with the Newtonian mechanics of the Enlightenment can be attempted only by leaving the "providences" out of an account of "Providence." As with Kendrick, this omission results in the mistaken perception that Milton's is an "individualistic rationalist world vision," which "precludes any sustained concern with institutional and/or organisational problems" (*John Milton and the English Revolution*, pp. 94, 101, 113). Problems of human collective action, however, are prominent among those subject to "the providences"—subject, that is, to the collaboration of human beings with each other and with God in carrying out God's purposes.

Thus, both neo-Marxist and radical Christian humanist readings find that Milton's poem faithfully figures all the "decentering" forces of human experience. But where the one sees at the deepest level of the epic a lack—"the lack at the heart of the form of capitalist labor," an "abstract internality" caused by "distance from experience" (Kendrick, *Milton*, p. 214)—the other sees a fullness—as experience itself in "providences" links all labor to its ultimate center in God's glory, the all in all.

29. Quoted in Henry Kamen, *The Rise of Toleration* (New York: McGraw-Hill, 1967), p. 177.
30. Cf. *CPW* 6:121, 7:246, 8:426, 436.
31. Berry, *Process of Speech*, p. 245.
32. For an excellent account of Milton's belief in "prelapsarian process," which offers many seventeenth-century analogues for Raphael's belief (5.497–505) and God's statement (7.155–60) that human beings "under long obedience tried" may ascend "ethereal," see Danielson, *Milton's Good God*, pp. 202–27.

FOUR. Milton's Antinomianism and the Separation Scene in *Paradise Lost*

1. Basil Willey, *The Seventeenth-Century Background: Studies in the Thought of the Age in Relation to Poetry and Religion* (1934; rpt. New York: Columbia University Press, 1967), p. 255.
2. See Maurice Kelley, *This Great Argument* (Princeton: Princeton University Press, 1941), p. 149, n. 21; E. M. W. Tillyard, *Studies in Milton* (New York: Macmillan, 1951), p. 13; Millicent Bell, "The Fallacy of the Fall in *Paradise Lost*," *PMLA*, 68 (1953): 863–83 and the ensuing correspondence with Wayne Shumaker, comments on Bell, "Fallacy," *PMLA*, 70 (1955): 1185–87, 1197–1202; A. J. A. Waldock, Paradise Lost *and Its Critics* (1947; rpt. Cambridge: Cambridge University Press, 1964), pp. 222–23.
3. J. M. Evans, Paradise Lost *and the Genesis Tradition* (Oxford: Oxford University Press, 1968), ch. 10; Barbara Lewalski, "Innocence and Experience in Milton's Eden," in *New Essays on* Paradise Lost, ed. Thomas Kranidas (Berkeley: University of California Press, 1971), pp. 86–117.

4. Tillyard, *Studies in Milton*, pp. 17–19. Fredson Bowers, "Adam, Eve, and the Fall in *Paradise Lost*," *PMLA*, 84 (1969): 264–73. Anthony Low also argues that Adam should have commanded Eve to stay ("The Parting in the Garden in *Paradise Lost*," *Philological Quarterly*, 47 [1968]: 30–35). Both critics argue well for the relevance of the claim by Milton's Samson that "Commands are no constraints" and point out that a command would not violate Eve's personal freedom, since it would allow for the possibility of freely willed disobedience. Low considers Eve's motivation in the same way that Bowers and Tillyard do: "Sweet" dalliance is in her nature; she expects and wants to be mastered (p. 35). This view of Eve's nature and motivation, however, undercuts for many readers the claim of these critics that she is fully capable of freedom.

5. Diane K. McColley, "Free Will and Obedience in the Separation Scene of *Paradise Lost*," *Studies in English Literature*, 12 (1972): 103–20; Elaine B. Safer, " 'Sufficient to Have Stood': Eve's Responsibility in Book IX," *Milton Quarterly*, 6 (1972): 10–14; Stella P. Revard, "Eve and the Doctrine of Responsibility in *Paradise Lost*," *PMLA*, 88 (1973): 69–78. These authors agree with Thomas H. Blackburn's discussion of liberty (" 'Uncloister'd Virtue': Adam and Eve in Milton's Paradise," *Milton Studies*, 3 [1971]: 119–37), and they receive reinforcement from John Reichert's reading of the scene in " 'Against His Better Knowledge': A Case for Adam," *ELH*, 48 (1981): 83–109. I commend, as well as qualify, all these analyses.

6. Wilding, *Dragons Teeth*, p. 229.

7. Kendrick, *Milton*, p. 207; Wilding, *Dragons Teeth*, p. 203.

8. Mary Nyquist, "Reading the Fall: Discourse and Drama in *Paradise Lost*," *ELR*, 14 (1984): 207.

9. Mary Nyquist, "Gynesis, Genesis, Exegesis, and the Formation of Milton's Eve," in *Cannibals, Witches, and Divorce: Estranging the Renaissance*, ed. Marjorie Garber (Baltimore: Johns Hopkins University Press, 1987), p. 200.

10. Kendrick, *Milton*, p. 217.

11. Nyquist, "Gynesis," p. 178.

12. See *Of True Religion* (1673), Milton's last publication, where, in the year before his death, the poet reentered the political arena in an apparent attempt to capitalize on Charles II's (Roman Catholic) inclination toward an increased religious toleration. Milton's faith in God's own tolerance of the variety of beliefs worked out by individual Christians had not changed in thirty years: "It cannot be deny'd that the Authors or late Revivers of all these Sects or Opinions, were Learned, Worthy, Zealous, and Religious Men, as appears by their lives written, and the same of their many Eminent and Learned followers, perfect and powerful in the Scriptures, holy and unblameable in their lives: and it cannot be imagin'd that God would desert such painful and zealous labourers in his Church, and ofttimes great sufferers for their Conscience, to damnable Errors & a Reprobate sense, who had so often implor'd the assistance of his Spirit; but rather, having made no man Infallible, that he hath pardon'd their errors, and accepts their Pious endeavours, sincerely searching all things according to the rule of Scripture, with such guidance and direction as they can obtain of God by Prayer" (*CPW* 8:426).

13. For studies of religious and political radicalism in seventeenth-century England, see Norman Cohn, *The Pursuit of the Millenium* (Fairlawn, N.J.: Essential Books, 1957), appendix; Leo F. Solt, *Saints in Arms: Puritanism and Democracy in Cromwell's Army* (Stanford: Stanford University Press, 1959); A. L. Morton, *The World of the Ranters: Religious Radicalism in the English Revolution* (London: Lawrence and Wishart, 1970); Christopher Hill, *The World Turned Upside Down: Radical Ideas During the English Revolution* (New York: Viking, 1972), *Milton and the English Revolution* (New York: Viking, 1977), *The Experience of Defeat: Milton and Some Contemporaries* (New York: Viking, 1984).

14. See John Saltmarsh: "It would be a matter of much Peace amonst Believers, if the names of *Antinomian*, and *Legal Teacher*, and the rest, might be laid down. . . . Surely, *carnal* suspicions and *jealousie* do much increase our differences. Some hearing the *Doctrine* of *Free-grace*, think presently there will follow nothing but *looseness* and *libertinism* and the other hearing of *holiness*, of *duties* and *obedience*, think there will follow nothing but *legalness* and *bondage*, and *self-righteousness*" (*Free-Grace; or, the Flowings of Christ's Blood Freely to Sinners* [1645; rpt. London, 1661], p. A4).

15. I hope that the following account of a radicalized right reason will help to address the concern expressed by John R. Knott, Jr., that "an overemphasis upon Milton's affinities with Hooker and seventeenth-century exponents of a rational Christianity" neglects "other aspects of [Milton's belief in] the operation of the Spirit," in particular "the affective dimension of his Christianity" (*The Sword of the Spirit: Puritan Response to the Bible* [Chicago: University of Chicago Press, 1980], p. 121). As I observed in Chapter 1, it is necessary, first, to distinguish Hooker's own richer (both Platonic and Aristotelian) belief in *recta ratio* from the narrower, skeptical and merely discursive "reason" of seventeenth-century Anglican "exponents of a rational Christianity." We may then watch the essence of Hooker's *recta ratio* take on a revolutionary identity.

16. They are surveyed in Gertrude Huehns, *Antinomianism in English History with Special Reference to the Period 1640–1660* (London: Cresset, 1951).

17. John Calvin, *Institutes of the Christian Religion*, trans. John Allen, 6th ed. (Philadelphia: Presbyterian Board of Publication, 1938?), I, 190; bk. l, ch. 16, sec. 7.

18. John Goodwin, *Redemption Redeemed* (London, 1651); quoted in Jackson, p. 162.

19. An extended account of such a tragedy can be found in *Walwyn's Just Defense*, where the Leveller William Walwyn discusses the depression and suicide of a woman who was "very religious after the way of Mr. Simpson All-hallowe's Thames-street" (Haller and Davies, pp. 377–80).

20. Solt, *Saints*, p. 101.

21. John Saltmarsh, *Smoke from the Temple* (London, 1646); quoted in Morton, *The World of the Ranters*, p. 60.

22. Dell, *Christ's Spirit, a Christian's Strength* (London, 1651), p. A.

23. Ibid., p. Av.

24. Dell, *The City-Ministers Unmasked* (London, 1649), p. 27.

25. Dell, *Right Reformation* (London, 1646), pp. 26–27.
26. Saltmarsh, *Free-Grace*, pp. A4v, 142, 148, 89.
27. Saltmarsh, *Groanes for Liberty* (London, 1646), p. 8.
28. Saltmarsh, *Smoke*, p. 20; quoted in Morton, *The World of the Ranters*, p. 60.
29. Saltmarsh, *Wonderful Predictions* . . . (London, 1648), p. 4. As interesting as Saltmarsh's "wonderful predictions" to the Army in 1647 is the antinomian reaction of the Army officer who recorded them. The test for this soldier of the genuineness of the spirit with which Saltmarsh was filled when he "appeared at the Headquarters as one risen from the grave" was that "he did not come with bitter revilings . . . but rather with wholesome admonitions to fly that danger which he apprehended was hanging over the Army." Therefore, "have we not," the soldier concluded with Saltmarshian antinomian moral reasoning, "more cause to suspect ourselves of failings than him of Melancholly in what he said: And may this not be a good memento to better things, though he perhaps mistake in the matter he delivered" (pp. 1–2). Saltmarsh might have been mistaken in his literal judgment, but the spirit of what he said was true. Once the Army had established its own positive laws, the individual soldier had still to judge the morality of his political and religious leaders, the generals, and even the preachers who had taught him. For a full discussion of the Army's confrontation with Levellers, see Austin Woolrych, *Soldiers and Statesmen* (Oxford: Oxford University Press, forthcoming).
30. See *A Defense, CPW* 4, pt. 1:535–36; *Second Defense, CPW* 4, pt. 1:673–75; sonnet to Cromwell.
31. Dell, *Christ's Spirit*, p. 12.
32. Jacob Bauthumley, *The Light and Dark Sides of God* (1605); quoted in Hill, *World*, p. 176.
33. *Fenstanton Records*, discussions in the 1650s between officers of the Baptist church at Fenstanton and members who had picked up Ranter views; quoted in Hill, *World*, p. 184.
34. Quoted in Hill, *World*, p. 176.
35. Morton, *The World of the Ranters*, p. 18. L. Clarkson, *The Lost Sheep Found* (London, 1660); quoted in Morton, p. 78.
36. On radical Arminianism, see Chapter 1, note 27, and Chapter 3, note 3; Hill, *Milton*, ch. 21; Dennis R. Danielson, "Milton's Arminianism and *Paradise Lost*," *Milton Studies*, 12 (1978): 47–73. An interesting, if unconventional discussion of the Arminianism of the right is found in William Lamont, *Godly Rule* (London: Macmillan, 1969), pp. 64–66.
37. Cf. Leo Solt, "John Saltmarsh: New Model Army Chaplain," *Journal of Ecclesiastical History*, 2 (1951): 73, n. 4. Saltmarsh held a non-Calvinist concept of universal laws of nature, as he reveals in such a claim as that natural law and the Mosaic law are "God's images" (see also Solt, *Saints*, p. 75, n. 12).
38. Quoted in Jackson, pp. 250–51.
39. It is significant that the "high" Presbyterians on the Puritan side of the revolution failed to support the trial and execution of the king. They did not hold a concept of the deity that allowed them to reason from signs to causes. For the nominalist, there are only the signs themselves, discrete events or commands

with no more general causes to reason back toward since, to their way of thinking, a natural law is a limitation on the omnipotence of God.

40. Woodhouse, p. 213. Goodwin's reference to the *salus populi* has a firmer philosophical base than Dell's because, although Dell argued that the soldiers followed a good higher than positive law, he could not demonstrate their rational interaction with natural law; he could only claim their obedience to God's direct command: "they were not at their own liberty, to do this, or not to do it, but their hearts were so inclined by God to this work, that they could not get off from it, though they had a desire" (*City-Ministers*, p. 28).

41. Goodwin, *Right and Might Well Met*, in Woodhouse, p. 219.

42. Goodwin, *Quaere*, p. 6; cf. Saltmarsh in Woodhouse, p. 185.

43. Goodwin, *Quaere*, p. 5; cf. Hooker: "Not that I judge it a thing allowable for men to observe those lawes which in their hearts they are stedfastly perswaded to be against the law of God: but your perswasion in this case ye are all bound for the time to suspend, and otherwise doing, ye offend against God by troubling his Church without any just or necessary causes" (33; *Pref.* 6.6).

44. Goodwin, *Catabaptism* (London, 1655), "Admonition," item 2.

45. William Cain suggests that Christ's rejection of Satan's offer of learning in *Paradise Regained* 4.322–27 denies the moral worth of all literary study, even the study of Milton's own works, that the poet "leaves only the inner authority of readers—an authority that is not required to exercise itself on texts like *Paradise Regained*" ("Learning How to Read: A Note on *Paradise Regained*, IV. 321–30," *Milton Quarterly*, 13 [1979]: 121). William W. Kerrigan makes a related suggestion in *The Prophetic Milton* (Charlottesville: University of Virginia Press, 1974), p. 180, n. 25.

46. Camille Slights shows casuistry as stemming from the vitality in seventeenth-century England of the doctrine of Christian liberty: "The casuistical view of morality as problematic action to be analyzed in terms of divine law, particular circumstances, and individual conscience permeates the ethical and political thought of the time" (*The Casuistical Tradition* [Princeton: Princeton University Press, 1981], p. 298). While it reflects the intensity of the English preoccupation with ethics, casuistry operated within a different dynamic from that of antinomian ethics since its attempt to maneuver logically among the multitude of positive laws led to stressing the process of ratiocination, thus reinforcing the restriction in meaning that "right reason" underwent during the seventeenth century. Slights recognizes that Milton's poetry reveals an ethic "more radical than any models offered by conventional casuists" (p. 295).

47. This belief is an assertion of the Christian humanist faith that a just God binds himself by his own laws. Goodwin gave the belief a radical formulation when, claiming that the revelations granted by God in Scripture are always consonant with reason, he asserted that if a doctrine of predestination "were to be found in, or regularly deduced from, the Scriptures, it were a just ground to any intelligent man to question their authority, and whether they were from God or no" (*Redemption Redeemed*; quoted in Jackson, p. 319). Goodwin did not doubt, as his Presbyterian opponents claimed, the divine authority of Scripture; rather he found that his faith in God's rational accessibility made it

impossible for him to accept the scriptural texts in an absolutely positivistic sense. Like the positive laws, the scriptural texts approximate and reflect the one Truth. They must be comprehensible as a whole; apparent contradictions must be reconciled, not accepted as divine paradoxes.

48. Empson, *Milton's God*, pp. 159–63.

49. *The Basic Works of Aristotle*, ed. Richard McKeon, trans. W. D. Ross (New York: Random, 1941), p. 958.

50. Their separation displays, as do all prelapsarian events, a "present radical undecidability" (Nyquist, "Reading," p. 206).

51. For a technical appreciation of their reasoning processes, see Lee A. Jacobus, *Sudden Apprehension: Aspects of Knowledge in* Paradise Lost (The Hague: Mouton, 1976), pp. 144–48.

52. See, e.g., J. Max Patrick, "A Reconsideration of the Fall of Eve," *Etudes Anglaises*, 28 (1975): 15–21.

53. "Milton's Alleged Ramism," *PMLA*, 67 (1952): 1035–53.

54. Quoted in Dell, *The City-Ministers Unmasked* (London, 1649), p. 27.

55. Quoted in Morton, *The World of the Ranters*, p. 78.

56. The interpretation of Aristotle's phronesis is that of Hans-Georg Gadamer, restated by Bernstein, *Beyond Objectivism and Relativism*, pp. 146–47.

57. Goodwin, *Triumviri* (London, 1658), pref., sec. 56, p. K3.

58. Northrop Frye, *The Return of Eden: Five Essays on Milton's Epics* (Toronto: University of Toronto Press, 1965), p. 65.

59. Marcia Landy, " 'A Free and Open Encounter': Milton and the Modern Reader," *Milton Studies*, 9 (1976): 22.

FIVE. Liberty under the Law: *Samson Agonistes*

1. In *Essays in English Literature from the Renaissance to the Victorian Age Presented to A. S. P. Woodhouse*, ed. Millar MacLure and F. W. Watt (Toronto: University of Toronto Press, 1964), pp. 169–94. Three essays by Samuel Stollman further develop background material for an understanding of Milton's belief in the relation between the Mosaic law and Christian liberty: "Milton's Samson and the Jewish Tradition," *Milton Studies*, 3 (1971): 185–200; "Milton's Understanding of the 'Hebraic' in *Samson Agonistes*," *Studies in Philology*, 63 (1972): 334–47; and "Milton's Dichotomy of 'Judaism' and 'Hebraism,' " *PMLA*, 89 (1974): 105–12. Northrop Frye ("Agon and Logos: Revolution and Revelation," in *The Prison and the Pinnacle*, ed. Balachandra Rajan [Toronto: University of Toronto Press, 1973], p. 154) and Mary Ann Radzinowicz (*Toward Samson Agonistes: The Growth of Milton's Mind* [Princeton: Princeton University Press, 1978], pp. 157, 246, 262) also discuss the fact that Milton used Samson as an exemplar of Christian liberty.

2. Goodwin, *Triumviri*, pref. sec. 69; cf. *CPW* 6:455.

3. See W. R. Parker, *Milton's Debt to Greek Tragedy in* Samson Agonistes (1937; rpt. New York: Barnes & Noble, 1968); J. B. Broadbent, ed., *Milton:* Comus *and* Samson Agonistes (London: Edward Arnold, 1961).

4. See John Huntley, "A Revaluation of the Chorus' Role in Milton's *Samson*

Agonistes," *Modern Philology*, 64 (1966): 132–45; Franklin R. Baruch, "Time, Body and Spirit at the Close of *Samson Agonistes*," *ELH*, 36 (1969): 339; Louis Martz, "Chorus and Character in *Samson Agonistes*," *Milton Studies*, 1 (1969): 115–34; Christopher Grose, " 'His Uncontrollable Intent': Discovery as Action in *Samson Agonistes*," *Milton Studies*, 7 (1975): 49–76. Anthony Low gives a balanced account of this line of criticism in *The Blaze of Noon: A Reading of* Samson Agonistes (New York: Columbia University Press, 1974), pp. 123–26.

5. See, e.g., Joseph H. Summers, "The Movements of the Drama," in *The Lyric and Dramatic Milton: Selected Papers from the English Institute* (New York: Columbia University Press, 1965), pp. 153–75, and Jon S. Lawry, *The Shadow of Heaven: Matter and Stance in Milton's Poetry* (Ithaca, N.Y.: Cornell University Press, 1968), pp. 350–96. Lynn Veach Sadler, in "Coping with Hebraic Legalism, The Chorus in *Samson Agonistes*," *Harvard Theological Review*, 66 (1973): 353–68, discusses the Chorus' role from the same theological viewpoint that I do and points out some similar instances of the Chorus' "carnal" vision. Although I agree that Milton's theological beliefs about Christian liberty, as noted by Barker, are relevant to interpreting *Samson Agonistes*, my reading of the dramatic significance of the Chorus' role in its relation to Samson's regenerative experience differs from Sadler's throughout. Sadler sees the Chorus as experiencing a regenerative growth paralleling that of Samson.

6. Arthur Barker, "Calm Regained Through Passion Spent: The Conclusions of the Miltonic Effort," in Rajan, *The Prison and the Pinnacle*, pp. 39–40.

7. For a complementary discussion, see Radzinowicz, *Toward* Samson Agonistes, pp. 254–57.

8. Arnold Stein, *Heroic Knowledge: An Interpretation of* Paradise Regained *and* Samson Agonistes (Minneapolis: University of Minnesota Press, 1957), p. 196.

9. George M. Muldrow, *Milton and the Drama of the Soul: A Study of the Theme of the Restoration of Men in Milton's Later Poetry* (The Hague: Mouton, 1970), pp. 220–21.

10. Martin Mueller, "*Pathos and Katharsis* in Samson Agonistes," *ELH*, 31 (1964): 168.

11. See Broadbent, *Milton:* Comus *and* Samson Agonistes; Empson, *Milton's God*, ch. 6; Charles Samuels, "Milton's *Samson Agonistes* and Rational Christianity," *Dalhousie Review*, 43 (1963): 495–506.

12. See Stanley Fish, "Question and Answer in *Samson Agonistes*," *Critical Quarterly*, 11 (1969): 237–64; Virginia R. Mollenkott, "Relativism in *Samson Agonistes*," *Studies in Philology*, 67 (1970): 89–103; G. A. Wilkes, "The Interpretation of *Samson Agonistes*," *Huntington Library Quarterly*, 26 (1963): 363–79; Mason Tung, "Samson Impatiens: A reinterpretation of Milton's *Samson Agonistes*," *Texas Studies in Literature and Languages*, 9 (1968): 475–92. John Carey, who finds no more logic in Samson's arguments than in those of Dalila and Harapha, concludes that Milton did not intend either Samson or the Old Testament God to be admirable; see *Milton* (London: Evans, 1969), ch. 9. Irene Samuel, on similar grounds, holds that Milton's God could not, in spite of the Hebrews' belief, be accepting Samson's violence toward the Philistines as valid service; see "*Samson Agonistes* as Tragedy" in *Calm of Mind: Tercente-*

nary Essays on Paradise Regained *and* Samson Agonistes *in Honor of John S. Diekhoff*, ed. J. A. Wittreich, Jr. (Cleveland: Case Western Reserve University Press, 1971), pp. 235–57.

13. These more orthodox readings of Samson's reasoning in his encounters with Dalila and Harapha are found in the following treatments of the play: Stein, *Heroic Knowledge;* Lawry, *The Shadow of Heaven*, ch. 6; Alan Rudrum, *A Critical Commentary on Milton's* Samson Agonistes (London: Macmillan, 1969); Muldrow, *Milton and the Drama of the Soul*, ch. 4; Low, *Blaze of Noon*, ch. 7; Radzinowicz, *Toward* Samson Agonistes.

14. This definition of government is based upon the Christian humanist concept of "right reason." The persistence of fideism and skepticism, current in Milton's day and in our own, has effectively abolished from our active vocabulary the concept of "right" reason and its corresponding definition of government. It has substituted a relativist view of human government, as of the universe. Nevertheless, to recognize that Milton based his political life and his art consciously on right reason in the face of growing relativism helps us to recognize the presence and function of the humanist world-view in ordering the world of his drama. For a useful history of the concept of right reason from Socrates through Reformation fideism and skepticism to Milton, see Robert Hoopes, *Right Reason in the English Renaissance* (Cambridge, Mass.: Harvard University Press, 1962).

15. Empson, *Milton's God*, p. 215.

16. Mollenkott, "Relativism," pp. 98–99.

17. Milton several times in his regicide tracts contemptuously compared the recalcitrant Presbyterians with the people of Meroz (see *TKM, CPW* 3:235). The Presbyterians themselves had relied upon the shame of Meroz as a goad to reluctant reformers at the outset of the civil war; see Stephen Marshall's sermon, *Meroz Cursed*, preached before Parliament in 1641: "and with *Meroz* all others are cursed, who come not out to the help of the Lord against the mighty" (p. 54). Thomas Edwards, Presbyterian author of a voluminous expose of sectarian heresies called *Gangraena* (London, 1646), was incensed to report that in one Independent tract he himself had been compared to Sisera while his opponent, the separatist Katherine Chidley, that "brazen-faced audacious old woman," had been "highly magnified" by being "resembled unto Jael" (*Gangraena*, Part III, 170–71; quoted in Morton, *The World of the Ranters*, p. 18).

18. For a helpful discussion of the difference between Milton's humanistic idea of God as a rational deity and the Reformation Calvinist and Lutheran "voluntarism," which regarded power, rather than reason or justice, as God's primary attribute, see Hoopes, *Right Reason*, chs. 6 and 10, as well as my Chapter One. Milton argued against royalist voluntarism that God himself is no tyrant, but subjects his will to natural law. Recall Milton's political application of this theological belief in his *Defence of the English People:* "It was not permissible and good to put a tyrant to death because God commanded it, but rather God commanded it because it was permissible and good" (*CPW* 4, pt. 1:407).

19. Stein, *Heroic Knowledge*, p. 182; Broadbent, *Milton*: Comus *and* Samson Agonistes, p. 53.

20. Cf. the similar discussion of David's public and private roles in Dell, *City-Ministers*, p. 27.

21. Don M. Wolfe, *Milton in the Puritan Revolution* (New York: Nelson, 1941), pp. 283–84.

22. The New Model Army's *Declaration* of June 14, 1647, that it was "not a mere mercenary army" but one "called forth . . . to the defense of our own and the people's just rights and liberties" was intended to reprimand the Parliament that had first relied upon the Army, but was now wavering in its pursuit of issues central to the revolution (see Woodhouse, p. 404). The *Declaration*'s similarity to Samson's claim to be a "person rais'd" even in spite of the "servile minds" of his compatriots leads Christopher Hill to view Samson as a symbol for the Army (*God's Englishman: Oliver Cromwell and the English Revolution* [1970; rpt. New York: Harper, 1972], pp. 190–91).

23. Joseph Wittreich, *Interpreting* Samson Agonistes (Princeton: Princeton University Press, 1986), pp. xxvii, 231, 113, 350.

24. Ibid., p. 273. See Irene Samuel, "*Samson Agonistes* as Tragedy," in Wittreich, ed., *Calm of Mind*, pp. 235– 57, and Wilding, *Dragons Teeth*, p. 254.

25. Helen Damico, "Duality and Dramatic Vision: A Structural Analysis of *Samson Agonistes*," *Milton Studies*, 12 (1978): 110.

26. Wittreich, *Interpreting* Samson Agonistes, p. 201.

27. Saltmarsh, *Free-Grace*, p. A4v.

28. Damico, "Duality and Dramatic Vision," p. 105.

29. See Wittreich, *Interpreting* Samson Agonistes, p. 320.

30. Samuel, "*Samson Agonistes* as Tragedy," p. 240.

31. Compare Wittreich, *Interpreting* Samson Agonistes, p. 353.

32. See Joseph Summers, "Response to Anthony Low's Address on *Samson Agonistes*," *Milton Quarterly*, 13 (1979): 106.

33. "*Samson Agonistes* as Christian Tragedy: A Corrective View," *Philological Quarterly*, 60 (1981): 176.

34. Madeleine L'Engle, *The Irrational Season* (New York: Seabury, 1977), p. 30, from the chapter "Rachel Weeping," a topic upon which—along with "Herod massacring"—Milton considered writing a tragedy (*CPW* 8:559).

35. L'Engle, *The Irrational Season*, pp. 31, 34.

36. Christopher Fry, *The Bible: The Screenplay* (New York: Pocket, 1966), pp. 166, 160, 168, 167.

37. Dietrich Bonhoeffer, *The Cost of Discipleship*, trans. R. H. Fuller, 2nd ed. (New York: Macmillan, 1972), pp. 106, 111, 163, 164; originally published under the title *Nachfolge* (Munich, 1937).

38. Typical is Goodwin's explanation, in the preface to one of his controversial tracts, of the difference he saw between patience and passivity: "If any man ask, why I could not be content to sit down by my charge, with . . . patience . . . I answer, though I do not *sit down* by it in patience, I *rise up* with it, and bear it upon my shoulder, with more than patience; even with joy and gladness; as I stand charged from heaven to do." Goodwin employed in

pamphlet controversies the same patience that the angels exercised in waging the war in heaven. "I trust," he remarks, "that the tenor of my answer doth no ways imply, that the least hair of the head of my patience is fallen to the ground" (*Sion-College Visited* [1647]; quoted in Jackson, p. 174).

39. Wittreich, *Interpreting* Samson Agonistes, p. 323.

40. Walwyn says, in *The Power of Love* (1642): "if you read over the story of our Saviours passion, and sufferings, you will finde [your salvation] was purchased at an excessive price. . . . I cannot suspect the most vitious man in the world, but that the hearing these things his heart will make strict enquiry, what he shall render unto the Lord for all his benefits? and his heart once moving in thoughts of thankfulnesse will instantly be inflamed with love, which in an instant refines the whole man." This new man will not seek worldly pleasures or security for himself, rather: "you will finde it nothing to hazzard your lives for God, in defence of his truth from errour; in defence of your brother or neighbour from oppression or tyranny; love makes you no longer your owne but Gods servants . . . and to be no respecter of persons . . . when tyrants and oppressors endeavour by might and force to pervert all Lawes, and compacts amongst men, and to pervert the truth of God into a lie, interpreting his sacred word as patron of their unjust power, as if any unjust power were of God, and were not to be resisted: I say, such insolencies as these will inflame your zeale, and set you all on fire manfully to fight the Lords battell" (pp. 35–40; rpt. in William Haller, ed., *Tracts on Liberty in the Puritan Revolution, 1638–1647*, 3 vols. [New York: Columbia University Press, 1933], II, 296–98); hereafter cited as Haller, *Tracts*.

David A. Hoekema, in presenting a case for Christian pacifism in the twentieth century, summarizes Christian "just-war" theory as follows: "The just-war tradition, rooted in the ethical theories of Plato and Cicero and formulated within the Christian tradition by Augustine, Aquinas and the Protestant Reformers, defends military force as a last resort against grave injustice. According to this view, when the innocent are threatened by an unjust aggressor and all other remedies have failed, Jesus' demand for sacrificial love may require us to use lethal force. . . . Pacifism and just-war theory reach different conclusions only in a narrow range of cases: both positions insist that Christians must strive always for healing and reconciliation and must act out of love for all, and both traditions unequivocally condemn the reasons—whether nationalism, territorial or economic gain, revenge or glory—for which nearly all wars have been fought" ("A Practical Christian Pacifism," *The Christian Century*, 103 [Oct. 22, 1986]: 917–18).

41. Dietrich Bonhoeffer, *Letters and Papers From Prison*, ed. and trans. Eberhard Bethge (London: Collins, 1969), p. 138; originally published under the title *Widerstand und Ergebung-Briefe und Aufzeichnungen aus der Haft* (Munich, n.d.).

42. Cf. Wittreich, *Interpreting* Samson Agonistes, p. 324.

43. Bonhoeffer, *Letters and Papers*, pp. 139–40.

44. Bethge, in his forward to Bonhoeffer, *Letters and Papers*, p. 10; Bonhoeffer, "Letter to a Friend, July 21st, 1944" in *Letters and Papers*, p. 125.

45. Bonhoeffer, *Letters and Papers*, pp. 137–38.

46. Ibid., pp. 124–25.

47. "Stations on the Road to Freedom," written on receipt of the news of the failure of July 20th (ibid., p. 161).

SIX. The Birth of Christian Liberty: *Paradise Regained*

1. Bonhoeffer, *Letters and Papers*, p. 161.

2. See, e.g., Douglas Bush, *The Renaissance and English Humanism* (Toronto: University of Toronto Press, 1939), p. 125.

3. Cain, "Learning How to Read," p. 121; Kerrigan, *The Prophetic Milton*, p. 180, n. 25.

4. Stanley Fish brings out this aspect of Christ's liberty in "Things and Actions Indifferent: the Temptation of Plot in *Paradise Regained*," *Milton Studies*, 17 (1983): 168.

5. William Walwyn, *The Vanitie of the Present Churches* (1649); rpt. in Haller and Davies, pp. 262–63.

6. John Saltmarsh, *A New Quere* (London, 1645), p. 8.

7. In his Epistle to the readers of the *De Doctrina*, Milton explains his idea of the "learned man" who is his intended audience: "if the very learned are not always the best judges . . . at any rate . . . mature, strong-minded men who thoroughly understand the teaching of the gospel" (*CPW* 6:122).

8. Peter F. Fisher, "Milton's Logic," *JHI*, 23 (1962): 40, commenting on Milton's *Art of Logic*, Preface, p. 11.

9. Saltmarsh, *Free-Grace*, p. 125.

10. Northrop Frye notes the relation between the meaning of the term "Son of God" in *Paradise Regained* and the meaning of Christian liberty ("The Typology of *Paradise Regained*" [1956]; rpt. in C. A. Patrides, ed., *Milton's Epic Poetry: Essays on* Paradise Lost *and* Paradise Regained (Baltimore: Penguin, 1967), pp. 301–21.

11. Barbara K. Lewalski, "Theme and Structure in *Paradise Regained*" (1960); rpt. in Patrides, ed., *Milton's Epic Poetry*, p. 328. For a complementary discussion of Christ's discovery of his mission in *Paradise Regained*, see Lewalski, *Milton's Brief Epic: the Genre, Meaning, and Art of* Paradise Regained (Providence: Brown University Press, 1966), ch. 7.

12. Lewalski, *Brief Epic*, pp. 198, 216–17.

13. S. B. Liljegren, *Studies in Milton* (1918; rpt. New York: Haskell, 1969), pp. xxxvii–xl.

14. *The Memoirs of Edmund Ludlow, Lieutenant-General of the Horse and in the Army of the Commonwealth of England, 1625–1672*, ed. C. H. Firth, 2 vols. (Oxford: Clarendon, 1894), I, 434.

15. Ludlow, *Memoirs*, II, 7.

16. Lewalski, *Brief Epic*, p. 270.

17. Saltmarsh, *England's Friend Raised from the Grave*, p. 4; quoted in Woodhouse, p. 81.

18. Quoted in Ludlow, *Memoirs*, I, 435.

19. Goodwin, *Peace Protected* (1654); quoted in Jackson, p. 405.
20. Stevie Davies, *Images of Kingship*, ch. 3, contains an excellent discussion of the meaning that Imperial Rome held for the English republicans and of the use Milton made in *Paradise Lost* of Imperial imagery to portray Satan's tyranny.
21. Howard Schultz, *Milton and Forbidden Knowledge* (New York: MLA, 1955); Lewalski, *Brief Epic*, p. 291.
22. Christopher Hill writes helpfully on this point: "*Paradise Regained* is about something far more fundamental than controversies about university teaching. The learned and cultivated Parliamentarians had won all the intellectual battles, but in 1660 they had lost the war. Milton had routed Salmasius, and in *Eikonoklastes* he had exposed monarchy; but kingship came back in 1660, opposed in print almost single-handed by Milton/Abdiel. Rational arguments were not enough. Moral commitment was in the last resort more important . . . the learning of the educated is nothing worth unless it is used to further God's cause" (*Milton and the English Revolution*, p. 424).
23. Bonhoeffer, *Letters and Papers*, pp. 139–40; Walwyn's *Just Defence*, rpt. in Haller and Davies, p. 363.
24. Introduction, *Leveller Tracts*, p. 22.
25. Bonhoeffer, *Cost of Discipleship*, p. 111.
26. Dell, *Right Reformation*, p. 136.
27. Milton also reversed a simile in which Charles had compared himself to Christ on the Pinnacle of the Temple and Parliament to Satan to say: "But it was . . . a Pinnacle of *Nebuchadnezzars* Palace, from whence hee and Monarchy fell headlong together" (*Eikonoklastes, CPW* 3:405).
28. Isabel Rivers, *The Poetry of Conservatism, 1600–1745: A Study of Poets and Public Affairs from Jonson to Pope* (Cambridge: Rivers Press, 1973).
29. Wilding, *Dragons Teeth*, p. 257.
30. Milner, *John Milton and the English Revolution*, pp. 147, 175.
31. Rapaport, *Milton and the Postmodern*, pp. 197, 196.
32. Hill, *Milton and the English Revolution*, p. 421.
33. Milner, *John Milton and the English Revolution*, p. 175; Bonhoeffer, *Letters and Papers*, p. 140.
34. Ludlow, *Memoirs*, II, 7.
35. Quoted in Jackson, p. 405.
36. My discussion of liberation theology is derived from Phillip Berryman, *Liberation Theology: Essential Facts about the Revolutionary Movement in Latin America and Beyond* (New York: Random House, 1986), pp. 152–61.
37. Walwyn, *The Power of Love*; rpt. in Haller, *Tracts*, II, 296–98.
38. Berryman, *Liberation Theology*, p. 187.

Index